GROWING UP ON AN ISLAND

OFF THE

COAST OF MAINE

Photo Anita de Laguna Haviland, 2008.

THE AUTHOR

Growing Up
on an
Island
off the
Coast of Maine

Carroll M. Haskell

Polar Bear & Company
An imprint of the
Solon Center for Research and Publishing
Solon & Rockland, Maine

Polar Bear & Company™
Solon Center for Research and Publishing
Polarbearandco.org, SolonCenter.org
GalleryFukurou.com

Retailers may order via Ingram, ISBN: 978-1-959112-07-5.
Contact: PO Box 311, Solon ME 04979; info@soloncenter.org.
Gallery & events: 20 Main Street, Rockland, ME 04841.
Copyright © 2011 by Carroll M. Haskell.
Library of Congress Control Number: 2011936845
Second edition: paperback, 2024
First edition: paperback, 2011

Cover art by Carroll M. Haskell
Cover design by Ramona du Houx. Illustrations: All photos courtesy of the
author, unless otherwise indicated.

Editor's Note: Where names of locations differ from official records, we have
deferred to the author's traditional usage.

Manufactured on durable, acid-free paper in more than one country.

CONTENTS

OLDEST BUILDING AND DOCK IN STONINGTON WITH LOBSTER BOAT *DALE DAY*.
THIS DOCK BELONGED TO FISHERMAN MAYNARD GRAY, SR. IN 1940. HOUSES ON
GREEN HEAD IN BACKGROUND. Photo Pam H. Haskell, 1999.

PREFACE

Why does one write an autobiography? My father was very good at storytelling, and before we Deer Islanders had electricity and television, yarns were a way of life. Sometimes, Dad would sit in his favorite armchair in the southeast corner of our little homemade house and play a hymn on his harmonica, and then he might tell a story about someone with humorous details or a punch-line ending. If our uncle Elroy, Dad's identical twin brother, happened to come visiting, the evening would become a real storytelling event. One of the subjects was our own Haskell family history. The twins recited our genealogy as far as they knew it, backwards it ran: Freeman, Peter, Cap'n Tristram, Solomon, and Cap'n Mark Haskell. Of course Solomon was not our ancestor.

Mrs. Estelle Noyes gave me a genealogy book that Dr. Benjamin Lake Noyes, the local historian, had got printed, with a complete record of Caleb Haskell's 1775 account of the battle in Dorchester, now known as Bunker Hill—and his trip to Quebec with General Benedict Arnold and the failed attempt to capture Quebec from the British, who invented the successful back-door entry, led by General Wolfe. There was also a Haskell genealogy included in the book. However, there was still a huge gap in my Haskell family genealogy.

Fifty-seven years ago, while I was working as a waiter on the eighty-two-foot houseboat yacht, *Antonia*, in Florida waters, I wrote to my father, Leroy Elmer Haskell, and asked him to write some autobiography, which he did on ordinary, lined, Woolworth, five-and-dime-store, yellow pad pages. I suspect that my mother, Charlotte Mildred (Torrey) Haskell, actually transcribed his scribbled notes for me on an inexpensive typewriter. I still have the original manuscript, which I have transcribed almost completely, word for word, for this book.

I started writing historical notes and sending them to my first cousin, Freda (Haskell) Barton, who suggested that I write to W. A. Haskell in Germany, and one day I did. He wrote back almost immediately and suggested that I write for the *Haskell Families Society Newsletter*. Win sent me the complete genealogy of my Haskell line. I was delighted. My genealogy is included in this book. About this time in American history, Alex Haley's, slave ancestors' story was being shown on TV, which generated some national interest in genealogies. Eventually, Win published most of my little stories, and Captain Arthur "Dud" Haskell of Deer Isle read them and liked them so much that he loaned copies to Robert Haskell, (Sunshine section of Deer Isle). As time went on, Win began having medical problems, and he had to give up publishing the newsletter. He encouraged me to write up all my stories into a book.

For almost a year I was having old Knowlton and Haskell family photos copied at Staples, which is almost handy on Germantown Ave., mere city blocks away. I was making up three loose-leaf binder books for my children and one for Judi and Bill Schoettle, and two others containing my collection of stories.

My brother-in-law, Dr. William A. Haviland, and his bride, Anita Haviland, read some of my stories and sent them to Paul Cornell du Houx, who liked them so much that he wanted to publish the whole works! All this has taken place since my first li'l story, "Growing Up on an Island," was published in Volume 10, Issue 1, page 11, of the newsletter of the Haskell Family Society (published quarterly since 1991 for Haskells worldwide).

I owe many many thanks to Mrs. Judi Schoettle who was supervisor of the library media centers and the social studies departments of Black Horse Pike Regional School District and previously also the supervisor of English and World Languages and Social Studies at Timber Creek Regional High School. Judi read and corrected many pages of my manuscript, and she continues to encourage me along the way.

Anita de Laguna Haviland has spent hours and hours organizing these stories and prompted me to do more writing to round it out as a whole book. I am immensely grateful for the care she has given to this project.

My bride of almost 53 years, Pamela Jean (Haviland) Haskell, is Dr. William A. Haviland's sister. She has patiently read my stories and made helpful corrections and/or suggestions, ever since I started with the first li'l story!

Dr. Melanie Martin, my ophthalmologist, has read some of my published stories and some that will definitely not be published, and she continues to encourage me to write!

Finally, Gordon "Gumper" Gray, who worked with me on the John L. Goss granite quarry from 1947 to November 1950, and Donald "Duck" Davis, who was tool carrier on the same quarry in 1950, have both read and approved of my stories about the stone-quarry workings.

Deer Isle, Maine
September, 2011

CMH

"My father, Leroy Elmer Haskell (above), was the tenth generation from William Haskell, who emigrated to Salem, Massachusetts, in 1635 from Charlton Musgrove, Somerset, England. He arrived with his brothers Mark and Roger, one sister, their mother Elinor, and her new husband, John Stone, who ran a ferry from Salem to Beverly in 1636."* —CMH

THE OLD HASKELL HOMESTEAD C. 1946, WITH THE WOODPILE OUT BACK AND A TALL RED-SPRUCE TRUNK TO ANCHOR THE CLOTHES LINE; 1929 CHEVROLET COACH; LEROY BOUGHT IT IN 1945 FOR $45 AND SOLD THE ENGINE AND TRANSMISSION TWELVE YEARS LATER FOR MORE THAN HE PAID FOR THE CAR.

1. FROM MY FATHER'S JOURNALS

On the 18th of March, 1899, in a small house perched atop a granite ledge, Mary Jane (Billings) Knowlton Haskell presented her fisherman husband with twin boys. Elroy was born first, and Leroy was cast into a slop pail, the midwife thinking it was the afterbirth. However, Leroy began to wail. The midwife bailed me out and cleaned me up, and I was soon suckling with my brother all nice and cozy.

Green's Landing had been renamed Stonington in honor of the new granite quarries in operation there. The Haskell homestead was about a mile and a half from the center of town and overlooked Webb's Cove, as it does today. Elroy's son, Melvin Frederick Haskell, and his bride of many years live there today.

*Opposite: Researched by Winthrop A. Haskell in July 1984, published in *The Haskell Family Anthology* (Digaprint Limited, Brighton, East Sussex, U.K., 2003).

The boys' parents were of poor means, and having twins made it most difficult. Of course the news was soon noised about, and people said, "That poor man, he married a woman with five children already!" She was a nice woman, widowed some six years back. Her first husband, Henry Knowlton, was a stone-cutter. He had a heart attack and passed away while holding his youngest son, Cecil Knowlton.

Freeman Charles Haskell [Leroy's father] was a lobster fisherman at the time, although he had been a sailor and captain of ships; his people were ship builders at Northwest Harbor, Deer Isle, Maine. Three of their ships were lost in the Spanish-American War.

There was plenty of noise at our house for several years. After a while we began to move out in time when we could remember some of our pranks, and it seems we got caught in this one. Mother owned a small three-acre lot on the shore, where she kept two cows, a pig, and some hens. She kept the pig in the barn, so one day my brother and I were standing on the pen, and of course we got some sticks and hit the pig. He started to run, grunting, making all kinds of noises. We thought that was fun, saying, "See that pig bizz!" So we kept at it until we heard a voice behind us say, "I'll make you bizz."

We looked around for a place to run, but it was too late. Dad caught us. We got our britches tanned, and struck out for the house, howling to the top of our lungs, stopping only long enough to say, "Didn't that pig bizz!" starting in howling again where we left off. Mother burst out laughing, and soon the crying stopped. It was all over.

Mother and Dad thought it a good idea to take one twin on the sloop with him, so that we would not be so much of a problem to her. Father agreed, and the next week I took the first trip with Dad down to York Island Harbor, just a little distance east of Isle au Haut. Mother got me some warm clothes, because at times it gets chilly out there, some quilts to sleep on, and some to wrap up in, and plenty of food to last a week. Off I went with Dad to York Island, where Dad stayed during the week, making it easier to fish, because it was about seven miles nearer to his traps.

We got under way on a beautiful morning just after daybreak. There was hardly any wind. Dad got out his big ten-foot oars and started to row, and I tried to help. The "old *Mildred*," I called her, wasn't old at all, about four years; she carried 125 yards in her mainsail, 45 yards in her hauling jib, the outer jib 65 yards, which he hardly ever used.

On these calm days he would get outside the islands, where he could see his sloop all the time, leave her to me, and strike out to haul his pots, in his peapod. Sometimes I would start fishing. Once Dad anchored on the upper end of the middle ground; I caught a couple hundred pounds of codfish before he came back. Then it was up anchor and row some more, to get to York Island, to anchor, to get something to eat, chat with other fishermen, and go to bed.

Imagine rowing that 45-foot Friendship sloop several miles with ten-foot dory oars, if you will. Freeman had to row standing up, using his weight to help move the boat along slowly into the York Island anchorage.

The next morning when I turned out, most all of the fishermen had left. One of the Billings boys had a launch, a boat with a motor in it, something new for these times. It sure made an awful noise. I was hungry, so I got into the breadbasket and found myself something to eat and started catching flounders and horndogs (sculpins) for bait for my dad.

The days went fast at first, but I missed the boys to play with at home. It was all-too-sudden a change for me, but soon the fishermen started coming into harbor, and things began to be a little more cheerful. I heard someone say, "Here comes Ol' Shag Nasty."

When Dad came rowing in, I asked him who Old Shag Nasty was. He told me that he was a poor boy who lived with his father in a sloop up the harbor. Dad said he thought that they shouldn't call him Old Shag, because he wasn't old at all. "He's a young fellow in his teens." Unfortunate, I suppose in a way, this may not be much of a life, but it makes you appreciate good things when they come your way.

As the days went by, I would row from one sloop to another, saying hello. "What's your name?" they would ask. I would tell them my name kind of proud-like. "You got a twin brother, haven't you?"

"Yeah, he's home. Dad had to take one with him, so he would

have a house to go home to," I said. "So he brought me the first trip."

"Well, how do you think you are goin' to like it?"

"Don't know yet. Maybe I can get used to it after a while."

Later on, I got more acquainted with the fishermen around the harbor; they would holler at Dad and say, "Freeman, I would like to send your boy in to the store." The store was up the harbor some distance, so Dad would let me go, cautioning me to "be sure to tie the peapod up good, so it won't go adrift" on me. "Yep," and away I would go to find out what the man wanted; bread, condensed milk, tobacco, were the usual order, and "Here's the money. And here's ten cents for you to buy some candy with."

I bought their order first, to be sure that there was enough money. Sometimes there was hardly enough to pay the bill, so when I got back they asked, "Did you get your candy?"

"If Dave Conley (the storekeeper) hadn't charged me too much, I would have had some left," I would say. Then they would wonder if I was fibbing and had eaten it already. I would hear them say, "Dave takes advantage of that boy some ol' quick!"

It wasn't long before the other fishermen would send me ashore after groceries too. It got so at times that I would have more orders than I could remember, so when I got back with the purchases, things got kind of mixed up. I got me a loaf of ginny bread,* a can of Eagle brand milk, some flounder hooks to fish with, and some hard candy, so I'd have something to chew on, something to fish with and all.

The next day after the boats began to come in, they would holler at each other and ask, "How did you do this day, Freeman?"

"Ah you, nat too good, you, and you?"

"Hardly nary a one."

I thought, "My, the language." They certainly had a dialect all their own. It would be something if one could go back in time with a tape recorder and tape their conversations. It sounds queer at times, and you can't keep from laughing at them.

Lobster fishermen were just beginning to use single-cylinder, two-cycle marine engines. John Billings and Elmer Billings had a gas engine. That was something to hear them tell about it, and it

*Gingerbread cake

soon became the topic of interest around the harbor. John and Elmer came alongside one day. They wanted to go down to Little Spoon Island after gulls' eggs, so Dad and I decided to go. We all piled aboard the launch and struck out for Little Spoon Island. That ol' engine made such a noise you couldn't hear a word the other fellows said. It pounded out more noise than energy.

Dad decided not to put an engine in his Friendship sloop. He said that he wanted to put her in the races which took place off Eagle Island each year, and it would spoil her for sailing. So he rowed for a long time, up to his death, which took place when I was twelve.

Dad tried some of those gulls' eggs—bah, I didn't like them at all.

My father told me quite a bit more about the gulls' egg hunt. When they ran down to Little Spoon Island in 1908, the island still had a virgin stand of white pine giants. They anchored the launch and went ashore in a peapod, which they had towed behind the launch. Since Dad was small, the Billings brothers sent him crawling inside the dead and hollow white pine trees lying on the forest floor, to throw all the gulls' eggs out, which were then destroyed. The fishermen and Leroy returned a day or so later, and all the new eggs were fresh, and they gathered them up to cook with on their sloops, which had tiny cast-iron cook stoves down below in the cuddy.

2. Deer Isle in 1900

On Deer Isle, Maine, there were several subsistence farms, a few small dairy farms, and a thriving sardine factory that employed housewives and young girls, who packed the herrings into cans to be cooked off in steam pressure cookers on the main floor below. Bradbury Island and Pickering Island, which lie a mile or so offshore west of Deer Isle's Northwest Harbor, were still subsistence farms supporting one family on each island.

There were several granite quarries on the nearby offshore islands: Green Island, Saint Helena Island, Scott Island, Russ Island, and Crotch Island, where there were at least four quarries but not all at the same time. As Dame Fortune would have it, further west there were granite quarries on Hurricane Island and Vinalhaven. Up the Penobscot River, there was a granite quarry at Frankfort, Maine.

With the invention of the steam-operated drill, followed by pneumatic drills, granite quarries could quarry blocks of stone quite quickly, compared to the older methods of drilling the holes by hand.

There were large public buildings, libraries, courthouses, state capitol buildings—some granite from Maine was even used in the Washington Monument. Maine granite was used in the footings and towers of the Brooklyn Bridge in New York City. Hurricane Island and Vinalhaven quarries secured some of these large contracts, where the stone-cutters earned as much as three dollars a day. However, quarrymen working there earned as little as a dollar a day.

Dix Island, just offshore from Rockland, Maine, had a monolith of gneiss, a distinctive red-streaked stone that quarried like granite, that was used as decorative trim pieces in the footings of the Bell Telephone Company central office on Broad Street in the Olney section of the City of Philadelphia. It was also used as trimming stone on the low outside stone wall borders of the public library on Arch Street in Philadelphia. Columns on the Insurance Company of North America (INA) building at 16th Street and Benjamin Franklin Parkway were turned out at the Bodwell Granite Quarry on Vinalhaven in the huge stone lathe that the future governor of Maine (Joseph Bodwell) had installed there. I believe that the granite for these columns was quarried on the John L. Goss granite quarry on Crotch Island, just a few minutes' row in a peapod south from Stonington, Maine.

Hurricane Island, once a nearly barren granite monolith rising above the waters of western Penobscot Bay, had as many as twelve hundred people living on the island, which had its own post office and grocery store and perhaps as many as fifty houses and temporary shacks. Only a few unused cut stones and a grout pile (broken granite) remained, on our infrequent marine picnic visits in the 1950s.

There were two quarries on Crotch Island, operating from some time in the 1800s to the late 1900s. Frank McGuire managed to buy the Benvenue Co. Granite Quarry, that was located on the north side of Crotch Island, directly opposite Billings Marine, which is still located on Moose Island at this time.

The granite-block dock and steel-framed loading derrick are still there and used by the latest owner, who has a stone finishing plant in Rhode Island. Granite blocks quarried on Crotch island in the 2000s were and are transferred to barges, then to flatbed trucks that load the blocks at what used to be the Settlement Quarry in Webb's Cove in Stonington. Possibly, very large barge loads are towed down the coast to Rhode Island. There were many large blocks of granite stored on the old John L. Goss loading dock in 2008, when we ran past on the Isle au Haut passenger-and-mail boat.

It is a little scary to see two or three of these loaded flatbed trucks on the Deer Isle-Sedgwick Bridge at once. The drivers are supposed to maintain five hundred feet between loaded trucks. Wise drivers of passenger cars should wait until these huge blocks of stone are off the bridge, remembering that the Tacoma Narrows Bridge fell down, and this bridge was designed by the same engineers.

In the early 1900s, shucked-out barrels of clams for fish bait were bringing three dollars and change, as credit from Fred Eaton's store. His granite-block dock still exists. But Fred's store (in Green's Landing, now Stonington)—the oldest business building on Deer Isle until late in the 1980s—has been rebuilt on the same location. The new owner generously lets the native lobster fishermen use the dock to load and unload lobster gear, so I have been told.

The large population of immigrant Italian stone-cutters gradually moved on to other states in the union, as granite-cutting work began to filter away. The John L. Goss Company, which thrived in the 1900s, declined and was bought by the Deer Isle Granite Company, which collapsed after the Kennedy Memorial job. My father, Leroy Elmer Haskell, still known as Dick Haskell, worked as yardman and derrick operator on the old John L. Goss quarry, which was still operating under the McGuire family's management in 1957.

In 2000 I went over there in my little outboard-powered skiff, and the cutting shed and gang-saw buildings had fallen flat to the ground. Vandals had set the old powerhouse on fire, and there is nothing left but rusty machines still sitting upon their granite-block foundations. The three Hodge steam boilers still sit forlornly rusting away. I was told that the old Number One Derrick, which had been the only one able to lift the huge, estimated-to-be fifty-ton granite block that became the Rockefeller bowl had simply fallen down one day. Fortunately, no one was hurt by the falling Oregon fir timber mast, the huge fir boom, and the massive cast-iron head block and attached steel guy wires.

In 1915 a German U-boat sank the *Lusitania* just a few miles off the South coast of Ireland, followed in 1917 by Germany declaring unrestricted U-boat warfare! The allied United States and Great Britain soon began escorted Merchant Marine convoys. In 1918 my mother's brother Ralph Torrey went to France to help fight the "Huns" and was gassed (mustard gas) at the battle of Château-Thierry. He survived and lived to be over 80 years old! The state of Maine took away Uncle Ralph's driver's license when he reached 80, but he told me that he had to drive in order to be able to work at carpentry. Garland and I called him Uncle Popeye. Stonington Entered the 1920s with both Crotch Island stone quarries working.

3. THE TWO DICKIES

My father was born in the Henry Knowlton house at the end of the Tea Hill Road, which at that time was down a dirt path on the south side of a granite ledge, where it sits today. In that small saltwater farmhouse my grandfather, Freeman Charles Haskell, lived with his "adopted" family after he married my grandmother, Mary Jane Billings Knowlton, who was recently widowed.

Freeman married Luella J. Eaton, 14 March, 1878. He was a sea captain, and I suppose he came into Northwest Harbor, Deer Isle, early, from one of his trips and took the tender to sail up to his house on Little Deer Isle. When he walked into the house unannounced, he found his wife in bed with another man, who escaped through a window. One can just imagine the squall that blew up after that discovery! At any rate, they became divorced, and at some later date Freeman was in Webb's Cove, most likely after a load of paving stone or pulpwood. Somehow, he met the newly widowed Mary Jane (Billings) Knowlton and fell in love. They were married on the 17th of December, 1894, in Green's Landing, Maine, renamed Stonington very shortly after their union. Personal note: I like the Green's Landing name better; it is almost more fitting.

There were five Knowlton children: three sons, Raymond, Albert, and Cecil; two daughters, Ethel and Florence. After four years, Mary Jane had an announcement to make. She was in a family way—with Elroy Freeman Haskell and Leroy Elmer Haskell, identical twins.

Elroy was born first on 18 March, 1899; Leroy was thrown into the aforementioned slop pail, as he was thought to be the afterbirth, but he began to cry, and the midwife bailed him out and cleaned him up. The boys both lived into their nineties.

The twins were soon followed by a daughter, Christie Mae Haskell, born on the 24th of September, 1900. Christie was not bright, and

Grandmother was disappointed in her. Christie married a man by the name of Charles Hooper, who abandoned her, leaving her with two young children and pregnant. Christie and the baby died in the subsequent childbirth, and grandmother Haskell carried on, mostly alone. Freeman had died on the 12th of May, 1912. Mary Jane did not marry again.

My father, Leroy E. Haskell, already known as one of the "two Dickies," went to work in the local fish factory to help support the extended family and never finished school.

Elroy had fathered Freda and Melvin Haskell and was constantly squabbling with his bride, who was formerly Christine Terry. At some point Freda lived with Grammie Haskell at Tea Hill, and Melvin joined the Navy the day that he quit school—he couldn't tolerate the school principal and teacher, Mr. Howells.

I was in the main room on the second floor where Mr. Howells was teaching trigonometry. Cousin Melvin was so frustrated with the mathematics that he threw his textbook at the genuine slate blackboard and it hit with such force that the lower right corner snapped off. The blackboard frame held that fragment from falling onto the floor. Melvin stormed out of the room and never came back. Shortly after that, he joined the U.S. Navy. His biography follows later in this book.

My father, Leroy Elmer Haskell, married Charlotte Mildred Torrey on May 7, 1927.

FROM LEFT, CHRISTIE MAE (HASKELL) HOOPER, CLARA KNOWLTON, ETHEL KNOWLTON, RAYMOND KNOWLTON. CLARA KNOWLTON, DAUGHTER OF JOHN KNOWLTON, HAD FOUR SISTERS; SHE MARRIED WALTER JONES AND HAD ONE SON, KENNETH, WHO MARRIED THE AUTHOR'S COUSIN, MARIE BUCKMINSTER. ETHEL AND RAYMOND WERE SIBLINGS.

4. EARLY HOMES

UNCLE JOE EATON'S HOUSE ON TEA HILL ROAD AS IT APPEARED MOST OF THE AUTHOR'S CHILDHOOD YEARS, AND WHERE HE WAS BORN.

I was born in midwinter of 1927 in an old saltwater farmhouse kitchen. The old house sat just about fifty feet off the north side of the gravel-surfaced Tea Hill Road. Legend has it that the colonial settlers banked up their houses for the winter with tea leaves, giving the name of Tea Hill to eight or nine houses and barns that sat close to the road. At one time the road ran down past my grandmother's house to meet a very rough wagon road from Clam City, which passed by the vacant Phoebe Thurston farm, Aunt Net Knowlton's small subsistence farm, and then downhill to make a tight right turn through the Ames Family's saltwater farm. The road from there to Green's Landing was maintained by Walden Ames and his team of oxen. These four farms were quite remote from the town that became Stonington, where wooden four-masted vessels came to load granite blocks to be sailed to New York and Philadelphia, to make footings for the huge suspension bridges that spanned their rivers.

The old kitchen was so cold that skim ice formed in the water pails resting on a wooden shelf less than ten feet from the woodstove that

AUTHOR (LEFT) AND YOUNGER BROTHER GARLAND HASKELL IN A HOMEMADE SANDBOX AT THE MCLEAN HOUSE, CLAM CITY, 1933.

provided the only heat in that old farmhouse. Dr. Noyes sat at the plain white pine table writing genealogy notes while he waited for my mother to give birth. She was lying on a camp-type folding cot close to the open oven door, and once I had entered the world I promptly pissed right into the oven! That so delighted my mother that she told me about it at times forever afterwards.

In April of 1928 Dad moved our small collection of household belongings to Clam City, where we lived in what used to be the McLeans' old house until sometime in 1938. It was a strange little house, perched upon granite blocks that were arranged in a rectangle upon the solid granite ledge that ran down hill to the Deer Isle Thoroughfare,* where there was a tiny rough sand pocket beach where my brother, Garland, and I played when we were older. The house was sited to let in the direct sunlight, and the kitchen faced the Thoroughfare with a magnificent view toward Isle au Haut and all the islands in between. There was a cast-iron cook stove, and Dad had a two-burner kerosene stove that was used in the summer. Pine stairs led up the east side, and there were two bedrooms and a winter larder above the first floor. There was a larger room on the first floor that faced the roadway. The house had a central brick chimney that had a westward lean from where it emerged from the

*A stretch of water off Deer Isle

roof. Somehow I think the house was shingled in the native white cedar, but all the houses in a little cluster were painted yellow with red triangle sections above the parallel sides. The house closest to the sea was also perched upon the same granite monolith, and was at that time owned by Henry Eaton and his family. The next one east of it was Otis Shepard's and was also close to the thoroughfare.

5. LEAN TIMES
FROM MY FATHER'S JOURNALS

The April we moved to Clam City, Carroll was four months old. We had to start all over, buying a stove, furniture and household goods to keep house. Uncle Joe Eaton's house had been supposedly furnished. We thought it was colder than any barn we ever saw. Plants froze in the next room on the first floor with a hot coal fire going in the stove and a five-burner oil stove going in the kitchen.

However, winters weren't like Florida's those days. Sometimes the temperature went down to 27 below zero Fahrenheit. Snow piled in ten-foot drifts, and there were no plows to clear the roads. Men got together and shoveled the roads so the mail could get through with a horse and buggy, sleigh or wagon. There weren't many cars in those days, and the roads were gravel.

Carroll was a year and thirteen days old when Garland arrived, a strapping baby of eleven pounds and some ounces, born at Sand Beach Farm. I kept house alone for three months before Garland was born, as "Mill" wasn't well. She stayed with Mrs. McGuffie and had Carroll with her.

A while before Garland was born, I was struck by a car and nearly killed. I was out of my head for a week with a concussion. My head was split open in two places. Jesse Stinson hit me with his car. It threw me over the top and down in front of the hood onto the road. Everyone thought I was dead for a while. Ruined the only suit I owned. My wife was outdoors scrubbing clothes on a washboard by the side of the house when my brother, Elroy, brought me home. I didn't know my wife for days. The house was full of neighbors, my wife told me. They sat on the stairs all night long the first night, she said, and I was raving like a madman.

The years that followed were hectic. The Great Depression

LEROY ELMER HASKELL HOLDING CARROLL MADISON HASKELL AT THE OLD MCLEAN HOUSE IN 1928, JUST BEFORE HE WAS RUN DOWN BY THE "VILLAGE IDOT." MARM'S LAUNDRY EQUIPMENT IS ARRAYED BESIDE THE HOUSE, AND CAP'N AL SHEPARD'S BREEZEWAY AND COW BARN ARE IN THE BACKGROUND.

came, with its bread lines miles long, no work for anybody, and no food either. We ate, such as it was, fish, clams, birds, and scallops. We had a garden at Tea Hill and raised vegetables. My wife took a baby on each hip, walking that way from Clam City to Tea Hill through the woods to dig in the garden. I used to take the boat and row off to the islands and cut wood to burn in the stove. These were the lean years that I hope nobody ever lives through again.

6. GOOD TIMES

Years before television was invented, the island folks entertained their families and visiting friends with stories. Sometimes Dick would play his squeeze-box accordion or play his harmonica, and some other times he would tell stories about his hunting trips or other events. One of his often-told stories was about going down to Isle au Haut in his peapod and climbing up the face of a cliff via a large spruce tree and looking out over an abandoned farmstead to see a small herd of deer eating apples that had fallen off the neglected trees.

He had purposely taken his Remington automatic .32 Special Model 8 rifle. If my memory is anywhere near correct it had a gas-operated mechanism, so that there was only one bang when fired, whereas a lever-action or bolt-action rifle would make a noise if the hunter tried for a second shot. Dick shot one large doe, and the cluster of deer merely looked up, giving Dad a second chance to bag another deer. He fired once more, and the remaining deer, now alerted, leaped and ran away very quickly. He climbed out onto the sloping field and gutted the two does, dragged them down into the brook that ran through the farm, and weighted them down with some large rocks that were lying in the stream bed.

It was late in November, and he suspected that the weather would come off cold and freeze the deer into the ice already skimming quiet little pools in the brook. He climbed back down to the shore, pulled in his peapod, which he had anchored fisherman-fashion with a killick stone tied to the boat's painter and a length of ground line fastened to the anchor stone and the painter.

After he had loaded his rifle and himself into the sturdy little boat, he cast the stone that he had found on the pocket beach back onto the shore, set up his homemade mast down through the mast hole into the mast step, unfurled the simple leg-of-mutton spritsail, pulled the sheet halyard down through a convenient gap between the inner clamp—which was fastened from bow to stern onto the oak rib ends—and the outside rub railing, which also ran from bow to stern. After all, peapods were merely easily-rowed workboats and did not have nicely finished hulls.

Dick started the return trip by pushing off with an oar that doubled as a crude rudder, as soon as the little cotton sail filled. He sailed downwind, passing west of Fog Island, skirting Merchants Island, and making between McGlathery and No Man's Land Islands, a long reach to just west of Devil's Island and on to Webb's Cove. As soon as he rounded Phoebe Thurston's Point, he lost his Sou'west wind and had to row into the outhaul mooring. Days later he and a second cousin went down and retrieved the two deer and brought them back to Stonington in the cousin's powerboat. Dick gave one doe to his cousin, and the other was hung in our woodshed-cum-saw-sharpening shop to provide meat for the winter.

Another frequently told story was about rabbit hunting on Devil's Island. Dad had a friend, Ed Hardy, who worked on the John L. Goss granite quarry. He was a blacksmith and taught Dick some of the blacksmith's craft. Together with uncle Elroy, they rowed down to Devil's Island in Dick's peapod. Ed had a foghorn that he blew into and Elroy and Leroy, the identical twins, each took a stand somewhere safely away from each of the other two hunters, while Ed blew into the foghorn. Pretty soon snowshoe hares were hopping all over the Island. The three of them shot so many rabbits that Dick had a pork barrel partly filled with rabbits, that he salted down like codfish.

But his all-time favorite story was about the trip that his father took with both twins to Rockland in the friendship sloop *Mildred*, possibly just to attend the Fourth-of-July celebration. In any event, the city was decorated with red-white-and-blue bunting, banners and flags. There were ball games and a marching band. Teddy Roosevelt's Great White Fleet had a destroyer anchored in the harbor, and the ship's boats were busy all day going back and forth with loads of sailors who were enjoying shore leave for the day's festivities.

The sailors quickly discovered the fireworks store and almost as quickly discovered that the trolley tracks that rose up the hill were just perfect to shoot off skyrockets by laying the rockets in the groove of the rail and then lighting the fuses. Another crew of sailors decided to try to make the ancient memorial cannon fire off a blast. Somewhere, they procured some black powder and managed to ram a charge into the ancient artillery piece, using crunched-up newspapers to seal the charge. And by dribbling a little powder down the touch-hole, they fired off the old gun with a smoking piece of punk, which produced a tremendous blast of noise, smoke and smelly fumes, accompanied by excited hilarity from the adventurous girls, sailors and youths standing near.

Eventually one of the skyrockets rose from the trolley tracks, and in its erratic flight rammed into the fireworks store; the exploding head sent flaming balls into the stock, and the store was ablaze in minutes! The horse-drawn fire apparatus came clanging down the street, and the steam-powered pump was connected to a hydrant, but by then it was much too late to save the fireworks store. However, the stalwart firemen managed to save the adjacent buildings.

Leroy and Elroy were so excited that they were jumping up and down, while their father, Freeman Charles Haskell, was simply aghast at the goings on. Sailing back to Webb's Cove in the *Mildred* was merely soporific sailing compared to the celebration, noise, and excitement of the day in Rockland.

7. At the Whiting Machine Works and John L. Goss
From My Father's Journals

Sometime during the winter and after my half-brother Cecil Knowlton came home from Boston, a man by the name of Graves in Vinalhaven, the next big island west of Deer Isle, was hiring men to work in the Whiting Machine Works in Whitingsville, Massachusetts. So my twin Elroy, Cecil, and I thought we would go and get a job. We hurried about, sawing wood for Mother and our sisters, and off we went to "Mass" for a job. I didn't know they didn't hire people who were only sixteen years old. When I got there, I gave the boss my birth certificate, which indicated I was seventeen. He said, "You're only seventeen, so you will have to get a work permit in this state," which surprised me, but I kept mum. Elroy and I went up before the school board to get a work permit and returned to apply for work. We were hired, and then we searched for a place to board. We started work the next day.

It wasn't like being home, where it was quiet; we didn't feel right, somehow, but we had to get used to it or go back home. I stayed and worked, getting along as best as I could. There seemed to be plenty of men no better-educated than me, I thought. I stayed nine months, and it was getting warm outside, past June, and I thought that I would go back home for a while. I didn't like working inside during the summer months. So I went back to Maine, leaving my twin and my half-brother, Cecil, there.

Back on the Island I was hired at the local fish factory again; I got some more firewood worked up for mother, then I got ready to go back to the machine shop again.

In 1914 war broke out in Europe, and in 1917 men were being drafted for the Army. Cecil, my half-brother, was drafted, and things were beginning to look bad all over. My half-brother, Albert Knowlton, enlisted his services as an expert accountant in the Navy. He was stationed in Buffalo, New York, as head paymaster, and I haven't seen him since the First World War.

As far as I know, Leroy never saw his half-brother again. Albert used to write, but very infrequently. Uncle Raymond, his other half-brother, came home on vacation every summer after his wife died.

The war went on, and I went back to work in Whiting Machine Works. The next year I went home and hadn't been there long when I got my call to go and be measured up for the service. I kept waiting and waiting. Finally, it looked as if the war was going to be over before I got my call. When it actually came, I went out to the main road at Tea Hill Corner to meet the taxi that was going to take some of the other boys along, and I could ride with them to Ellsworth for the physical examinations. A Model T Ford touring car came along with some young fellers in it, and they were blowin' the horn and hollerin', "The war's ovah!" So I didn't get any farther than the side of the road. I walked downtown to see what was cooking, and the cab driver said the draft board had cancelled the call for more recruits.

I soon found work, when people realized the draft was over. So I went to work in the stone industry, working part of the year and loafing winters. If I thought it would be a long wait before the quarry opened again, I would up and go away, usually to Whiting Machine Works.

I think it was in 1918, I got a job yachting out of Neponset on the yacht *Robin*, a steel sailboat, Cap'n George Hatch. She did a lot of racing, and I soon found out it was all work on a sail yacht, so I switched to a steam yacht, the *Swastika*, out of Nyack, New York. We ran up the Hudson River a ways. The captain's name was Irving Harbour. I didn't like him too well, so the job didn't please me. I left when we got into City Island, New York, a New York City suburb. It was in the fall of the year, so I went back to Whiting Machine Works, where they always found a job for me.

One day when it was cold in the shop, I put on a sailor's suit to keep warm and soon had plenty of visitors from every boat in the American Navy fleet. They started asking me what ship I was on and all the other things they could think of. Some of them I kidded along; others I told something else.

After a while the shop foreman saw all those gobs calling on me, so he came over to see what was up. I told him, "This sailor suit is drawing gobs like a new piece of flypaper!" He asked, "You been in the Navy?" I said, "No, I hope the boss don't fire me, 'cause I am a sailor." So off he goes. Next day the boss came to see me and asked, "You been in the Navy?"

"No, Sir!" He looked at me awhile and asked me over again the same question. Then I said, "I hope you're not going to fire me, sir. I am a sailor."

"Well," he said, "it will make some difference in your pay." After a spell, the foreman came and talked with me quite a bit. Finally, I got a better job by wearing my sailor suit.

Uncle Sam's sailors didn't know the difference between U.S. Navy uniforms and yachting uniforms, so that's one the boys didn't know or find out. I got ten cents' raise and transferred to a Norton O. D. grinder instead of a lathe to run.

I worked all winter in Whiting's, got better acquainted with my boss, came to learn his name was Mr. Bragg, from Port Clyde, Maine, south of Rockland. It got so he came up and talked to me quite a bit. He wanted to talk about fishing and lobstering, and that was right up my alley. So I could brag to Bragg and not get off course.

Life, in and out of the shop, was dress up for every meal, keep as clean as the stuff in the kitchen all the time. It soon wore to a frazzle, so when the month of May arrived, I think it was on the sixth, I got through and went home.

I went to work for John L. Goss Corp. in the granite industry. I worked in the quarry and on the company's steam tug, *Eugenie Spofford*, from Stonington to Boston and back, then to Calais, Maine, and back to Stonington. I got these trips real often. Sometimes they lasted three weeks. We never had any stormy ones, a rather nice adventure. The trip to Calais, which is on the Maine-New Brunswick border, was rather beautiful.

It was in the fall, and the leaves were turning colors, yellow and red all along the shore. It was beautiful to look at and especially when we started up the St Croix River to Calais. We were towing a barge loaded with coal. We had to wait for it to be unloaded, so we docked in St. Stephens just across the river, because there wasn't water enough to lie afloat on the low water in Calais. We towed the empty barge to the John L. Goss dock, to reload with random-sized granite blocks.

We returned home, and I worked in the quarry a few days, then left on another trip to Boston. We took another light barge in tow at Portland and went in to Newburyport, Massachusetts, about nine o'clock at night and got a barge so big you could jump off the rail right down into the smokestack of the *Eugenie Spofford.*

The barge's name was *Myrna.* Captain George Knowlton asked the barge captain if he could put up a bit of sail going down by the South Ledges off Cape Ann. He said, "Yep." It wasn't long before we were on our way out of the harbor. I looked out astern once in a while to see how things were, because now we had two barges in tow. The little one of a thousand tons was being towed astern of the *Myrna,* which helped to keep her straight. I looked aft and saw the old *Myrna* coming with the smaller barge in tow, and I said, "Cap'n, I think the barge is going to beat us 'cause it's right abreast! Look to starboard and maybe you can see her."

Cap'n George took a peek, and sure enough there she was. He said, Tell Guptill to stand by with the fire axe. That old barge is heavy, and if she fetches up on that hawser, she'll tear the bitt right outta this tug!"

I guess the chief saw it and he put a few more revolutions on the compound steam engine. Anyway, she never got by and we went into Boston sometime around three in the morning, left the barges at anchor and struck out for Rockland, Maine. We steamed into Rockland before dark, got the barge in tow and struck out for Stonington. We anchored the barge around 9:30, tied up at the Eastern Steamship dock, and we all went home. It wasn't too hard work, but long hours. I had a trick at the wheel, four hours on and eight off. I couldn't sleep much; there was so much noise and activity.

I was back in the quarry the next day. The boys didn't like it too well, 'cause I got all the paid vacations, they thought. I told them that they could get the next trip. "Where have you been?" one asked me. So I told them all about the trip, the four hours on and eight off, working right around the clock, about the poor sleeping conditions, and after a while the story got to be old, and they didn't ask about it anymore.

8. THE BIG BLOW
FROM MY FATHER'S JOURNALS

One morning, sometime in August, 1911, when my father left
home he went straight to York Harbor, without hauling any of his
traps. The weather was bad and seas were rough, and some of the
fishermen were still beating down the Bay and through Merchants
Row on their way from Stonington to York Island Harbor, which
lies between Isle au Haut and York Island, just east of the High
Island and parallel with it. I would stay with Dad this week, and
my twin brother, Elroy, would accompany him on the next trip.

A heavy sou'west wind developed into a storm that kept the
fishermen in the harbor. The sea was very rough even in the lee of
Isle au Haut, and sloops were tossing and bobbing up and down
so lively you could hardly stay in your bunk at night.

The fishermen were talking back and forth about what they
thought the weather was going to be like. No one thought it was
going to last so long at this time of the year, but it was making
up for a real storm. The wind didn't bother you much in York
Island till the sea rolled in from the east through the mouth of
the harbor on the high water. Those sloops really bobbed it out.
Some of the men had to put out more anchors and keep watch to
see that they didn't bump into each other, as the anchorage was
so small.

It came on night fast and early, and rained. I didn't have any
oilskins so stayed in the cuddy about all the time. The night was
long. I hardly slept a wink. Next morning Dad was up getting
something to eat out of the basket of provisions Mother had
so carefully and thoughtfully prepared for our welfare, when
I heard someone say from some other boat, "I guess this is
another day in port. You, Freeman, you hear me? Air you up, you,
Freeman?" They started to gossip about the weather, first two,
then another, then another would bob up until finally about all
the fishermen were jabbering about the weather. Old King Hutch,
who lay outside of us, looked out his cuddy, took one gander at
the weather, never said a word and disappeared below again. Old
Koleson lay just inside of Freeman. He was a Norwegian; you
could hardly understand a word he said. Cap'n Stevie Gray lay

just ahead of Freeman, and I suppose I could go on naming the biggest part of the men anchored there after thinking about it.

After a while things quieted down, and they all went below to get some breakfast. They spent the days visiting each other for two long, rainy days, their sloops pitching and rolling in the confines of York Harbor. Sometime in the afternoon of the third day it let up raining, and some of the fishermen decided to set sail for home. It was still too rough to haul. Some of the men formed an exploration party to go ashore on York Island and climb to a high seat, so they could look off to the south'ard. Dad and I went ashore with the rest of the curious and climbed the slope to look out.

It sure was rough. The Middle Ground would break in nine fathoms of water. The Black Horse and Red Horse reefs were just breakers, and the sea was breaking on Little Spoon Island, the wind taking the spray the entire length of the island. Way Ledge was just a bed of spray. Freeman said, "It's no use to haul, we might as well go home. What traps are left after this storm won't have a lobster in 'em."

Some of the fellers went home after taking a look at the sea from the top of the island that afternoon. Dad stayed until the fourth day and then decided it still wasn't fit to haul. He hoisted the sails, hauled in the anchor and headed east, out through the harbor's mouth, swinging her north after he cleared a bunch of rocks in the entrance, giving her a full heading for home.

The storm was severe, and some of the men had to have a whole new string of traps after losing most all of theirs sitting on the bottom of the bay. It was a terrible cost to a fisherman to replace so many traps right in the middle of the fishing season, and impossible to catch up on the loss just experienced, this year anyway. If he doesn't lose any more traps for a couple years, he may catch up a little. Pot-warp [rope or line] jumped from twelve cents to sixteen and then to eighteen in a year's time, but the price of lobsters to the fishermen was still very low. They got about twice as much as when they sold them by the piece, about twelve or thirteen cents a pound. Selling by the piece, lobsters would bring four to nine cents, depending on their size. About this time a new device was introduced that, instead of measuring the full length of the lobster, measured just from the eye socket to the back end of the body shell.

It was a very exciting year for me, and loads of adventure.
I soon had to rough myself into new shoes and clothes to get
ready for school. I heard Dad say, after some of the fishermen
had their traps wiped out entirely, they would have to start all over
again building a new set. Most of the men haven't been very far
in schooling or ever traveled extensively, but they are the best kind
of sailors.

It was from this small island that the sailors were selected to win the
yacht race between the challenger, *Valkyrie II* from Scotland, and the
Vigilant. The *Defender*'s crew, under Captain Hank Haff, were all from
Deer Isle, Maine. *Valkyrie II*'s crew all came from Wivenhoe, Essex,
England, under Captain William Cranfield. In 1899 "Sir Tea" (Sir Thomas
Lipton) sent the *Shamrock* to challenge the defending yacht, *Columbia*.
Again, members of the two crews came from Deer Isle and Wivenhoe.

I could go on for some time telling about the different
fishermen and lobster dealers at that time of my young life, I
suppose, but I'll go on with my story and tell about my Dad, his
accident, and the tragedy that soon took place.

This same year, 1911, late in autumn, November or December,
my father was hauling his traps when his peapod broke loose and
went adrift. So he turned the sloop about and shot up alongside,
catching the tender with one hand. When he did, the sea fell away
from under it, letting all the weight fall on Dad's ribs, breaking
two of them. He kept on hauling, until finally he had to give up,
feeling sick. He wouldn't have any doctor, so it took a long while
to recover. Finally when he did feel better, Mother thought she
would go up to Little Deer Isle to see her people.

After a while Dad thought he would take the trip, too, so he
struck out to walk to Little Deer Isle. He got all sweaty walking.
It's about fourteen miles, and he had to catch the tide just right
in order to cross on the bar between Deer Isle and Little Deer
Isle. So he most likely was cuffing right along. As a result he came
down with pneumonia, and then he was awfully sick. Finally it
set him into the quick consumption (tuberculosis) and he passed
away on the 28th of May, 1912. It was a sorrowful day for me. It
affected me so much that the next school year I hardly passed.

About my age: I was born in 1898, by the town record, but
the people next door (John Knowlton's family) said we were born

in 1899. So we always said we were a year older than the calendar year at present. I said I was 14 when the record showed us as 15. Anyway, time went by and another year of school was coming up shortly. It was a struggle to get ready for high school in about three or four weeks' time.

Then influenza struck our town, and people were sure getting sick fast, all over. My brother got sick with influenza and paralysis symptoms. I wrapped him in hot blankets and kept changing them during the night to keep him steaming hot. In the morning he could move his legs and arms pretty well. My half-sister Ethel was sick. The girl next door, Etheny Knowlton, died from the flu. People were getting no relief from the doctor, and they were beginning to die all over town. I wasn't sick, so my other half-sister, Florence, and I lived in a little bait house down on the shore for a month to six weeks.

I got a job working in the fish factory for a while. It was long after school started that my family got the quarantine tag taken off the door, so they could go about town and other folks could come to visit and help out a bit. My twin brother looked terrible, thin as a rake, and I didn't think he would live, but after awhile he began to gain a bit. He weighed ninety pounds, and Sis didn't weigh more than eighty-five.

I kept working, and it seemed things were on the up when Mother got blood poisoning in her hand, losing the left forefinger. The operation took place in Knox Hospital in Rockland. Seems so trouble was following me all the way, giving me a real shakedown.

I figured I was too far behind to start school now, so maybe I had better keep right on working. I worked all summer until the factory closed in the fall. My half-brother Cecil came home from Boston, and we went clamming all fall, selling clam bait to Fred Eaton for $3.20 per barrel for store credits.

Regarding the $3.20 per barrel of clam bait: Roy "Van" Jones told me a story, years ago. It seems that his wife's father was digging clams and selling them to the same Fred Eaton. "One has a lot of time to think about things while digging furiously down in the cold almost freezing clam-flats, so one day he rowed in to Fred's dock with his barrel-load of clam baits and hollered, 'Fred, come out here!' Well, Fred was as curious as anyone else, so he walked out onto the dock. The digger shouted, 'Now you're out of th' store, damn ya, gimme my three dollars!' Fred was so surprised and amused that he paid the digger three dollars in cash. But of course it only worked once!

It took twelve to fourteen bushels of clams shucked out to make a barrel of bait [Approximately $840's worth at today's prices, in the shell.]

Boy, that was cold, rugged work. We dug clams all over, wherever we could find them thickest. We would get about half a barrel a tide around the home place, but when we went to the islands close by, we could do better.

Once we got a barrel apiece digging in Burnt Island Thoroughfare. By the way, there are 128 islands in Jericho Bay.

Leroy told me he and Cecil went down to Marsh Cove on Kimball Island and got into a patch of sand where the clams were in tiers, the largest on the bottom, and Cecil was digging faster than Leroy could wash and bag them; he just kept tossing the clams out in front of him, digging as fast as he could. When the tide came in and forced them to quit, they had gathered nine bushels in one tide.

9. THE MCLEAN HOUSE

Sometime in April of 1928, my father, Leroy Elmer Haskell, and his identical twin brother, Elroy Freeman Haskell—known as "the two Dickies" to the townsfolks and nearby neighbors—had decided that Uncle Joe Eaton's house on the Tea Hill Road was too cold and had moved us to Clam City using his relatively new 1924 Model T Ford,* which had a homemade pickup-truck platform fastened behind the tall coupe body.

The entire contents of the house consisted of a cast-iron Home Clarion woodstove, a newer kerosene stove, a plain white pine wooden kitchen table and several used wooden chairs; a factory-painted brown steel double-bed frame with mattress was erected in the upstairs north bedroom. There was a Victorian-style enameled white iron crib set up facing the view southward, directly opposite from the other bedroom.

*Footnote: A "phone booth coupe," according to *Hemmings Motor News*.

This smaller room had a double-hung window. The view from this room was out over the Deer Isle Thoroughfare. There were deep green conifer-clad islands as far as the eye could see. The gaps between these islands showed the ocean waters, which were every shade of blue depending on the day's weather. Sometimes the sun reflecting off the water was bright enough to dazzle, and other times the water seemed to be an ice-cold gray. A narrow staircase led to the second floor directly from the kitchen, and there was a long, narrow storage place with two plain white pine shelves at the head of the stairs, where Dick stored two large bags of flour, a wooden tub full of salted butter, all of the household's canned goods, a hundred-pound bag of sugar, kitchen salt, and a hundred-pound burlap bag full of coarse salt, used for preserving fish and game.

Downstairs there was another room facing north that was used as a sitting room. Eventually there would be a Sears and Roebuck's battery-operated radio that sat upon a wooden orange crate that Dad had obtained free from Ted Boyce, who had a grocery store on Main Street in Stonington. The two large radio batteries were stored in the orange crate, which lay sideways on the floor; the radio sat upon the longer flat side, which then served as a table. There were two double-hung windows facing north in the sitting room. The only door to the outside was on the southeast corner of the kitchen, and there was a wooden platform along the east side of the house, where our mother stored her clothes-washing rain barrel, galvanized washtub, scrub board, and other laundry equipment. Dick drilled a hole in the very top of a massive granite erratic boulder that sat upon the thin soil about twenty-five feet east of the kitchen door. He drove an iron rod into the hole and used it for an anchor point for the cotton clothesline, the west end of which was secured to a homemade spruce cleat fastened to the corner trim board of the house. A slender dry spruce sapling was trimmed very nicely smooth with a drawshave to serve as a clothesline prop.

Dick—as my father may be identified in the remainder of the book—constructed a little workshop out of salvaged lumber and driftwood timbers. The building ran north and south, and there was one salvaged window facing west. The northeast end had a coal bin for anthracite that contained our meager supply of hard coal for winter heat. The very south end was a privy, and there was a Sears and Roebuck's catalogue for toilet paper. (We recycled things long before it became fashionable.) The night soil was used for Marm's flower gardens. She had some beautiful dahlias.

The McLean house sat directly upon a granite ledge. The east end of the house rested directly on the ledge; the sills were shimmed with granite chips to make them level, and the west end was supported and leveled upon granite blocks. All the houses and outbuildings in that little cluster were painted yellow on the lower eight feet or so and barn-paint red above the yellow. The roof was merely weathered eastern white cedar singles. A central brick chimney that leaned westward completed the structure. Dad made a driftwood sandbox, and brought the coarse beach sand up to the house in a salvaged and recycled burlap bag. The sandbox was placed on the north side of the house. There was a Tolman sweet apple tree just a few feet northwest of the house. They were winter apples that kept well into March, becoming a little shriveled but still useable to make applesauce or pies.

The large Shepard family across and uphill from the Clam City Road had an extensive apple orchard on the south side of the Clam City Road. Otis Shepard had a square hip-roofed house right down on the shore below Captain Al Shepard's large house built by Thomas Eaton. Captain Albert Shepard bought it after Thomas died.

The old saltwater farmhouse still sits there in its original colors, very much faded at the present time. The apple orchard has not been cared for in nearly sixty years. Otis Shepard's house has been enlarged, almost beyond recognition. Otis's old cow barn fell over and was later demolished. Henry Eaton's house was sold out of the family, and the tiny hay field north of the house has grown up in a mix of maples and conifer trees. It is still visible from the Lobster Co-op dock. By 2000 our little rented McLean house had been torn down. The rough old cow pasture lying south from the Indian Point Road has nearly completely grown up in pasture spruces and alders, obscuring the magnificent view of the islands south of that point on the Clam City roadway, which has been renamed Indian Point Road.

The old Ames saltwater farmhouse has been extensively changed. A large flat-roofed dormer was built upon the north-facing roof, which increased the size of the upstairs bedrooms. The apple orchard down by the Ames family cemetery has been removed. Further east, the house and studio of sculptor William Muir and his bride Emily Lansing Muir has been torn down, and an elegant summer home has been built upon the same site overlooking Camp and Russ Islands, which lie directly south across the Deer Isle Thoroughfare, presenting a splendid view toward Isle au Haut and all the islands in between. Further east, on Phoebe Thurston's point, there are at least five new summer homes; most are facing south to present the owners with views toward Hell's Half Acre,

AUTHOR AT THE AMES FARM, 1954, BEFORE RENOVATIONS.

Devil's Island, and Bold Island, and for the most easterly of these new houses, a view toward Shingle Island and much further east, Swans Island. Webb's Cove lies north of the point, and some of the new summer folks keep boats in its protected waters.

10. CHRISTMAS AT THE HASKELL HOMESTEAD

Our mother, Charlotte Mildred (Torrey) Haskell, was very fond of Christmastime. I happened to be born four days after Christmas in Uncle Joe Eaton's house on the Tea Hill Road in Stonington, located on a tiny island just an hour's row across the Eggemoggin Reach from Sedgwick. There was no bridge or State-run ferry in those days. Most of our freight and food supplies came by steamboat from Rockland, approximately twenty miles west of the island.

Marm was determined to have a Christmas tree, and she even went out into the very nearby Tea Hill woods where she found a small balsam fir, chopped it down and dragged it home all by herself, an annual event that she performed until I was old enough to accompany her. My brother was

From left: Garland, Leon, the author, Clam City, late 1934.

born on January 13, 1929, in the Sand Beach Farmhouse in Stonington, on the west side of Deer Isle, close enough to the great Christian holidays to be named Garland for the decorations at Christmastime.

We lived in the McLean House on the Clam City Road at that time, although Marm wanted to go to the Sand Beach Farm to have her second and third baby boys. At Clam City she had to climb the steep and rough wagon road that ran west and uphill behind Great-Aunt Rhoda Shepard's house to the conifer forest that lies between the Clam City Road and the Main Road. It was a mere half-hour's walk northwest of the houses strung along the Clam City shoreline of the Deer Isle Thoroughfare, which was the major marine traffic route from Rockland to the Fox Islands, North Haven, and Vinalhaven, then further East to Stonington, and on eastwards to Swans Island, and beyond that to Bar Harbor on Mt. Desert Island. We didn't have electricity, but Marm decorated the tree with tinsel and popcorn chains and glass ornaments that had survived from her father's house on the Reach Road in North Deer Isle.

The great depression had just manifested itself, and our father was recovering from being run down by the "village idiot," so he was out of work. A great mystery enters our lives at this time: Why did Theodore "Ted" Boyce offer my father a job cutting pulpwood in the Long Cove Woods? Of all the storekeepers in Stonington, why was Ted the only one to offer any help during my father's injured state of health? Was it because Ted was a generous, caring person, or was it because the young man who ran our father down on purpose was the son of Ted's wife, before she married Ted? I can only surmise that is the case.

One of my early memories of my father was that he was lying in bed, very ill with appendicitis, and he was unable to work for a while after he was operated on. He looked haggard and frail, but he walked to Long Cove every good working day, cutting pulpwood for Ted Boyce.

In any event, it was the most impoverished time of our lives. Ted let Dick (Dad) run up a grocery bill all that winter of 1928-1929 and every winter until FDR's relief programs began.

Our youngest brother "Wink" was born on July 23, 1934. Marm named him Leon, which is Noel spelled backwards, rounding off all three of our Christmas-season names.

Dick had gotten a job working on the public roads in the WPA program. He always maintained that Leon was his lucky baby because that was when he got a job. Dick would be working on the WPA projects until World War II broke out in Europe. Then he and his identical twin brother Elroy—also known as "Dick" by the townsfolk, since they couldn't tell one from the other—went down to Connecticut and were both working in Pratt & Whitney in East Hartford.

However, our mother had a younger sister, Franscene (Torrey) O'Leary, living in Boston's suburb of Brighton. Her husband was a trolley operator on the B.M.T. line from Boston city center to Watertown, and he was working all through the Great Depression. Aunt Franscene rescued her sister at Christmas by sending toys for Marm's little boys in 1934 and for several more Christmases while we lived in Clam City.

In 1938 we moved to a tiny house that our father had built. It became a prime example of affordable housing, "Great Depression style." There were just two rooms, each eighteen by twelve feet. It had a barn-type roof, so that we could walk around upstairs without banging our heads. There was an outhouse inside Dick's tiny workshop, and there was a picture of the president hanging on the wall, which Dick always said was laxative enough, to put his exact words into more delicate language.

By this time, Garland and I were old enough and big enough to cut a balsam fir all by ourselves, but Marm usually came out to oversee the selection. There were quite a few balsam firs that were always nearby in the woods. It didn't seem to matter to our neighbors if we cut one of their trees. A six-footer was just right for our tiny house, and it was usually erected in the northeast corner of the house, which was oriented east and west to take advantage of solar gain in the wintertime. For

"Affordable housing Great Depression style on a snowy winter c. 1945, from left: Dick's saw-sharpening shop, the old henhouse, our 1938 new home, and the 1929 Chevrolet coach. Dick cut down all these magnificent red-spruce trees shortly after he returned from Connecticut." —CMH

Christmas, our first cousin Erma (Howard) Weed gave us some hand-knitted woolen socks, which should have made us very pleased, but little boys wish for toys! The woolen calf-length socks were very warm in our L.L.Bean leather-topped rubbers, which we wore to school on the coldest winter days.

11. THE 1930s

Franklin Delano Roosevelt's cabinet of thinkers would try something, and if it worked, fine! Let's keep it! Under the WPA, many projects were begun. Bridges were built connecting islands in the Northwest to the mainland. The results of many projects are still in use. "It wasn't all peaches and cream": the Tacoma Narrows bridge fell down!

Frank McGuire, R. K. Barter and his brother were instigators to have a bridge built connecting Little Deer Isle to the mainland. There was at that time a rudimentary causeway connecting Deer Isle to Little Deer Isle. The suspension bridge idea took hold, and the Deer Isle-Sedgwick bridge, designed and engineered on the same model as the Tacoma Narrows bridge, is still standing; the Bucksport-Prospect suspension

CAPTAIN GEORGE KNOWLTON'S THREE-MASTED SCHOONER AT BARTER'S WHARF UNLOADING COAL ABOUT 1936. THE SCHOONER *WEBSTER* LIES ALONGSIDE, AND THE LOCAL LOBSTER FLEET LIES WEST OF THE TWO SCHOONERS. From a note written by Leroy E. Haskell on the back of the photo on Photo Post Card.

bridge was under construction a little earlier than the Deer Isle Bridge. The new Deer Isle–Sedgwick Bridge was dedicated in 1939.

Lobster fishermen were still using single-cylinder marine engines and homemade wooden traps. "Skeet" McDonald on Isle au Haut called them "poverty crates." Herring fishermen were catching large amounts of fish by shutting off a cove with "twine," sometimes several dories full of nets. Then the fish were "pursed up" in purse seines and loaded into dories by pulling the heavy nets into the dories by hand. My father was part of a crew that caught over fifty thousand bushels of herring in Marsh Cove on Kimball's Island, and he quit because his cousin who owned the "gear" (boats and nets) cheated him out of his fair share payment of the catch. Dick didn't finish school, but he was good at mathematics.

On weekends one of my cousins, Elston Hooper or Dennis Buckminster, my brother Garland and I rowed to one of the nearby islands in the large homemade sixteen-foot, flat-bottomed, white pine skiff, painted "brindle" gray, to explore and sometimes to dig clams for flounder bait, or to take home to add to the family larder.

Robert Carlton Hutchinson, known as Hutch, and I used to crawl into Dad's locked shop down on the shore of the old Knowlton-Haskell homestead through a trap door in the floor, and once we fired up Dad's forge and broiled some snappers (short measure lobsters) on a brass plate over the coal fire. I don't recommend that method, because I got sick enough to throw up! Where did we get the illegal lobsters? We hauled someone's traps down by Devil's Half Acre Island. We didn't take the "keepers," as that would be stealing!

School started right after Labor Day and for a while "Hugh" Barbour brought ice-cold milk to the school, and we children drank it right out of the bottles. That luxury didn't last long. Someone had to pay for it! After that early morning school-day treat, we trudged all the way home for lunch, and back again—till the end of the school day.

Cap'n George Knowlton came into R. K. Barter's Wharf in Stonington with his three-masted schooner, and R. K. Barter had local laborers unloading the anthracite (hard coal). For a short while, Stonington folks tried heating with coal, as it would keep the un-insulated houses warm all night long. However, the coal gases had to be burned off carefully before banking the fire for the night. Our misadventure with anthracite is related later on in this book.

Arthur Barter had many acres of woodlands clearcut for lumber and pulpwood, providing jobs for some of the island folks. He had a sawmill in Deer Isle and produced rough boards for home construction purposes. At that time two-by-fours were nearly exactly two inches by four inches, honest measurements!

Some of the herring carriers were powered by huge Fairbanks and Morse two-cycle diesel, crude-oil engines. Dick went as engineer on the *Christopher*, and someone had introduced bedbugs to the boat. They thrived in the crew's quarters, and Dad brought some home with him. Marm was outraged. She asked around amongst the trusted neighbors and found out how to rid the house of the pestilence. She painted every board on the inside of the upstairs with Kem-Tone, a water-based interior house paint that smothered the bedbug eggs, and after a while we were cleansed of the pests. Dick didn't last long as engineer on the *Christopher*, and Bill Jones tried his hand next at the same job. It was during the time Dad was on the *Christopher* that we got to know Cap'n Ed Knowlton; his little prank is included here later on as well, as published in the *International Haskell Family Society Newsletter* sometime between 2000 and 2006.

At some point in time during the 1930s, the two Dickies tried their hand at lobstering with powerboats. Uncle Elroy had a Hudson Super Six in his lobster boat, and he bought a converted sailing sloop for his brother Leroy, who put a Model T Ford engine in it. My father used telephone batteries that Mr. Murch, the telephone man, gave to him, as they were too weak to operate the old magneto-type hand-crank telephones that were used on Deer Isle into the later years. These batteries were strong enough to operate the Model T Ford ignition system. Once the engine was started with the hand crank, Dick switched it over to run on the magneto. "Jimmie" Gray shimmed up the crankshaft in his Model T Ford boat motor to provide just a tiny clearance between the field coils and the whirling magnets that were the heart of the Ford magneto and produced the electricity to fire the sparkplugs on the Ford engine. Gordon "Gumper" Gray told me about his dad's engine, as he visited us in late June of 2009. We sat on the fog deck and told stories for an hour or so. I saw that Gumper's feet were itching back and forth on the decking and realized he was ready to leave. He promised to come back and pick some blueberries, but the weather was wet and foggy ever since his visit.

12. THE DEPRESSION YEARS

In less than five months after I was born, our little family moved to what used to be the McLeans' tiny house (already referred to above) on the gravel-surfaced Clam City Road, which is now called the Indian Point Road—but for all the folks who grew up there, it will always be Clam City. Eventually I knew everyone who lived there in the 1930s, except "Underbrush" Sawyer, the local game warden. He lived high up on a granite monolith upthrust surrounded by tall red-spruce trees. Only the very top of the roof's pointed tower was visible through gaps in the treetops from the road below. There was a small wooden garage near the bottom of their gravel-surfaced driveway, and in the garage was a beautiful red 1931 Pontiac coupe. Across the Clam City Road there were at that time three small red buildings that belonged to the town of Stonington, and in the very west one, lived Bill Jones and his bride Evelyn (Knowlton) Jones and their three children, Herbert, Vera, and Collis. Herb was building model airplanes, and eventually he became a pilot, flying military versions of the Piper Company planes in Korea during that forgotten war. Vera married my distant cousin, Owen Billings, who descended from John Jackson Billings and his wife, Rhoda Ann Eaton. Collis was two months older than me.

Collis and I used to walk to school together, down Thurlow's Hill. Sometimes we climbed on the quarried granite cliff that was created by removing granite blocks to make a roadway down the hillside. We passed along Main Street, which had an open sewer that ran down the hill under the wooden sidewalk and emptied into Stonington's harbor. There were several stores along the street. The most memorable was a drugstore that was run by Linnie Billings; then next was Crockett's clothing store, then Marion Haskell's house sitting high above the street behind a granite wall which retained the front lawn. "Maid Marion" never spoke to us children; she was almost aloof and appeared to be very serene! I recently learned that she was a bird watcher. Next, west of her house was Jewett Noyes's drug store, then Ted Boyce's grocery store. We turned right by Ted's store and walked up what is now Pink Street past some tiny houses and Mr. Lumquist's abode. He was a stone-cutter working on Crotch Island. He used to walk up to Webb's Cove on the weekends and fish for flounders from a granite ledge that had a vertical face that was about ten or twelve feet above the clam-flats directly below. He had made a long fishing pole out of a red-spruce sapling, and he hid his fishing gear very carefully up against a red-spruce tree so that it was almost invisible to passing children, or anyone else. He came from Sweden and spoke with a heavy accent. We were somewhat in awe of him. He walked with a limp, due to a skiing accident in his youth. On the left side of Pink Street stood the old red barn which was used later as a basketball gymnasium and dance hall. The street petered out and became a rough wagon road uphill to a yellow house that sat off by itself, and the school children passed right by, intent upon watching their footsteps in the rough pathway that continued uphill and finally emerged in the southeast corner of the schoolyard. There were two very ancient, large white spruce trees at that point in the pathway. Collis and I started school in 1933. I was five years old until December 29th.

There were other schoolchildren living in Clam City; my distant cousin Carolyn Billings lived with her grandparents, Charles Barter and his wife Ida. They had a saltwater farm close to the shore of the Deer Isle Thoroughfare with its beautiful scenery of the islands lying south of the farmstead. Charlie had a lobster boat that seemed to spend most of its time tied directly to Charlie's bait-house dock. The old house is still there, but the ancient cow barn has been replaced with a newer one. There is a neglected henhouse east of the barn, but there haven't been any hens in it for years and years. Carolyn worked in Massachusetts for years and managed to keep the property for her retirement; she lives there alone.

Almost directly across the Clam City Road from Carolyn's driveway there is a house that was built by Myron Shepard, son of Otis and "Nealy" Shepard. He tried lobster fishing. His father built two lobster boats in a little shop that he erected atop the grout pile of broken granite blocks next to Ralph Cook's house that sits near the bottom of the slope downhill from old Cap'n Al Shepard's house. The road turns slightly right at that point and runs along the shore upon granite blocks to make it nearly straight and level.

Otis went lobstering after his wife died. Myron's boat was nearly identical to his father's. It had a Chevrolet six-cylinder car engine for power and a pot hoisting gear made from a Ford or Chevy rear axle assembly. Lawrence "Lump" Cousins converted many of these for lobster fishermen. "Lump" removed one side of the differential housing with an acetylene torch and then welded the differential gears directly to the ring gear, so that it would always turn the remaining axle shaft. He closed the opening with a metal plate welded in place. There was a brass winch head attached to the remaining drive axle, and the driveshaft torque tube was secured to the deck; it ran forward to be driven from the Chevy's water pump and cooling fan crankshaft pulley, which had been modified by welding on another pulley so that the drive belt could be removed while the hoister was not being used to haul lobster traps. I went lobstering with Myron about three mid-winter trips in 1952, I think. He really wanted my father to go as stern-man, "because Dick knew the bottom."

In 1934, sometime after Dick had started working on the roads in FDR's WPA program, there was enough income to afford a forty-cent weekly trip to the movies in the old Opera House for Garland and I. Dr. Lewis Tewksbury ran the movies, and "Iron Man Don Webb" ran the projector. There was a raffle once a week, and anyone who put their name in the raffle can had a chance to win the prize money. However, the person whose name was drawn had to be in the audience. If they were not, I seem to remember that the prize money was increased for the next week's drawing. Dr. Tewksbury climbed up onto the stage and shook the bejabbers out of the large can to make a show of the drawing process; someone from the audience would go up and reach in to withdraw one slip of paper, and Dr. Tewksbury would read off the name. Of course the audience attendance would greatly increase as the monetary amount grew larger!

Dr. Tewksbury retired to California in his old age, and he and his wife drove all the way across the country. The last time I saw him, he had just returned to Stonington in an Oldsmobile, which was limping on a couple of its eight cylinders and smoking as if it was ready for the junk pile.

He had joined with Frank McGuire and others to lobby for a suspension bridge to the mainland, and in 1939 it was completed and dedicated. He must have felt proud and pleased as punch to have had some influence in getting it built.

Stonington didn't have fluorinated water, and Dr. Tewksbury was always busy filling and cleaning teeth for the island's natives. They had two daughters, Norma and Marjorie, who were older and ahead of Garland and me in school.

13. MORE DEPRESSION STORIES

The Great American Depression was at its lowest economic and emotional point during 1933, and about that period of time I have some clear memories. Our family lived in the small four-room wooden house that perched on a granite ledge overlooking the Deer Isle-Stonington Thoroughfare. I fondly recollect watching the marine traffic passing through on its way east to Mt. Desert Island, Swans Island, Frenchboro, and points downeast. I remember a particular sardine carrier that had an enormous Fairbanks and Morse crude-oil engine that made such a loud noise you could hear it for nearly an hour before it came into view. It was one of my favorite childhood nautical noises.

There was a small shed that served my father as a workshop, coal bin, and potato storage area, and the family as a privy. My father was unemployed, as were most of the island's menfolk, except those who worked on the stone quarries or fished in their powered lobster boats. Dad had a fifteen-foot peapod, with which he tended his lobster traps by rowing from trap to trap. He removed the lobsters and crabs, and sometimes he caught a codfish, but usually it was a sculpin, which he used for bait. A healthy man could manage fifty traps with a dory or peapod. The legal-sized lobsters were sold to lobster dealers, and the short lobsters (illegal-sized) sometimes found their way to our kitchen table. They tasted just as good as the legal-sized *homards*. On other days he cut firewood for one of the lobster fishermen who owned a huge woodlot. Father cut the wood on shares, which means that if he cut ten cords of wood, half of it went to the property owner and the other half belonged to my father to do with as he pleased.

My great-aunt Rhoda and her husband owned the little house we lived in. During the spring and summer months, she would bring one cow down to browse on the grass that grew amongst the glacial erratic boulders left during the last glaciation. She tethered the cow to a metal bar, driven into the ground in a different spot each day, and bossy effectively mowed the grass in a circle around the crowbar. Therefore, we had an excellent view out over the field and beyond to the many spruce-forested islands that lie south of Stonington. Some were and still are as barren as a Newfoundland southwest hillside.

My favorite birds were the song sparrows. They arrived in the spring and sang beautifully while perched in the pasture rose bushes and scrub surrounding the little house.

My brother is thirteen months younger than I, and we explored the granite ledges at the edge of the sea, played imaginary boats using the empty half of mussel shells to plow through the gravel on the mini beach at the bottom of the field. The playing was accompanied by sound effects imitating the engines of lobster boats. Sometimes we fished for flounders from an old stone quarry wharf, which belonged to a family that lived along the shore, east of us.

During the spring and summer months, we sometimes explored along the waterfront, beachcombing for any item that took our fancy. In the fall, some boats were hauled up on the bank of a small stream, where they rested clear of the winter's ice. The family who owned the saltwater farm used oxen to till the soil and to do a lot of the heavy work. The menfolk rigged tackle to haul the boats, and the two oxen pulled them slowly up the slope, where they rested in cradles all winter. Sometimes the three brothers erected snow houses on the vessels to keep snow and ice out of the bottoms, where due to freezing, expanding bilgewater could start a plank (force it away from its fastenings).

My distant cousin (we had the same great-grandfather) lived in the old, rambling house next door (to the east). I sometimes picked my way through the many granite boulders on a rough and irregular path to play games with her on the lawn. Her grandfather had a lobster boat with a motor, and he liked to work on jigsaw puzzles, which were glued to a large piece of cardboard when they were finished, framed and hung on a wall, just like a painting. I remember that they ate in the continental style, and after dishes were washed, the cups were put back on the table upside-down in their saucers, and the plates were placed at each place setting, upside-down as well.

That fall I started school in the first grade and walked to classes along the gravel road that wound around the shore. In places it was very uneven and rough. There was and still is a place where the granite ledges at the side of the road had been drilled, the holes filled with dynamite and blasted to bits in order to make a cart-way. The whole journey was approximately thirty minutes in duration. I soon emulated the other children and walked up through the woods to enter the school

grounds from the rear. The building was erected on quarried granite
blocks, which were hoisted and mortared together on a granite ledge to
form a very solid foundation, I'm sure. The first classroom was located
in the southeast corner of the first floor. I remember experiencing the
effects of solar gain, as the warmth of the sun's rays through the very tall
windows could be felt on sunny days.

Our first-grade teacher was tall and thin. She wore her dark hair in
a bun. She was the daughter of Charles Dority, the senior blacksmith
who worked on the John L. Goss granite quarry—which was located
on Crotch Island, a massive monolith, which at one time rose over two
hundred feet above the surrounding waters of East Penobscot Bay.

Summer waned, and with the arrival of fall weather Dad brought out
and cleaned his shotgun. Equipped with his lunch pail, twenty-gauge
Remington, and warm clothes, he went duck hunting. He would swap
a duck for shotgun shells with his friends and some trusted neighbors.
There was absolutely no money in the family coffers, and barter was a
way of life for most of the residents on the island.

My father's half-sister gave an old woolen coat to my mother, who
"cut it down" with scissors and with needle and thread made a winter
coat for me to wear to school. I remember that somehow I had a Lind-
bergh-type aviator's helmet, which had earmuff flaps that fastened under
my chin. One very cold day I trudged off to school, wrapped up like a
mummy, in a woolen scarf and homemade mittens. I walked my solitary
route to school, and when I arrived there were just five other children
in attendance. These children lived in the cluster of houses immediately
west of the schoolhouse, called Gray Town. After a while someone decided to send us home, as there weren't enough pupils to start classes.

Meanwhile, my great-aunt Rhoda had walked down to our little
abode to gently admonish my mother, "Gracious, Mill, you didn't send
that child to school today, did you? It's twenty-nine below zero, deah!"
(The island's natives had a particular cadence and rhythm in their speech
pattern. It will gradually disappear as the effects of national television's
standardized speech are adopted by the newer generations.)

The Settlement Quarry, located in Webb's cove, was trying to get a
shipment of stone out on a barge for the "Fuller job." The Thoroughfare
was frozen so thickly that the tugboat couldn't tow the barge in to the
dock. Workmen blasted a channel with dynamite, and the tug and barge
inched into the wharf. The derricks and hoisting engines ran on steam,
and the barge was soon loaded for the trip to New York, but the channel
had refrozen, and a new passageway had to be blasted.

Normally, the quarries were shut down in winter. The lobstermen kept busy during the winter months building new traps and hunting for suitable red-spruce limbs, out of which they made the lobster-trap bows. Dad bent the roughly hewed limbs around a homemade form and forced the ends into holes bored into spruce-bottom crosspieces. Once he had made three crudely uniform bows and cross pieces, he fastened them to the bed logs and set the trap bows onto a spruce sapling, which was fastened to the wall of the shop. The free end of the sapling was then supported by a forked branch, one end of which fitted into a hole in the floor, making a sort of horse. Spruce laths were nailed to the green wood parallel to the bed pieces and spaced evenly using a wooden gauge. A door was constructed of pieces of spruce crudely hewn to a curved shape to match the radius of the bows and fastened to the trap with pieces of old tires or leather to serve as hinges. The lobster fishermen knitted bait pockets (bags, closed with a drawstring) and pot heads (the funnel-shaped entrance nets which were laced into the traps with twine).

Not every day was spent building traps. Sometimes snowstorms left the town roads impassable in places, where the drifted snow packed in very solidly. The trucks of that time didn't have the enormous power of today, and these places had to be shoveled out by hand. My father and the young man next door walked down to the nearest snow-drifted area and shoveled the snow into the ocean, which was right at hand. Then they walked "downtown" to shovel the sidewalks and other areas clear. Perhaps they earned fifty cents each!

In the wintertime one could dig clams if one knew how to get a little open area of clam-flats next to a tumbled ice cake. My father walked up to Tea Hill, where his mother lived, and went down to the shore and eventually found enough clams for a meal. He wrapped the clams in burlap sacking to keep them from freezing while he walked home again. Sometimes Dad would chop a hole in the saltwater ice and spear flounders that were hibernating in the mud on the bottom of the cove. He threw them onto the ice to freeze, which made them easier to skin.

Eventually spring arrived; the ice broke up in Webb's Cove, and there were clams and mussels to be harvested and more flounders to be speared, as their outline was easily seen while we glided along in the peapod searching for these succulent fish. In May, smelts came into the brooks to spawn, and we caught them with our hands. They were delicious sautéed in butter, which Aunt Rhoda gave us. She was truly rich with three cows.

In 1935 the Roosevelt administration started the WPA program (Works Progress Administration), and Dad got the job working on the roads. The local economy stuttered along; coasting schooners came into Barter's Wharf and unloaded coal. All the work was done by hand except the hoisting, which was accomplished with the aid of a stationary engine banging away on deck. My brother and I were mere spectators of these industries. Coasting schooners carried great loads of firewood to be unloaded onto wharfs made of the local granite shored up with spruce pilings driven into the ocean bottom by pile-drivers, which were powered by the ubiquitous stationary engines.

14. THE LOCAL BANK FAILURE

Months after Dick (my father) was hit by the car, he walked across the Shepard Family's apple orchard to see our Clam City neighbor, Henry Eaton, to ask Henry to take him back on the quarrying gang. But the boss quarryman said, in a scolding tone, "You can't work, you're still sick!" Ironically, Henry died a little later, and in 1937 Dick bought his 1928 Chevrolet coach for five dollars. The Chevy had since been in a tiny wooden garage. His widow and daughters didn't know how to drive. Dick pumped up the nearly flat tires and fussed and fussed with the little four-cylinder Chevy. Finally one day he cranked it up with the hand crank, and it belched smoke and noise. Dick put the transmission in gear, and the old car lurched out into the driveway.

We subsisted on dandy-lion greens, wild berries, wild apples, clams, mussels, periwinkles, lobsters, odd jobs for dad, and fish. At any rate, Dick cut pulpwood for Ted Boyce, one of the local grocery-store small businessmen who let our grocery bill accumulate over each winter all through the Great American Depression. Somehow, Dick could find enough odd jobs and income from lobstering, using a rowboat and homemade lobster traps. He earned just enough money to pay off his accumulated winter's grocery bill each summer.

Meanwhile, after the stock market collapsed in 1929, some of our relatives who were yacht captains and/or crew members were also out of jobs. In 1933 our new president, Franklin D. Roosevelt, declared a four-day bank holiday and shut down the nation's banks. Grammie Haskell lost her entire savings. The local bank asked the depositors to surrender their life savings, so that the Bank could recover. From that time onward, she kept what meager savings that built up over time in an empty coffee can, which she hid away for safe-keeping. My great-uncle Arthur, Grammie's brother, kept his entire life savings in his pocket, and one day he lost his wallet with a considerable amount of cash. It was almost comical to see him walking around looking at the ground in hopes that his treasure would suddenly reappear. That particular bank recovered somewhat when President Roosevelt's Banking Act created the Federal Deposit Insurance Corporation, which guaranteed individual bank deposits up to $5,000.

Meanwhile, some of the town's money disappeared. My uncle Robert McGuffie, by marriage, was the first selectman. He was framed and sent to jail in Ellsworth, Maine. Amazingly, citizen Calvin Ames, the last one you would expect to go out of his way to help anyone, went around from house to house, gathering signatures on a petition that pleaded that our uncle's trial was not fair. Eventually my uncle was released, after the petition was presented to the court. My uncle's reputation was nearly worthless; he was dismissed from the Stonington school's mathematics teaching position and could not return. So he rigged up to go lobstering, with help from the two Dickies, Leroy and Elroy. My uncle by marriage continued to fish for the rest of his working days, until a stroke felled him. No longer able to work at lobstering, he shortly passed away.

Some of the townspeople who had lost their savings in 1933 felt that once burned, if you will, they never deposited a penny after that. In the late 1940s, my uncle Elroy had returned to the island and become the night fireman at the John L. Goss granite quarry. He cruised over to the quarry on Crotch Island in his home-built, sixteen-foot, outboard-powered skiff. He kept the three boilers' fires banked all night and had steam up in the morning, so that when Howard Haskell stepped off the *J. Douglas* quarry boat, the boilers were ready for Howard and me. Also ready were the steam-powered air compressors, the steam turbine to generate direct current to power the gang saws, the overhead crane, circular stone saw, and other pieces of equipment.

One day Uncle Elroy and I were driving somewhere in his new Buick Super, and he bragged that he had $7,000 in his wallet. So I demanded that we drive to Bar Harbor and deposit the whole works in that bank, which had not failed in 1933. Of course, he was reluctant to do that, so I said, "If someone hits ya upside th' head, ya won't have a penny left." Finally convinced, he drove to Mt. Desert and on to the Bar Harbor Bank and presently "Uncle Dunk" was a depositor with a brand-new savings book. I had to remind him that his uncle had lost his wallet and all his savings in one shot! At the present time there are two banks on Deer Isle, the Union Trust in Stonington, and Bar Harbor Banking and Trust in Deer Isle.

15. THE SWING

When my father's older half-brother, Raymond Knowlton, came all the way from Los Angeles, California, by train to Rockland, Maine, then by the local Eastern Steamship Line to Stonington in 1932, he brought his son Drexel with him; my father and Drexel made a swing by tying a large spruce pole between two tall red-spruce trees. They cut off all the branches on the opposing sides so that there would be a clear path for the swing to operate. The pine board seat was suspended from the horizontal beam on three-quarter-inch manila line, sturdy enough to support any human being. I was four years and eight months old about the time they decided to hoist me into the swing. They hauled the wooden board seat way up the hillside and let me go. I swung in an arc and was catapulted out over the hillside like a stone from David's sling. My trajectory flight ended in the brush pile created by their limbing-up operation, which cushioned my fall somewhat. But to this day I remember the terrifically numbing pain that immobilized me for a moment or two. Meanwhile, Dad came running down the hill to see if I had been killed. Of course, as feelings returned to my numbed little body, I began to wail! Dad picked me up and hugged me to him, but I kept crying because I was in pain. From that day to this I was never happy to be in a swing.

16. THE BEAR AND ME

When I was about three years old, my mother, Charlotte Mildred (Torrey) Haskell, kept telling me, "Don't go up into the woods; there's a bear up there." Marm used to tie me to the clothesline like a tethered cow, and I could move back and forth with the loop of tether sliding along the length of clothesline. Eventually I was allowed to roam about. There was almost no automotive traffic on the Clam City Road. Once in a while Walden Ames would trundle noisily by with his ox team carrying a granite foundation block on a crude two-wheeled cart. The destination of these quarried stones is covered in a story about Lewis Sawyer's house foundation later in this book.

Little folks are apt to be curious enough to go find out what a bear is, and true to form, one day Marm didn't hear me making boat noises or humming; she couldn't see me outside anywhere, and she soon began to search high and low. She eventually enlisted the neighbors, and still I was not found. Myron Shepard, who lived in the house south of ours and right upon the shore just a

AUTHOR C. 1930, LOOKING FOR BEAR, IN FRONT OF CAP'N AL SHEPARD'S HOUSE AND BARN.

few yards up above the Thoroughfare and high spring tides, searched along the shore to where the high granite rock formations ended in steep nearly vertical cliffs. Still I was not found.

Eventually someone ventured a query, "Did anyone look up in the woods?" There I was found, sitting on a flat-topped spruce stump. When I was asked why I was up there all alone, I replied, "I wanted to see th' bear!"

We lived in a time of rural innocence; children were allowed to roam unchallenged by the neighbors, who quietly accepted our adventures and explorations, noting carefully that so-and-so went down to the shore with another child—and they might also make sure that they knew when the children returned or did not return. We never ventured very far from home.

Ida Barter frequently warned us, "Do not go near that well in the field, because if you fall in, we can never get you out!" So Carolyn Billings, my brother Garland and I would lie flat on our bellies and crawl over to look

GARLAND (LEFT) AND AUTHOR, 1935.

down into the well. I seem to remember that just one peek was enough to quell any curiosity of what a well really was. It was very deep and very, very dark down there.

We did venture as far as the Ames Brothers granite quarry, which was surrounded by alders, and the quarry hole was filled with dark-brown water, which looked deep and forbidding. We were quite content to peer over the plant growth and never tried to get down into the quarry hole. There was a granite block wharf south of the quarry, where the Ames brothers might have shipped paving blocks or other stone workings by coasting schooner. But by 1933 all signs of a loading derrick were gone. Possibly, the crew of a coasting schooner could load granite blocks using a boom and backstay rigging. By that time most of the schooners had single-cylinder gasoline stationary engines for such purposes.

Marm, on the other hand, had to wash diapers and clothes with a wooden scrub board, a large galvanized tub, a rain barrel, and another wooden tub to which a hand-cranked wringer was attached. We were amazed to see cousin Amy (Shepard) Morey doing her laundry with a Maytag washer powered by a tiny single-cylinder gasoline engine. However, FDR's Rural Electrification Act changed everything: stay tuned for further developments.

17. PLAY AND WORK

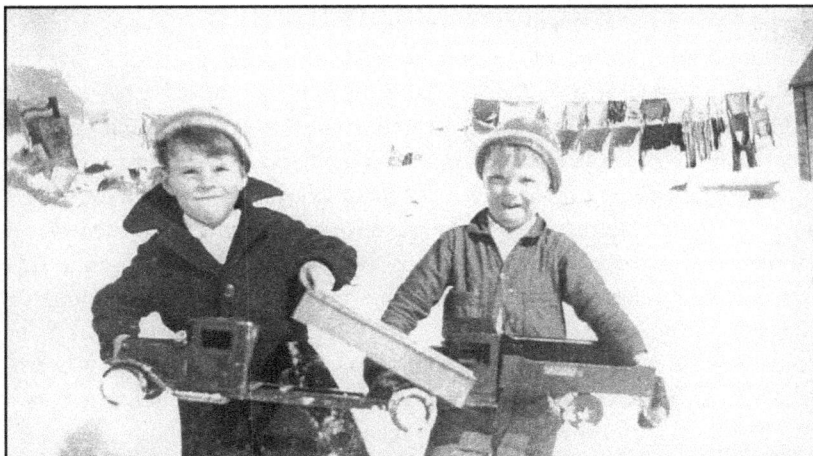

AUTHOR WEARING AUNT ETHEL'S CUT-DOWN WOOLEN COAT WITH THE HUGE
LAPELS STICKING OUT SIDEWAYS. GARLAND WEARING SOME SEARS ROEBUCK
CLOTHES, SHOWING OFF OUR CHRISTMAS 1934 PRESENTS FROM AUNT FRANSCENE
O'LEARY AT THE OLD McLEAN HOUSE ON THE CLAM CITY ROAD. THE LAUNDRY
HANGING OUT BETWEEN THE OUTHOUSE AND THE McLEAN'S TINY WOODSHED.

FOUR LITTLE COUSINS, ALL DESCENDED FROM JOHN JACKSON BILLINGS (FROM
LEFT): CAROLYN BILLINGS WITH A HUGE RED BOW IN HER HAIR, CARROLL AND
GARLAND HASKELL, SHIRLEY SHEPARD. ALL FOUR ARE SITTING ON A WOODEN
LADDER, APPLE TREES IN THE BACKGROUND.

My distant cousin Carolyn Billings (we descended from the same great-grandfather) lived in the old rambling house next door; I sometimes picked my way through the many granite boulders on a rough and irregular path to play games with her on the lawn. Her grandfather "Charlie" Barter had a lobster boat with a motor.

Illumination in the old Barter homestead was by oil lamps. Usually houses had at least one Aladdin lamp, which had an asbestos mantle; once it had become thoroughly heated, it glowed with a much brighter light than the older and more common cotton-wicked oil lamps.

There wasn't any refrigeration in most houses, because there wasn't any electricity. There weren't any vacuum cleaners, or powered water pumps. Almost everything was done by hand. I think that once this family had owned a cow or two—but not when I was a youngster. Carolyn had a swing in the barn, where she could entertain herself on cold or rainy days. There was an old tobacco can up on top of a beam, which held some crystals that had been collected and saved; one was a large amethyst, and the others were yellowish quartz crystals.

In the late summer of 1933, my mother realized that I would need a winter coat to wear to school. My father's half-sister Ethel had a long navy-blue coat which Marm "cut down" and modified to fit me, using her new Singer foot-pedal-operated sewing machine.

Sometime during 1934, a man came and repossessed the sewing machine. My mother was outraged; she owed five dollars on it, and there wasn't a penny in the house. Years and years later the same man, selling something door-to-door, knocked and introduced himself. Marm was angry in an instant. "I remember you! You came and took my sewing machine, and it was all paid for except for five dollars! I'm goin' to get on the phone, Mistah! An' you won't sell anythin' on this island!" She took great pleasure in telling him off.

18. THE NEW DEAL YEARS
FROM MY FATHER'S JOURNALS

After a while I got a job on John L. Goss granite quarry again, working in the quarry while waiting for the *Eugenie Spofford* to be assigned a barge or something to tow. The quarry wasn't getting many orders for stone, and it shut down during the winter.

Working in the quarry was brutal, and the air was always full of stone dust. If one smoked, his lungs soon filled with the dust, which then adhered to the nicotine tars and exacerbated the threat of silicosis, a certain death, the same as black lung in coal mines.

I got sick with appendicitis. I hadn't felt well for some time and after lying on my bed for four days had to be taken to the hospital. I was there twenty-one days before they got me on my feet. I had spent what money I had, which wasn't much, because I hadn't worked since autumn. I had just $42 when winter set in and didn't know where the next meal was coming from. When I went to the store after stuff to eat, I could only look at it.

Finally, I got a job cutting wood for Ted Boyce in the woods off Long Cove in Deer Isle. It was about a five-mile walk each way. It was difficult, but I accepted it. I thought I could cut enough so we could eat anyway. I worked almost every day all through the winter, and in the spring I found that we had eaten all winter. I didn't owe too much, but I had no money at all.

I had to go looking for a job. I hunted the house high and low to see if I could find two or three pennies to buy a daily paper to look up want ads. There wasn't one penny down behind the furniture or anywhere in the house. I found nothing and no job either, so I dug clams and did numerous other odd jobs.

Winter came on again. I was lucky that my boys liked rolled oats. I went down to the Town Office and got some Federal Aid stuff: cornmeal, rolled oats, flour, and bacon. I was so ashamed to be seen getting relief food that I didn't go back for anymore.

On July 23rd, 1934, my youngest son, Leon Curtis Haskell, was born. On May 6th 1935, the Franklin D. Roosevelt administration created the Works Progress Administration (WPA) by executive order, and shortly after that I got a job working on the roads. "Wink" was my lucky baby!

Leon, "Wink," was born at the Sand Beach Farm. My mother went over there to have Garland, and Dick stayed in the McLean House alone for both Garland and Leon's births.

Dick's wonderful 1924 Model T Ford "telephone-booth coupe" was stored in the forge-cum-boathouse-and-shop on the Webb's Cove shore of the old Knowlton-Haskell Homestead until long after Wink was born.

I remember riding on the homemade pickup-truck-type wooden

cargo bed and peering out past the sides of the coupe and having to duck in again as alders whipped past the Ford's hurtling progress along the rough graveled roadway, because an alder slapping into our faces stung quite painfully. We were going to visit my mother's father, Madison Torrey, who had a steer!

Garland and I were afraid of the big black beast! Grandfather invited us to stay for "suppah" as he hauled a cast-iron spider (frying pan) out from under a bale of hay. Dick declined his offer, and we were soon bouncing and jolting along the rough Reach Road again toward home.

I only remember seeing my mother's father once more, when he was very ill with diabetes and staying with his oldest daughter, Geneva (Torrey) Howard, in 1938. Madison passed away there and was interred in the Reach Cemetery, downhill behind the Forest Hill Cemetery, which is very close to the old Reach Road.

19. Grammie Haskell and the Auld Knowlton Homestead

The "auld" Knowlton-Haskell Homestead was built upon a granite formation. I assume that Walden Ames and his brothers laid up the granite block foundation directly onto the granite formation which sloped downhill southward toward Clam City. Gravel from the Ames gravel pit was hauled up to the foundation and backfilled on the north side of the foundation to make a nearly level yard between the house and some granite boulders that roughly formed the north property line.

The east side of the foundation had a rough granite wall, which was erected about eight feet east of and parallel with the house foundation, and the void between this granite wall and the foundation's east wall was also filled with gravel.

A set of granite steps was built into the retaining wall and is still used today to get down to the sloping subsistence garden. The western and southern sides were also filled with gravel but were not level by any means. A set of granite steps let into the west wall provided access to the basement, and a roughly-built cover kept the rain and snow out of the basement. A rude granite wall kept the steeply sloping south embankment from running down into the apple orchard. The apple orchard had a damson plum tree and three pear trees planted in a north-to-south line. My favorite apple was the Red Astrachan, which was the second tree south of the retaining wall. There was a sour apple tree just south of this retaining wall. I suppose Grammie fed its fruit to the pig, which resided in a crude little barn that was built south of the retaining wall. Grammie (Mary Jane [Billings] Knowlton Haskell) kept a Jersey cow and one pig in the tiny barn. Hay was stored in the loft of the barn for the cow's winter feed. A little south of the barn, there was an even cruder chicken coop, where nearly two dozen mostly Rhode Island Red hens were kept to provide eggs for the subsistence farm's kitchen; any surplus eggs were carried down to Stonington's main street stores for credit toward kitchen supplies. Thanksgiving dinner was almost surely a large hen. Only Leo Turley on the North Main Street farm had a turkey, which was a family pet when Garland and I were exploring the neighborhoods. Mary Turley was especially fond of children and would ask us to come see the "turkey gobbler."

The Knowlton-Haskell house had a tiny bedroom on the first floor in the northwest corner. There was a rudimentary kitchen under the

OLD HASKELL-KNOWLTON HOMESTEAD C. 1908, FROM LEFT, FRONT ROW: ELROY FREEMAN, CHRISTIE MAE, LEROY ELMER HASKELL; BACK ROW: FLORENCE AND ETHEL KNOWLTON, FREEMAN CHARLES AND MARY JANE (BILLINGS) KNOWLTON HASKELL; IN FRONT OF THE HENRY ALBERT KNOWLTON HOUSE, WHICH BECAME THE HASKELL FAMILY HOMESTEAD ON 17 DECEMBER 1894, WHEN FREEMAN AND MARY JANE WERE MARRIED IN GREEN'S LANDING (RENAMED STONINGTON).

stairway to the second floor. This stairway was very steep, built onto the north inside wall, and ran from just inside the northeast corner's outside door, which provided the main entrance from the gravel-surfaced road that ran uphill to Ralph Knowlton's cow-fence gate. There was also a gate at the north fence line of the Knowlton-Haskell homestead.

There was a parlor in the southeast corner of the house, where there was a parlor organ, which our first cousin Marie Hooper played while pumping on the foot-pedal bellows. Dick had bought an Atwater Kent crystal radio set, which was built into a handsome wooden cabinet. The cabinet now serves as a pots-and-pans storage place at our old homestead. There was a larger room west of the parlor where a cast-iron kitchen stove resided, and its sheet-metal smokestack was sealed into the centrally located brick chimney.

Tucked onto the south side of the house was a washing shed, where the laundry was done by hand in wooden tubs equipped with a hand-operated wringer, and there was an ironing board. Flatirons were heated on the woodstove and would retain heat for quite some time. My aunt Ethel made soap using saved cooking fat and lye. She put the ashes from the woodstove into a V-shaped wooden trough and poured hot water over the ashes, which leached out into an iron pot. The whole works was heated on the cast-iron stove, and eventually she turned out a dark, russet-colored mass that when cooled could be broken into roughly shaped hunks of laundry soap. This soap was not recommended for tender skins!

I don't remember eating at Grammie Haskell's house very often, but when we did we soon learned not to reach for anything, as Grammie would give us a sharp rap on the knuckles with a table knife and the admonition, "You must say, 'Please pass the butter'!" or whatever we had reached for. She was a tiny person and could not leave well enough alone. I remember one day Dick had gone to the grocery store for supplies in his shiny black 1924 Model T Ford. Dick was carrying in some things and Grammie just had to help and somehow a half-gallon glass jug of molasses fell onto the floor and broke, molasses thickly spreading across the wooden flooring. Grammie quickly scraped it all up into a wash pan and saved almost every drop, broken glass and all.

At that time, about 1932, Uncle Elroy had separated from Christine (Terry) Haskell, and Freda, their daughter, was living with our Grandmother. I remember Aunt Ethel's sourdough bread. We really enjoyed the coarse, crusty bread, whether it was buttered or not. There were dried fish stored up in the hayloft, and we boys would grab a handful of dried smelts and run off to the shore to play in the old *Squid* or romp around on the Old Indian Trail, which ran out around Phoebe Thurston's Point all the way to the Ames' subsistence farm.

Garland and I walked up from Clam City through the woods to find Grammie lying in a coma on a couch in the dining room. Aunt Ethel wanted us to kiss Grammie goodbye, but we were too young to understand the situation and declined. Mary Jane Billings Knowlton Haskell passed away on November 5th, 1937, and Aunt Ethel found herself volunteering to raise the two orphans, Elston and Marie Hooper, by herself. She must have had a difficult time. I remember her making soap and doing the laundry in the shed-like extension on the south side of the house. She kept a vegetable garden and watered it from a spring, which was a long walk down the hill and through a path in the spruce forest. The spring was located under a granite ledge and about ten feet above the salt water in the cove. We used to drink from it every time that we passed along the Indian Trail. Sometime after the 1950s, someone bought the property where the spring is located and had it deepened and walled up inside with imperfect paving stones taken from a "paving motion" quarry somewhere on the island.*

He built a house on the high ground above the high tide line and had the spring water piped into the house.

Grandfather Freeman sent the two oldest stepsons to Rockland, Maine, where they studied to become accountants. Upon graduating they both traveled by the new transcontinental railroad to California, the Golden State, and became very successful.

Eventually, sometime after 1938, both Turleys passed away, and

---

*The term "paving motion" was earned in the early colonial period. Some of the new settlers quarried granite and made paving blocks from the quarried stone, which were carried as payload or as ballast on trips down the coast to be sold in Boston, New York, and even as far south as Philadelphia. The stones were hauled out to the Green's Landing docks by the easiest route, which wasn't necessarily the shortest. There is at least one abandoned paving motion in Webb's Cove, so conveniently located in relation to the water that the paving stones could be loaded directly into the ship by hand. Some industrious families built a small sloop of shallow draft and wide of beam to carry their load of stone to market. Money in the colonial period was very hard to come by. Perhaps their loads of stone were paid for in letters of credit to more local Maine banks. In any event, the small family paving motions were abandoned, sometime after larger quarries were opened on several of the offshore Maine islands. See Chapter 96.

Will Saunders lived on that tiny farm after that. The north end of the farmhouse was rented out to Peter Billings and his bride, Helene (Burns) Billings. Helene came from Swans Island. Sometime after 1947, the old Turley farmhouse burned to the ground, and Peter and Helene Billings moved to a house just off of the Oceanville Road, very near her sister Charlene, who married Ralph Carter. To this day they have lived side by side in separate houses, both houses facing toward the inner protected harbor formed within Webb's Cove. Ralph's house is up on the side of a hill and lies southwest of Helene's house.

But I digress. Downhill toward the westerly side of Webb's Cove, my father built a boat-shed-cum-blacksmith's forge, which was equipped with a woodworking vise and long pine-board work benches, with empty dynamite boxes serving as storage places for salvaged marine-engine parts. There was a rough driftwood platform overhead, where Dad kept blacksmith's flux in a paper bag, which was also stored in a wooden box. Also he kept a supply of fuller's earth to make sealing putty for boat planking seams, when mixed with a little linseed oil and a dollop of Japan dryer. Dad would make knives and tools using his forge, which was fired with coal salvaged from the railroad tracks on the remains of the Settlement Quarry.

Eventually all the tracks were removed and carried over to the Deer Isle Granite Quarry. The old steam launch, *Minnehaha*, had been hauled up onto a nearly flat-surfaced granite ledge that sloped down to Webb's Cove. The ledge is just east of the Settlement Quarry's grout pile. The old boat was laid up there on two parallel railroad tracks. We little boys used to climb up into the boat and make imaginary trips while steering the old boat with its seemingly huge steering wheel. There was a single-cylinder steam engine located about midship, and a vertical boiler provided the steam. There was a photograph, which appeared in the *Island Ad-Vantages* at some time—possibly in an article by Clayton Gross, one of our local authors—of the *Minnehaha* floating astern of a large schooner, loading stone at the old Settlement Quarry's dock.

20. THE FIFTY-CENT PIECE

In April of 1928, Dick (Leroy) thought that he would do better in a house that was at that time owned by Captain Al Shepard. It was that tiny thing perched upon a nearly-flat granite monolith (a "ledge" for the natives). I was just over three months old. Cap'n Al had married my great-aunt Rhoda (Billings) Shepard, and she was very kind to us. There was a substantial apple orchard between Henry's driveway and Otis's cow barn. We had a terrific view out over the rough pasture toward Isle au Haut. There were other islands just across the Thoroughfare: Scott, Green, and Russ Islands.

My brother Garland Leroy was born in January 1929 at the Sand Beach Farm, as stated, which overlooks a beautiful view of the islands west of Stonington, on the south end of Deer Isle. It was an excellent spot to watch the beautiful sunsets over the Camden Hills quite some distance west of Stonington.

The Great Depression settled in around Deer Isle, and Christmas in 1933 was especially bare, but Marm had a sister Franscene in Brighton, a suburb of Boston. She had married the Irishman from County Cork, and he had a job all during that economic hard-times period. Aunt Franscene sent inexpensive toys for boys for several Christmases. Then along came the WPA, and Dick got the job working on the roads, exclaiming when my youngest brother was born in July 1934, "Leon Curtis is my lucky baby, because I got a job!"

The causeway from Deer Isle to Little Deer Isle was improved and raised high enough to be useable at any stage of the tides. Dick advised the foreman to follow the natural lay of the sand bars, "because if you make it straight, it will be used as a racetrack!"

"Well o' course," as Hez Robbins would say, it was used as a racetrack anyway! There have been several accidents on the causeway, and sometimes the vehicles ran off the roadbed down over the rough stone foundations into the sea water.

Global warming has raised the sea level and the Deer Isle to Little Deer Isle causeway will have to be raised again, possibly in my remaining lifetime! We will soon see!

Garland and I were taken up to Aunt Geneva Howard's while Marm was at the Sand Beach Farm. Aunt "Geedy" was a great cook and loved little boys; she had two daughters, Erma and Delma. Erma Howard married Fulton Weed. Delma Howard married Raymond Weed. I remember that Delma showed us how to catch lightning bugs out in the pasture behind their childhood home.

It had a kitchen hand pump that drew water from the well quite some distance behind the house. We were fascinated with the cast-iron clanking and banging noises as Uncle Harold pumped water vigorously into a pot or bucket in the sink below the pump spout.

The house had an attached cow barn, and Aunt Geedy milked her little Jersey cow all by herself.

Across the street was a house built by Cap'n Mark Haskell, Jr. in the early 1800s (I am told), and it stands today, a little worse for wear. Ralph Haskell lived there in 1934 with his wife and two daughters, Judyth "Peg" and Janice Haskell.

One day after we had returned to Clam City, I wanted to go downtown and buy a milkshake. Dick had left his pants on a chair, and I rummaged around in his pockets and found a half-dollar coin. So I trudged down to Jewett Noyes's drugstore, which had a nice serpentine "marble" soda fountain. Possibly the stone came from the "marble quarry" on the Reach Road. It was a beautiful addition to the store, at any rate. I asked Vera Shepard to make me a milkshake and passed her the coin. She immediately looked at it and asked me where I had gotten it. I didn't have a convincing story, and she kept the fifty-cent piece, which she returned to Dad after he came home. Of course I was dismayed and didn't realize that I had stolen it. So I traipsed all the way back to the little house, pausing to admire the coasting schooners in the cove just east of what is now the Lobster Co-op and dilly-dallying along the way. Marm was only curious as to where I "had disappeared to." But I was soon lectured on taking anything without permission from anyone.

21. SECOND GRADE AND SURVIVING

At that time children started school in the first grade, and I walked to class along the gravel road that wound along the shore for a short distance, providing a view of the three beautiful coasting schooners and out past the islands of Stonington harbor. Rugosa roses grew wild in spots, and there were still some late blossoms. There was the place where the granite ledges at the side of the road had been drilled, the holes filled with dynamite and blasted to bits in order to make a cart-way. The evidence of this work may be seen today, opposite what used to be "Cookie's house" (Ralph Cook). I'd walk along the gravel-surfaced road for a few minutes, turn right at Boyce's store and on up through the woods like the rest of the children, past a small single-story house which may no longer exist, to enter the school grounds from the south and rear. The old Stonington school was finally closed and the classes all moved to North Deer Isle in February, 2001.

It was on a fall day of 1933 that my dad, his brother, Elroy, and the blacksmith by Ed Hardy, who worked on the stone quarry, rowed down to Devil's Island for rabbits. They had taken a fisherman's-style foghorn and stationed themselves in spots to favor clear shooting. There followed the story that was often repeated, the snowshoe hares hopping around, and the shooting began. There may have been daily bag limits, but we never forgot that Dad brought home a huge pile of rabbits, which he cleaned and then salted down in an empty salt-pork barrel that he scrounged from Ted Boyce.

We didn't have any money, but we did have food. We islanders didn't know how good our lives were compared to the rest of the country. We had short lobsters once in a while, lots of flounders and salted codfish, an occasional freshly-caught haddock, crabs, scallops, mussels, and periwinkles, dandelion greens, wild apples, dried codfish, homegrown potatoes, turnips, and other vegetables that could be canned in Mason jars.

Truly, subsistence farming required long hours of labor, weeding, and irrigation by carrying water in pails to the gardens during the dry months of July, August and September. Food from the sea was available by digging clams, gathering mussels and periwinkles. Flounders could be caught from the shore using a long sapling for a fishing pole. But anyone who had access to a seaworthy dory, peapod, or Whitehall rowboat could row out to the nearest shoals and with clams for bait and some luck catch enough codfish to feed the family all winter.

There was an immense amount of labor involved in drying codfish. Some folks made drying racks out of old spruce limbs and driftwood. The codfish were split open and the backbone along the length of the stomach cavity was removed. The fish were then soaked overnight in a strong "pickle" made of a large amount of salt and fresh water. The split fish were laid out on the homemade drying racks and had to be watched over all day long in case a rain squall threatened. In that case the fish had to be carried in under cover as fast as possible.

One day, possibly in 1937 or 1938, the hay in Aunt Rhoda's barn caught on fire due to spontaneous combustion. Al happened to be home. He drove the cows out into the barnyard; then he pushed his brand-new Terraplane sedan out of the burning barn and scorched his hands on the hot metal. He burned the palms of his hands badly but recovered nicely after a while with applications of Aunt Rhoda's home remedies. Leroy was also home, and he grabbed an axe and went up the sloping granite ledge that the barn was built upon to chop the breezeway in two, so that it

MARM IN HER NEW KITCHEN WITH NEW COMBINATION GAS
AND WOOD STOVE, FLUORESCENT LIGHTS, 1956.

wouldn't act as a chimney. It's amazing how quickly the neighboring men assembled to form a fire line, passing the buckets along to be thrown on to the roofs of the attached woodshed and breezeway. The well in the field next to us was sorely taxed to keep up with the need to extinguish the fire. The barn burned to the ground, but the house was saved. Marm kept a tight hold on my brother and me, so that we wouldn't get hurt. I remember the excitement of watching the men pass the water along in ten-quart pails across the road and up the embankment, to be thrown onto the walls and roof. Eventually a new cow barn was built, which is presently used as an artist's studio.

My mother's sister, Franscene Torrey O'Leary, had three daughters: Janet, a year older than me; Renee, Garland's age; and later Natalie, who never married. Dan worked on the trolley lines in Boston as a trolley operator. When the 1934 Christmas season arrived, we were overjoyed to receive toys from "Aunt Scene." That summer the O'Learys came to Maine. Dan drove up on the graveled roads in an impressive Gardiner touring car, to enjoy a short vacation. Janet was appalled at the thought of using our privy. Renee soon became our favorite cousin; she was so lively and funny. Natalie was just a baby.

There was a New England aviator, Wincapaw, who was called the

LEON "WINK" BUILT THE NEW CABINETS; PUMP IS UNDER
THE CABINET.

"flying Santa Claus." He flew out over the remote island lighthouses
and dropped Christmas packages by parachute from his airplane. Mr.
Wincapaw flew a bright red Stinson equipped with pontoons. In 1935
The Stinson Company began building the famous SR5 Stinson Reliant,
a single-engined, high-winged monoplane. It was powered by a nine-
cylinder Wright Cyclone, similar to the very famous engine in Charles
Lindbergh's New York-to-Paris *Spirit of St. Louis*, a Ryan Company
airplane. The red Stinson flew into Stonington and came alongside of
Barter's lobster car. Soon a crowd of curious people gathered on Barter's
Wharf. On the spot, Dad bought me a barnstorming flight for five
dollars. That was enough money to buy groceries for a week, at least. At
seven years I didn't realize how dear that flight had to be. The big radial
had an electric starter and clattered into action after we were all aboard. I
sat in the back seat, on the right hand side. The crowd was happy to push
the big plane away from the float, and we began to idle out past what is
now the Co-op #2 dock. Once clear of obstructions, the pilot opened
the throttle, and the big radial pulled us along; the floats were pounding
on the crests of the choppy waves. Very soon the pounding became a
rippling feeling, and all at once we were up on one wing, and then she
was clear and flying free, climbing rapidly to level off at a comfortable

height, so that we could see all the roads and houses perched in seemingly random locations on the granite ledges, which were the solid base of the south end of the island. All too soon we came down again and taxied in to the lobster car. That was a thrill that would last me for a lifetime.

We moved from the little house on the Indian Point Road to Tea Hill Corners sometime before the surprise attack on Pearl Harbor. My father had bought some land, and had started to build a workshop. My mother walked up through Aunt Rhoda's woods and examined the construction. She said to Dad, "We could live in this." Eventually we did. Imagine a family of five jammed into a tiny house just eighteen feet long and twelve feet wide. Dad started to build a larger house on another piece of land that he bought for a very small amount of money on the road that ran past the Stonington cemetery. He dug the foundation trench by hand, but for some reason, most likely lack of funds, the house was never built. There seemed to be a "this house is good enough!" attitude. Sometime later he dug another foundation hole just south of our house, and it eventually became a small victory garden.

Sometime after we had moved to Tea Hill Corners, Garland and I discovered a fallen red-spruce tree, the roots of which had formed a perfect crotch for making a huge slingshot. We rummaged around in dad's workshop and found two Model T Ford inner tubes. We cut one into two, then into two strips of rubber the entire length of the inner tube. Further examination unearthed an old work shoe with a tongue large enough to make the leather pocket of the proposed slingshot. We went back into the woods and fashioned our super slingshot, securing the rubber strips to the tree roots and to the leather pouch with twine. The test shot was made with a stone about the size of our fists, and it sailed in a nice arc out over the spruce trees. We fired off several rounds and eventually became sated with the experiment. Much later in the day we walked down town and discovered that out artillery had landed in the main road. We never heard that any cars or pedestrians had been hit; I'm sure that the local grapevine wireless would have been buzzing about any maimed pedestrians or damaged vehicles. Our invention would have made a dandy grenade launcher in the war that lurked just over the future's horizon.

In the early 1950s my mother decided that we needed a bigger house, so she started to dig out a cellar hole. Eventually we excavated down to the granite formation, merely four feet below, and she built the foundation walls all by herself. She went all around the neighborhood with a wheelbarrow searching for fieldstones, which she loaded one at a time and wheeled home, then mortared them in place to form the foundation. Dad and I erected the framework and sheathed it with spruce boards, paper, and cedar shingles. The resulting structure was to become the new kitchen with a small bedroom above. My brother Wink built the kitchen cabinets. Garland had enlisted in the U.S. Marines at this time, I believe. Dad bought a large combination stove that used wood on one end and had four propane burners on the opposite end; the oven would bake on either fuel. The old kitchen that had been built onto the north wall was removed, and that wall was re-paneled with "beaver board," a very flammable material, favored locally because it didn't separate in the extremes of Maine weather. The old Home Clarion was loaned to our new neighbors, Ethelbert and Emily Shepard Morey, who had built a small house across the road from us; both little houses still stand today. Long after World War II there were six new houses built from Tea Hill Corner south to the intersection of the main road and the cemetery road, a section that I call Tea Hill Corners. There is another new house built further back from the road, which cannot not be seen from the highway; this house was built on or near an old cart-way that went down to a small gravel pit and an old paving motion.

My brother and I continued to explore the shore in Clam City, and one day before the United States entered World War II we saw a flight of Lockheed Hudson bombers being ferried to Halifax to be loaded onto ships leaving in convoy for England. We waved to the pilots, but they were too engrossed in their task to notice two little boys. But one day, much later, two Canadian Spitfires flew over, and their pilots responded to our waves by doing wing waggles. We jumped up and down in excitement. I read an article just recently that some of the pilots ferrying bombers were females, and at some point during World War II the bombers were flown to Gander, Newfoundland, and then flown across the ocean to England.

22. ADE AND ME

Adrian Gray and I got along like a house afire sometimes: I remember that he walked all the way over the Clam City Road from school with me, and we explored the tidal pools on the ledges east of what is now the Lobster Co-op and the granite grout pile that lies below what used to be Henry Eaton's house in the 1920s. Since it was low tide, we played on the tiny sand beach there, until the incoming waters drove us to climb up over the discarded broken granite pieces, and we straggled through Great-Aunt Rhoda Shepard's apple orchard to the little red-and-yellow house where I lived. I built up a fire in the old cast-iron woodstove, and we mixed up a batch of dough. We had flour all over the kitchen. We baked the biscuits on top of the stove in a cast-iron frying pan. My mother came home sometime during this culinary adventure and was very surprised to see us trying to cook something. I don't remember if Adrian went home hungry or not.

Our next adventure, years later, was a clamming trip to Webb's Cove. Adrian had a clam hoe but no clam roller. So I loaned him one of Dad's fine wire-mesh-sided and -bottomed rollers, and we plodded up to the cove, taking the shortcut past Ernest Snow's chicken farm. We straggled down the slope to Ralph Knowlton's shore-side cow pasture to begin digging on the sandy flats along that shoreline. I had nearly a full roller of nice clams and poor old Ade had a small collection of broken-shelled things in the bottom of the roller. He declared that he had enough and we carried our bounty along the Tea Hill Road, down past "Ernie's little house," and I deposited my clams in our work shed. I accompanied Adrian all the way to his house in Gray Town, where he threw the clam roller into the mud room with a crash.

Ade graduated with my class in 1945, with Merrill Allen, Collis Jones, and me. Adrian went off to New Hampshire, where he worked in a hardware store or something on that order. He came back to the Island for vacations, but I only saw him twice after we graduated. Merrill Allen married Charlie Cleveland's daughter. He passed away with heart trouble. Collis Jones passed away on December 28, 2008, leaving me as the sole living male graduate of the class of 1945. There were four girls in the graduating class. Norma Eaton married my first half-cousin, Donald McGuffie, and they have two daughters, Donna and Jeanie. Mary Gross moved to Arizona, and I haven't seen her since 1950 or so. Linnie Dunham married and remarried; she was at the Stonington High School alumni banquet last summer (2008) along with Marie (Buckminster) Jones, a cousin on my grandmother's side. She married Kenneth Jones, and they have two sons, John and Frank Jones.

Adrian had an older brother, Walter "Punk" Gray. He was a needler, and we didn't get along well at all. A bunch of us youngsters were down on Ames's Pond ice skating, and Walter, Shirley Shepard, George Boyce and Jack Billings began throwing snowballs at us younger lads. Then they changed to snowballs with rocks inside, A couple of belts with one of those, and I exploded off the ice, climbing right up Walter's side and bit him on the cheek! We were left right alone for the rest of the day.

Years afterwards I was home on a week's vacation from the Bell System, and Walter and I had a very pleasant conversation. The very next day I was down to visit my father, and he said, "Punk Gray is dead!" I couldn't believe it. He looked perfectly well the day before—I never did get that clam roller back!

23. ON THE WAY HOME FROM SCHOOL

Somehow, I don't remember the details exactly, one of the school kids wanted Wilbur Fifield to beat me up, and I managed to climb the most southerly of the two ancient skunk spruce trees that marked the southeast corner of the school property. But Wilbur was right behind and gaining on me, as he was older and stronger. In desperation I jumped right out onto the spruce limbs, and by holding onto the outer tips in succession I slid very rapidly down to the ground and ran off along the path that the Snow lads used going back and forth to school, which came out near their house. I continued going east until I came out on the main road and eventually got back to Clam City unharmed.

Another adventure was when Everett Billings and I ran down Russ's Hill and fooled around with his red bicycle for a while. Then I started for Clam City along the north side of Main Street. Someone chased me, and I ran along past the Stonington Power Company garages, which at that time were west of Ben Sturdee's store. Bobby Hutch or someone spooked me, and I began to gallop along right through five or six brand-new squares of concrete sidewalk, where Herb Carter was in the process of putting on the finishing touches. There were the usual old-timers sitting in a congenial cluster on the stone wall west of the steps, where the wall was just about a comfortable height to sit upon and gossip with their friends. As I suddenly appeared, sprinting along the sidewalk, unmindful of Jack Reid, Jason Gross, and Charles Ferguson, slapping my new brogans into the soft concrete, as one of them shouted, "Hi!, Hi, Hi!" Herb was too startled to trip me up, and I managed to put a footprint in each square, as I hurtled along. Herb was not pleased that he had to smoothen out the concrete once more. The old-timers were amused, and my new shoes were stiff as boards until the cement wore off. I was careful to go down Pink Street after that.

One nice spring day before school let out for the summer, a 1939 Cadillac limousine drove onto Frank Webb's dock, and the *Red Wing* lobster boat was waiting for Massachusetts Governor Saltonstall, who was going out to Isle au Haut for a little vacation, I suppose. The Cadillac was driven by a black chauffeur. I had never seen a black man, and I shouted to the other boys. "Look at that black man!" We all ran over to take a peek. But we were too shy to try to talk to him. Dennis Eaton took the governor's party down to the island by the scenic route, past the islands lying between Stonington and Isle au Haut.

Jack Reid almost always sat upon the stone wall, passing the time of day and waiting to talk to anyone who could understand his Scots brogue. He lived with his daughter, Estelle Noyes, until he passed away. He flew to Aberdeen, Scotland, every summer for several years. (Pam and I flew to England in 2004 to attend the International Haskell Families Reunion in Dorset. After the reunion we went on a two-week Trafalgar Bus Tour of Scotland and were delighted to see what I thought were eider ducks walking on the soggy beach in the rain at Aberdeen.) Jack Reid had a subsistence farm, the only house on the main road north of Tea Hill Corner at that time. The property bordered Burnt Land Pond, where Hutch and I played boats in the pond. There was a Scotts plum tree in the back of the farm near the woods, and Hutch and I raided it for the delicious fruit when they were very ripe. My father, Dick, was sitting on the wall one evening after school, and Hutch and I were roughhousing back behind the wall; Hutch made a wild charge at me, and I doubled over, and Hutch slammed into my backside, and I grabbed his sleeve and tumbled him over my back. Hutch fell onto his back with such force that it knocked the wind out of him. Dick was so amused and pleased that he talked about it for years afterwards.

24. CLAM CITY WINTERS

The Deer Isle Thoroughfare's salt water froze so solidly in the winter of 1934–35 that the U.S. Mail had to come into Stonington on the *Kickapoo*, a big steam-powered ice breaker. It stopped in the harbor in the main channel. Dr. Noyes had a Model T Ford snowmobile, a conversion that had caterpillar tracks driven from the rear axle by toothed gear wheels; another set of two-toothed gear wheels which kept the caterpillar tracks on the vehicle were on an idler shaft in front of the driving geared wheels

SOPHIE ROSE HASKELL HOLDING TWO CAPE RACERS MADE BY AUTHOR'S DAD, LEROY HASKELL.

(I believe that these conversions were manufactured in New Hampshire). Dr. Noyes drove it out on the ice to bring in the mail and other freight that had come over from Rockland on the ice breaker. Some of the townsfolk walked out onto the ice to get a good look at the *Kickapoo*, up close.

Someone in our family went out onto the ice and took pictures of the ice breaker with a Kodak Brownie box camera, and these photos survived in Marm's little box of snapshots until now. I was told that courageous souls drove to Rockland on the ice in Model T Ford touring cars. They simply tied two thick planks across the car, so that if it happened to drive into a soft spot, the crew could escape or possibly lever the Ford across the soft spot, saving the car from sinking into the ocean. Anyway, there were regular crossings of the Eggemoggin Reach to Sedgwick by automobiles on the ice.

Our father made a kite-shaped sail, and he scooted down the bay on the ice on his ice skates, carrying his Remington twenty-gauge shotgun slung like a rifle from his shoulder. Dick came back with a bag full of ducks that he had shot. Marm said that the ducks were frozen into the ice. (I have been challenged about this story all my life, but I remember eating those ducks!) He came up the bay and clambered into the *Kickapoo* on her starboard side, and some of the crew chided him as he stumbled down onto the ice on the port side, while the ice breaker was stopped momentarily in her work. Garland and I watched through the kitchen window as he skated ashore onto the tiny ice-covered beach that lies between two huge granite ledges.

Earlier in the day we had watched Bert Tracy sailing about on his homemade iceboat rig that he had concocted using a Cape Racer sled and some kind of rudimentary sail. Garland and I walked down through the glacial-debris-littered field and out onto the ice to get a better look at Bert's iceboat. Marm suddenly noticed that we had escaped, and she rushed down to the shore calling to us to come back. We were quite a way from shore by the time that she got down to the saltwater-ice-cake-covered beach.

Great-Aunt Rhoda Shepard's sons had two or three nice homemade Cape Racer sleds that were kept in the woodshed that was attached to the kitchen, New England style. This arrangement made bringing in the seasoned, fitted, stove-wood lengths very easy in the deep snowy winters that were almost standard in my childhood years. There was a breezeway from the woodshed to the cow barn. There was fitted firewood piled all along the north wall of the breezeway. I think that the sons brought the firewood in from the breezeway first, and as the winter progressed the piled wood in the breezeway diminished daily, until by late May there was only a small pile remaining in the immediate woodshed. The Cape Racer sleds were hung on large nails driven into an exposed wooden beam that was high enough to keep these sleds hanging vertically against the rough, bare wooden north wall. The Cape Racers were made out of the local red oak wood, which was sawn into three-quarters-of-an-inch pieces about six feet long by one inch deep, as seen from the side. The bottom runner was curved up to meet the top length, and the gap was maintained by rungs, hand shaped about five inches long, that were fitted tightly into holes drilled by hand with a brace and a small bit. They were sometimes fitted in rows of three and spaced almost a foot between each set of three vertical supporting rungs. The two curved bottom runners were each shod with a flat steel strip that was secured to each bottom runner with wood screws through countersunk holes, all of which were drilled and reamed by the countersink tool, by hand. The two sides were held together to form a sled that looked something like a fragile ladder. Holes were drilled in the inside surface of the top oak side pieces at an angle so that the steel runners would cut into the snow or ice on their edges first. The whole contraption was held together by two loops of heavy-duty cod line, one loop at each end of the row of oak rungs. Each loop of cod line was twisted Spanish-windlass fashion with a thin but sturdy oak piece that was kept in tension by being forced under an oak rung. The rungs were a little over a foot long, whittled out of red oak and fitted loosely into the bored holes spaced about three inches apart for most of the length of these sleds. Cape racers were especially fast on frozen, crusted snow or on ice. In deep soft snow, they were not much better than ordinary red flyers made in Philadelphia and sold in most general stores in rural Maine at that time. My father made three Cape Racers, one large one that we used as a sledge to haul clams home over the packed snow surface of the Tea Hill Road. Dick also made a small Cape Racer for Leon, our youngest brother. Years later he made one for Melinda, our first-born child. We have them both here in West Mt. Airy at the present time.

Harold Robbins lived just south of the Clam City Road, west of the present-day Lobster Co-op, and he was very inventive. I first remember Harold towing a homemade wooden boat around in a rain-filled puddle hole that formed after every large rainfall, in a shallow depression in a large granite ledge that was part of the granite hillside formation that ran parallel to the Clam City Road. Harold had a slender alder stick with a length of twine attached to the toy boat, as he played atop the granite ledge next to the house were he lived with his parents. His father was known as "Frankie Robbins," and he was a lobster fisherman. Frankie's bait house still exists, perched upon a sloping granite ledge. But now it serves as a summer camp for "folks from away."

Harold made a crude bobsled using two Cape Racers as runners. The front one was attached to the driftwood-plank main body with a wooden pylon that was fastened to the sled at midpoint. The other sled was fastened more securely parallel and at the rear of the driftwood-plank main body. A loop of pot-warp served as a tiller, tied to each front runner, so that by pulling on the left or right runner he controlled the direction of the crude sled. We local children eagerly helped tow the heavy rig up to the top of the hill. By experimentation we discovered that sleds would not slide all the way from the top of Thurlow's Hill to the "Valley," the lowest point on the Clam City Road east of Thurlow's Hill. However, we did manage a long slide from the top of the hill by "Mel" Stinson's down to the Valley, whooping and hollering all the way down. Eventually, we tired and towed the heavy old thing over to Harold's place. Then we trudged home, dragging our little tin sleds. Harold became a lobster fisherman, and he had a large wooden boat with a World War II surplus Cadillac V8 engine in it for power. I seem to remember that Lump Cousins rigged it up for him.

Years later Harold was also the caretaker of the cluster of summer houses on Grog Island. My bride, Pamela, all three of our children and I rowed down to Grog Island in Dick's old peapod for an early spring picnic on the northwest beach of the island. Harold walked over to see who was there, and as soon as he saw me he said, "OH! its you—I am havin' trouble with these kayakers!" Then, without another word, he turned right around and walked back through the alders and red-spruce trees, leaving us to enjoy the beach and the day. Nathan was just beginning to learn to row the peapod. Melinda and Jennifer were quite content to play boats in the sand with empty mussel shells.

25. THE *HINDENBURG* AND OTHER CRAFT

In early May of 1937, I was nine years and five months old, and on the sixth the neighborhood was surprised to hear something approaching from the east. It made a whining noise, and after a while the entire population of Clam City was outside looking up into the sky to see whatever it could be, coming towards us. We soon saw a huge, silver-colored zeppelin floating along through the air. It was swinging slowly, something like a pendulum, from side to side, its motors churning away and the huge propellers making the whining noise. It wasn't very high above us, and we could see passengers inside. We waved to them and some waved back. My brother and I jumped up and down with delight and excitement. Little did we know that it was on its way to total destruction at Lakehurst, New Jersey, that very evening.

We moved from the little house on the Indian Point Road to Tea Hill Corners in 1938. My father had bought some land and had built an even smaller house, which still stands today.

One morning during World War II, long before daylight, we were awakened by the sound of airplane motors. The sound seemed to be stationary, and my brother and I climbed out of our little bunks to peer out of the east-facing window to see two huge silhouettes floating above the trees. They were blimps signaling to each other with Aldis lamps. Eventually they flew out over the ocean, and sometime during the day our dishes rattled on the shelves as depth charges exploded in the ocean. That following weekend, my cousin and I walked along, exploring the shore in Webb's Cove and discovered that the rocks and gravel beaches were coated with heavy oil. There were dead ducks and cormorants mixed in with the debris.

26. WINTER AND WAR

When winter arrived, we entertained ourselves by jumping saltwater ice cakes in Little Webb's Cove. One very cold winter day, there were several of us Tea Hill boys jumping ice cakes, and I happened to jump onto an ice cake that had no firm center and went straight down to the bottom through the void and managed to resurface through the same hole—the other lads stopped laughing long enough to haul me out. I was soon on my way home, up through the old colonial abandoned farm's apple orchard and along the Tea Hill Road to a path forming the hypotenuse of a right triangle, a shortcut that emerged by Ernest Snow's; by then my clothes were frozen and only bending in the joint areas. I stripped off right next to the Home Clarion woodstove, and Marm bundled me up in a warm flannel blanket while I warmed up. I seem to remember that my first cousin Dennis Buckminster accompanied me all the way home. I never even caught a cold from that misadventure!

Shortly after that, Germany invaded the Ruhr and none of the peace guarantors even blinked, so Hitler invaded Czechoslovakia, Hungary, and Poland, and World War II was under way. Presently, Pratt & Whitney Aircraft Motors in East Hartford, Connecticut, was advertising for engine assemblers, and Dad and Elroy went down to Connecticut to try for a job. Elroy was hired and working in the engine-testing room all through the war. Dad was also there, at first assembling the 1800-horsepower series air-cooled, double-row engines. After a while, he was assembling the larger 2800s that were used in the famous P-47 Thunderbolt fighters, and eventually he was assembling the huge 4900s used in some of the B-29 bombers. He came home once in a while, and one day he came home in a 1940 Nash Lafayette four-door sedan that he bought in Connecticut. On one of his trips home he bought a 1929 Chevrolet two-door sedan from Malcolm Williams for $40 so, that we boys could learn to drive. After a while, he discovered by osmosis, I suppose, that he could do as well economically by working at Billings Marine in Stonington as he could working at Pratt & Whitney in Connecticut, and he came home; by then Garland and I were in high school.

27. OLD FISH MARKET STORIES, 1938

When Garland and I were quite young, years before television changed the world forever, we used to walk over the Clam City Road to "go downtown" (Stonington). There were several grocery stores, a drug store, a crude machine shop, Bill the barber's shop, and right next to it was "Shorty" Webster's fish market, which had a tiny dock on the back side, which was useable at any stage of the tides. A few of the seafaring men used to gather there evenings in a sort of an informal club and talk about the latest radio news and gossip, and swap stories tall and short, mostly true, but truth is elastic in Maine, and some tales would definitely stretch one's imagination. Dad would sometimes tell a story adding sound effects. His identical brother, uncle Elroy, would come in and spin a yarn. On nights when the stories got just a bit too racy, the men would shoo us out to preserve our delicate ears and also to save our morals.

All the while tales were being told, Guy Seefus (his nickname) and his fishing partner George Gross would be icing down saltwater-caught smelts in wooden barrels to be shipped on the *J. T. Morse* or another of the small steamboats that ran along the coast to the islands from Rockland to Mt. Desert. Almost all the daily commerce was carried to the Fox Islands (Vinalhaven and North Haven), Stonington, Isle au Haut, Swans Island, and Mt. Desert by Eastern Steam Ship company boats.

One night Dad felt compelled to tell a tall tale that has entertained us ever since.

Pop had me on the *Mildred*, a forty-five foot Friendship, haulin' traps off th' eastern side of York Islan', and sea ducks an' drakes kept flyin' by. Dad said, "I would like to have one of them to bake in th' oven tonight."

So he went down in th' cuddy and brought out an old muzzle-loader. He loaded a charge of black powder but could find nary a bit of lead shot, not even a handful of trap nails, so he took the sounding lead and stuffed the line into the barrel and then the lead, rammed it down with the ramrod, and brought the gun up to await the next flight of eider ducks.

Along came a big flock with a drake in the lead. Pop took a lead on that feller and touched off the muzzle-loader. There was a terrific blast, and black smoke obscured everythin'!

Our father was waving his arms as if to clear the skies, and he continued,

> When that smoke cleared away, there were fourteen sea ducks and drakes strung out on that sounding line, an' all we had to do was haul 'em in!

The fishermen clapped their hands and laughed at his outrageous story.

Just about then Fred Smith slid a cherry salute (fireworks) out under Guy Seefus's feet, and when it went off with a loud bang, Guy jumped right up into the air and landed feet first inside the new barrel that George had just rolled into the shop. Garland and I were delighted that he could jump so high and so quickly.

Of course we grew older and grew out of listening to their stories. The old fish market became a tiny motel many years after World War II, and its tiny dock became what is now called a sundeck, so that the tourists can sit out there on deckchairs with a lunch of fish and chips and watch the marine traffic, quite enjoyable I am sure!

28. CATCHING FROGS WITH EDWIN

The first day of school in 1938, we walked up to Tea Hill Corner to wait for Charley Barbour to come along in his 1934 Ford school bus. He stopped for the li'l crowd of Tea Hill Children, and Garland and I climbed on. We were no sooner sitting down than Alley Webb piped up from the back, "Hey! you guys live close enough to school that you can walk!" So we did, rain or shine, snow, sleet and hail; we walked every day, two round trips, home for lunch and back to classes.

Sometime after we moved to Tea Hill Corners and after school started, I met Edwin Thurlow and his older sister, Callie. She gave me an Edgar Rice Burrows book, *The Land That Time Forgot*. I read it so many times that I still remember the plot. Only Rosamunde Pilcher's books have enthralled me that much. However, this little episode involves a tiny flat-bottomed skiff, Edwin and me, and a galvanized washtub.

Edwin liked to catch eels, so we would fish for them in Burnt Land Pond; a bit east of the town's water pumping station there was a granite ledge where we could sit and fish. After we had caught an eel or two, we walked to his house, where we skinned the eels by driving a large nail right through the eels' heads into a stout workshop doorpost. And then with the creatures securely anchored, we could peel the skins right off, using a sharp knife and a pair of pliers to grip their slippery hides. We then fried the eels in a large cast-iron spider, and it produced a squirmy feeling watching the eel sections writhing in the pan. Eels never became high on my epicure's list. Sunfish either, but small-mouth bass are excellent!

One night, Edwin thought it would be fun to carry his tiny skiff out to "Crystal Lake," a large puddle hole next to the main road. So we put a galvanized washtub into the skiff and two short oars, and carried the boat over to the pond and shoved 'er in. Edwin rowed on the stern thwart seat, and I captured frogs with the aid of a flashlight; the washtub was jammed in behind me and between Edwin's legs. At some point in th' search, amidst moments of delight, laughter and excitement, we swamped, then upset the craft, lost all our frogs, but saved the flashlight and oars; we decided that since we were already wet, we might as well wade around waist-deep in the water and capture more frogs. After a while we had as many frogs as we were going to find and we were getting itchy feelings below the waterline, so we clambered out of the pond and went back across the road and down through the woods to Edwin's house, where we cleaned some frogs. They were not to gain a place on my delicacies list.

Edwin's father had a steamboat-sterned lobster boat that he kept moored in the small cove in between Atlantic Avenue and Sea Breeze Avenue in Stonington. It has since then silted in so much that one cannot get over the sand bar that has formed between what used to be Colwell's lobster dealership and granite ledges west of that granite block foundation, unless the tide is at east halfway up.

Sometime during the sixth grade, in the fall session, Edwin and I were walking home and emerged onto the "Heater," the road that passed by the town's cemetery. Edwin became enraged about something and mashed me in the face with a rock as big as a softball, which he'd grabbed up in his hand. I retaliated with a stout wild-cherry branch that had broken off a tree in a storm or something. I whaled away as fast as I could pound on his head and shoulders, and he ran away down through the woods. I continued along the asphalt roadway to our house, where Marm was really upset that I was injured. I was crying, "Marm, you better go down to the Thurlows' house to see if I killed Edwin." Through my tears and anguish, I told her about our little battle. As it turned out, I hadn't killed him, and he was back in school the next day, but we were never close friends again after that.

Edwin did not finish the sixth grade; he went to sea as a deckhand, and in 2004 he returned to the Island and now lives in the Island Nursing Home in North Deer Isle. His sister passed away in 2007, and I remember seeing her at the local grocery store in 2006; she had the same intense blue eyes and was delighted that I remembered her.

29. The Tarzan Adventure and Other High Jinks

Sometime after the WPA projects began, my brother and I were allowed to go to the movies in Stonington. Dr. Tewksbury ran the new Tarzan movies on Saturdays in the Opera House, and we were inspired to try swinging through the trees. The only vines in all of Stonington grew on a huge old oak tree behind "Cad" Gardiner's house, and she drove us away every time she caught us swinging on them. So we tried swinging from spruce tree to spruce tree.

We rigged some pot-warp up in a tree that grew close to a granite ledge near the gravel-surfaced road that served all of Clam City.

We tied a loop in the end of the line, so that our little feet could stand in the loop. Somehow, I slipped right through the loop and fetched up in a hangman's noose fashion. Garland was quick to see the impending disaster and hauled me right up over the edge of the ledge, just like hauling in a lobster trap.

We didn't try swinging on pot-warp again. However, we did make quick little commando raids on Cad's Tarzan vine. She must have had very good hearing, because within a minute or two she was out on the back porch steps, shouting at us in her thin little voice to go play somewhere else.

The next movies that stimulated us were the Flash Gordon serials. Buster Crabbe was the actor who played the Flash Gordon role, and he had a magic cape that enabled him to fly through the air in his war against Ming, the evil emperor. We had just moved up to the new little yellow house below Tea Hill Corner by the time this Hollywood series appeared in our modest movie theater.

Marm had some black flannel blankets, and we tied the corners to our ankles and held onto the other two corners with our hands to emulate

Flash Gordon's dramatic leaps into the air. Thus equipped, we launched ourselves off the small ledge in front of the house into the weeds, and that exercise kept us happily entertained all one afternoon.

We roamed the shoreline of Webb's Cove, beachcombing for treasures, like sea-polished pebbles in various colors. Sometimes we found hermit crabs, which were a great source of entertainment. The creatures immediately withdrew into their temporary homes, and we would set them down in a tidal pool and wait until they started to move again. Eventually we grew tired of that amusement and began a more serious activity: digging clams to take home to eat.

Dad had made a clam knife out of an old kitchen table knife that he called a "case knife." It had a thin blade with a half-circle shaped point, and, when shortened to about an inch and a half protruding from the homemade handle, was just right for opening the mollusks. I have one of Dad's clam knives to this day.

30. The New House and Adventures in the Woods

It was sometime in 1938 when we moved to the new house just south of Tea Hill Corner on Route 15. There were new woods to explore and an interesting swamp with a new-to-us species of yew, a huge stand of tall, spar-growth red-spruce trees, and a new "forest" of red-spruce saplings growing so close together we used it as a secret retreat.

Our father was an old string saver. There were spare rear-axle parts for the old 1928 Chevrolet coach that Dad had bought from Henry Eaton's widow for $5. It sat in their family garage for years and wouldn't run. Leroy worked on the old engine for days and eventually got it to working. Then he ruined the clutch trying to pull stumps out of the ground using a length of tree stump and a chain for increased leverage. It was an interesting rig and with a modern torque converter transmission would probably have worked better.

We eventually uprooted the stumps with shovels, axes, and crowbars, in that order. There were four lovely red-spruce trees that provided shade for the house, but dad only saw trees as a source of lumber or firewood and cut them all down.

In 1939 the new Deer Isle-Sedgwick Bridge was opened for traffic, and dad drove the family up to the dedication. The clutch was slipping badly, so we children walked across the bridge, where we climbed into the old two-door Chevy for a short ride on the mainland.

Not long after that, Dad went down to work in Pratt & Whitney, while Marm soldiered on by herself, trying to make ends meet with her two-dozen Rhode Island Reds and her vegetable garden. I dug clams and caught flounders for the larder. We dug dandelion greens in season and picked blueberries, which our mother preserved as blueberry sauce. The Second World War was in progress in Europe, and defense plants in Connecticut were hiring workmen, including Leroy and Elroy. Soon some of the Stonington lobster fishermen were working at Electric Boat in Groton, Connecticut. My cousin Evangeline (McGuffey) Knowlton was working in Connecticut along with her husband, "Bud," who also worked at Pratt & Whitney.

My brothers and I stayed in Stonington in th' tiny house that Dad had built to use as a workshop. My mother had walked up through the woods to see the progress and said, "We could live in this!" So eventually we moved from Clam City to make the tiny yellow house our new home. Dad sent home some money every payday, and I dug clams and brought home fresh flounders to stretch out the food budget.

31. THE GREAT WHITE HUNTERS

My brother Garland was a crack shot with a rifle and fast at shooting ruffed grouse as they rose from cover with a startling noisily furious beating of wings. Some days during hunting season he came home with as many as four partridges. He would never clean his game, but I liked to eat, so I cleaned the birds and rabbits that the "Great White Hunter" brought home. Somehow, these meals tasted ever so delicious cooked slowly on the back of the Home Clarion woodstove.

One day we decided to row down to Saddleback Island to try to shoot some black ducks that Garland knew were feeding in the cove on the southeast end of the island. Three of us set out on a foggy morning rowing Dad's thirteen-foot peapod. Dad had made a set of stand-up oarlocks, and we moved easily using these, standing up to push with one's weight instead of pulling the oars and rowing while facing aft.

We had almost reached Bold Island when we heard Uncle Harry Buckminster coming up from Swans Island's Seal Cove. His big "Novi" boat had a Chrysler marine engine with a reduction gear and made a distinctive noise we all recognized. He saw us rowing along and shut down the big motor to shout across the water. "Don't you boys go down the Bay today. It's gonna' clear off and blow up nor'west." We just waved and kept on rowing, as the big seiner got under way again.

As we approached the northwest beach on Saddleback, we told Mike, the third "man," to drop us off and row very slowly down the east side of the island, while we sneaked down through the woods to try to get a shot at the ducks.

Garland and I went trotting up through the scrubby field and were soon threading through the skunk spruces toward the cove. Just as we got close to the shoreline, we could see Mike rowing full speed standing up, into the inlet. The black ducks were already climbing away from the intruder! Garland rushed out and fired two shots with his Remington automatic, and I managed to knock down one duck with the ancient double-barreled Meridian. We scolded Mike for charging down to the cove as fast as he could. One of the ducks that Garland had knocked down rose up and escaped before either of us could bring our shotguns to bear on the fleeing bird. "Well, two is better than none," I said, and we loaded our game into the boat and shoved off for home.

Meanwhile, Mother Nature had quickly been making up some ground swells and one hit the little rowboat broadside, as I was pushing away on the oars while standing up. The sea flipped me right over the side. I managed to keep a tight grip on the oars as I went down and passed them to Mike when I surfaced and grabbed the gunwales. I clambered back into the boat, bringing in a lot of seawater with me. Mike was so alarmed he was up in the bow crying like a baby. I said, "Shut up and keep her into the wind while we bail her out."

Garland was bailing with a little aluminum dish that someone had discarded, and I wrenched off one hip boot and bailed with that. We soon had her bailed out and began to row in earnest, as Uncle Harry had been right. The wind was making up and, she would slide off a foot sideways for every two feet we rowed forward.

We sidled along to the lee of Millet Island and labored up to the Shivers, a tiny granite ledge with some trees growing in the thin soil on top. With two of us rowing, we were bending the oars at every stroke as we emerged into the open area northwest of the Bold Island bar. Dad had told us to load the boat with rocks, and that would reduce the wind resistance. Perhaps with one person on board, but three of us made a very large surface. So we tossed the ballast overboard and in desperation dragged the peapod across the mussel bed at Devil's Half Acre. We worked our way across the narrow stretch of water to the lee of the two Coot Islands, where we found "Kelp" Dunham and his brother Eugene hunting for mink. They had a trained beagle and were quite successful. Kelp towed us up to Clam City with his lobster boat, where Mike and I abandoned ship and scuffed up through the woods to the little yellow house by the side of the road. We left Garland to row back to Webb's cove in the lee of Deer Isle.

Amazingly, I never got sick from my immersion and remaining wet all the way home. Kelp always reminded me, "I saved your life that day, 'ol son."

32. MARM'S COMPASSION

When we moved to just below Tea Hill Corner on the main road, there were only our neighbor's daughter and two much younger boys as playmates. Robert C. Hutchinson (Hutch) lived "up th' road" with his grandfather and his older sister Clemina (Meanie), who was still alive in 2008. We became lifelong friends and sometimes got mischievous. Bob's grandfather, Jack Reid, had a large farmstead that ran all the way back from Route 15, west to the pumping station road and north to the south shore of Burnt Land Pond, the town's water supply. And we roamed all through the dense spruce-forested grounds. We liked the granite ledge that ran along the south shore of the pond, and there was a large white pine that had been broken off by lightning or a really strong line gale. The granite ledge was quite level and flat for as much as a hundred feet, covered with reindeer mosses and other plants that will tolerate stone dust and leaf mulch as nutrient-bearing soil. The last time I was on that spot our son Nathan was learning to row, and we sneaked in there on the old Noyes ice-house roadway with our ancient station wagon, with a little plywood skiff sticking out of the tailgate. We rowed across the pond from where the old ice-house ramp used to be located and climbed up onto the ledge. And I was pleased to find that the big old pine had dropped many viable seed cones, and there was a large stand of white pine saplings, some as tall as twenty feet at that time (approximately 1978).

Edwin Thurlow has returned to Maine after a life at sea and other things, to live on Little Deer Isle on the Haskell District Road. He and Douglas Haskell have become friends and work together at times.

Earlier, I wrote about Edwin and me wallowing around in a swampy puddle hole chasing frogs. I'm sorry to report that I didn't find frogs' legs as appetizing as the French do. So, some sixty years later, I was surprised to meet Edwin again, as I came out of the Little Deer Isle post office in the summer of 2003.

I remember that during the early days of World War II in America and between sessions of school, Edwin and I rowed over to Russ Island, and I dove for scallops using large stones to help me get to the bottom faster. I scooped up one or two scallops on each dive and returned to the surface. We had perhaps ten or twelve scallops on the bottom of the flat-bottomed skiff, when—ancient to us mere boys—Bob Smith came rowing over from Clam City in his lapstrake peapod to rant about someone pulling his traps and that he was going to "lay on the island some night with his rifle and shoot 'em." I guess that he had rehearsed what he was going to say, as he would have had to be blind not to see that I was almost naked and wringing wet. At any rate, he had spoiled our adventure, and I got dressed; then we went ashore and ate our scallops raw. We picked some wild raspberries on the sheep-pastured island, and they were our dessert.

Edwin's mother developed cancer, and my mother walked down to their house and helped with the laundry and cooking and was a great comfort to her. Their daughter had married by then and lived on Little Deer Isle. After his mother died, Edwin left school, and I didn't see him again until he climbed out of Douglas Haskell's little pickup truck, asking if my name was Carroll Haskell.

Our mother had a quilting frame, and she worked and worked making little panels which were sewed together laboriously until the entire quilt pattern was ready for batting and a backing. Then she would invite neighbors who lived within walking distance to come and help sew. She would have homemade cookies or cake, and they would all have tea, as Marm didn't drink coffee.

If we boys came into the house when they were all gathered around the quilting frame, we would almost immediately go out again, so that they could talk without being interrupted. Those quilts were very welcome indeed; during the cold windy winter nights after the woodstove fire had gone out, they kept us warm until Marm or Dick had built the breakfast fire again. Sometimes she poured in a little too much kerosene, and the old stove's fire box would burst into flames with a barely-muffled "kerwump," and Dad would be on his way downstairs hollering good-naturedly, "Give it to 'er, Mill!"

Marm's subsistence garden was right in front of the house. She planted it with tomatoes, pole beans, cucumbers, green Swiss chard, and beets. She watered the garden plants, carrying a ten-quart pail and dipping into the pail with an empty tomato can with tiny holes punched into the bottom. When our hand-dug well (started by Marm in a fit of pique) ran low, there was an almost inexhaustible supply across the road behind the Will Saunders's small ice house. "But it didn't look to be fit to drink," as the water was always dark; possibly from roots of the bordering spruce and hatmatack trees.

I used to walk up to the shore, down in front of grandmother Haskell's subsistence farm and dig enough clams to make a chowder, and sometimes there were enough left over to steam and serve as a special treat. In the winter I would turn small saltwater ice cakes over and dig every square inch of exposed sandy mud to get enough clams for a chowder. Sometimes I would get lucky and find an ice cake up on edge with a bit more area exposed to dig into. And after the ice had drifted out to sea, my cousin Elston and I would drag the big flat-bottomed skiff down the homemade ramp and launch her, then pole around looking for flounders hibernating in the mud. We would spear just enough for two meals, knowing that the number of fish were finite.

33. MARM'S DISCIPLINE

When Garland and I were little tykes, we usually could do anything that came to mind. However, if we got out of hand and were specially naughty, "Super Nanny," our mother (not to disparage the current TV program by that name), would go out and cut a little switch. It might be half an inch in diameter on the big end and perhaps two feet long, tapering to a mere leaf stem.

She would snap that thin end against our ankles, and she would have immediate compliance! Did that ever smart, stung like a hornet's sting! We would do anything to make her stop. I don't think that she had to apply the rod very many times during all our childhood years! But the threat of the switch was always used by Marm to get some activity to stop or to get some request immediately fulfilled. Dad, on the other hand, would give me a backhanded cuff, if he was angry or annoyed beyond his patience!

34. CHILDREN'S DRIFTWOOD PLAY BOATS

Most of the Island boys grew up in and around boats. Our Stonington neighbors and friends' families had at least one usable rowboat; some had as many boats as their work required. In the days of fish weirs, the fishermen used dories. They pulled up the "twine," cotton nets that captured the herrings inside the weir, right into the dories, unless there was a huge catch, when several dories might be required. Eventually, someone invented a powerful pump that sucked the fish up into a scaler. The fish went into the hold of a sardine carrier, and the fish scales were collected for commercial use.

My brother Garland and I "rammed around" the nearby shore, towing homemade boats by attaching a piece of twine to an alder switch or something to use as a towing stick. The string was then fastened to the bow of these crudely made craft with a shingle nail, and we proceeded to maneuver them around rocks and into imaginary coves, all the while making motor sounds. One day I tried to make a square-rigged model ship, having just returned from a swashbuckling Errol Flynn movie about pirates. I worked and worked with Dad's drawshave and other tools, shaping the hull to conform to my memory of the pirate ship.

Once we reached the shore, I launched the clumsy looking pirate ship. The square sails filled by the so'west breeze, but the craft simply rolled over and lay on its side, near immobile. Meanwhile Charlie Barter, our neighbor just to the east of us on the Clam City shore, quickly made Garland a very smart sailboat out of a driftwood shingle, two gull's feathers and a thin sliver of stone that served as ballast and rudder at the same time. Garland sailed this driftwood craft all afternoon. He would set it on a course, and after a while it would "fetch up in some rockweed" or on a half-tide ledge. He would wade out to retrieve it, then send it off again and again.

I left my inferior square-rigger on the rocky shore, temporarily defeated. I copied Charlie's design but could "only find a solitary bedraggled crow's feather" and my attempt to fasten a sliver of stone into the driftwood shingle was clumsy. My little cedar shingle sailed, but not as fast as Charlie's splendidly simple sail-away boat. Charles Barter was my cousin, Carolyn Billings' grandfather. Her mother lay dying of tuberculosis in a tiny room off the kitchen of the old saltwater farm (a term invented by Tristram Coffin, I think). At any rate it fit. There was an old barn, and at one time there were two or three cows.

Garland and I continued to play boats along the Clam City Shore. And sometimes we walked up through the woods to Grammie Haskell's little saltwater farm, avoiding the graveled road that passed through the Ames family's yard, as our mother didn't want us disturbing them. Our two Hooper cousins lived there, and Freda Haskell also lived there. She was uncle Elroy's daughter, and the house was again full of children's voices and restless energies. Cousin Melvin Haskell lived with his dad in a tiny house on the Clam City Road.

From Grammie's house, cousin Elston Hooper, Garland, and I roamed the shore around Webb's Cove, looking for treasure or playing with our homemade boats. We knew that the sun was a reliable clock; but it was usually low in the sky before we were hungry enough to straggle back through the woods to the Clam City cluster of houses.

Eventually I married Pamela Jean Haviland, and our three children enjoyed my homemade sail-away boats. We had a small wooden outboard-motor-powered skiff that carried us to many island picnics, and a feature of these summer events was my making driftwood sail-away boats. However, the children made such a fuss that I had to crank up the Evinrude and chase these little boats and take them home, where they were shortly forgotten, as wheeled toys were more attractive once we were back on land.

In 1995 Garland came up from Texas with his new bride, Betty, and we all piled into the sixteen-foot skiff and motored over to the Chain Links, a series of tiny islands west of Deer Isle, about a twenty-minute run. The old Evinrude was near the end of its usefulness, but it ran faultlessly that day. We rigged a fisherman's anchor by tying the painter to the anchor's ring and then a length of line to the fluke ends of the anchor, perched the anchor on the top of the stem and shoved the boat off downwind, paying out line until I tripped the anchor overboard after the skiff had blown away from the beach far enough to stay afloat all through our picnic hours, as the tide in Penobscot Bay rises and falls through an average of nine feet.

After we had enjoyed our picnic lunch, Garland made a sail-away boat out of a foam picnic plate. He forced two gull's feathers down through the foam well ahead of the center and stuck a bit of driftwood into the rim of the plate to serve as a rudder, and with a tiny stone as ballast it sailed away very smartly, while my driftwood shingle with two crow's feathers wallowed along behind. Our children were old enough by then to be quite happy watching the fragile things disappear downwind.

35. GARLAND'S CHERRY SALUTE

The Fourth of July rolled around in 1940, and we could buy fireworks in Harry Friedman's store in downtown Stonington. Garland came home with a cherry salute, and he took a good-sized potato, hollowed it out with a knife, and jammed the firework item into the void. He lit the fuse and lobbed the "grenade" right up over the roof of our little house, and it hit the ground just a bit south of the neighbor's porch, where their two dogs were temporarily sleeping. The cherry salute bounced once and landed under the porch, where it exploded. Those two dogs came out from under the house, the foxhound braying and the Labrador barking furiously to the full length of their restraining chains that were fastened to the wire clothesline. Our neighbor came out looking all around and said, "My lands! That must have been a car backfiring!" Garland was so amused that he was rolling on the ground laughing.

36. MARINE TRAFFIC AS SEEN FROM OUR CLUSTER OF RED-AND-YELLOW HOUSES

Before World War II, almost all heavy freight came to Maine's offshore islands by coastal schooners, and later cargoes were shared with the newly invented steamships. Tillson's Wharf in Rockland became the western terminus for Penobscot Bay marine traffic. My grandfather used to sail his big forty-five foot Friendship sloop, *Mildred*, over to Rockland to bargain for winter supplies. My father used to tell me about those trips. Grandfather would buy a barrel of broken crackers, a barrel of flour, and hundred pound bags of sugar, possibly to be divided on a barter system for a return of favors or labor instead of money amongst the other families living along the shore of Webb's Cove, or possibly in the town of Green's Landing, which became renamed Stonington shortly after my grandfather, Freeman, married Mary Jane (Billings) Knowlton.

Eventually, most of the freight and cargo business was carried by the steamers, and the largest four-masted schooners, like the *Luther Little*, were gradually retired to die on mud banks or in a quiet cove away from marine traffic—but some of the smaller schooners became cruise ships.

I remember that Fulton Weed and his brother Raymond had coasting-schooner loads of firewood come into the tiny cove between Sea Breeze Ave. and Atlantic Ave. to unload on the dock behind Thomas Warren's ship chandlery store. The hardwood stock was sawn into fitted firebox lengths with a stationary sawing machine rig by the Weed brothers for the ubiquitous cast-iron woodstoves in Stonington and nearby homes. I gamely started splitting the mixed hardwood lengths with an axe, and it was all to be sold to local customers. One day the axe bounced off a maple knot and made a painful gash in my left thumb, and I walked up to Dr. Brown's office, where he cleaned the wound and bandaged my thumb. I was exempt from wood splitting for a while.

Many of the offshore islands gradually lost year-round residents and became summer retreats. Life on subsistence farm islands must have been lonely. There were no doctors available. Should an emergency occur, the family would have to row or sail to Rockland on the mainland or to a larger island, Deer Isle or Mt. Desert. The colonial family that settled on Bradbury Island nearly starved when the patriarch died suddenly, and his widow slaughtered and butchered the farm's only steer. Signal fires alerted the townsfolk on Deer Isle, who managed to cross the saltwater ice and rescue the rest of the family after the ice was thick enough to support a team. The island was farmed until 1925.

Garland and I used to watch the coastal schooners gliding by under sail, and sometimes the schooners would be moving along pushed by the jolly boat, which was a short stubby thing usually powered by a single-cylinder, two-cycle marine engine. They barked away very noisily with their cushioned bows against the schooner's transoms. Some of the sardine carriers had huge Fairbanks and Morse two-cycle oil engines, and they were so noisy that they could be heard coming from miles away. But the steamers were very quiet except when the captain blew the steam whistle.

When we grew older we sometimes walked over to the Eastern Steamship dock to watch the steamships come in to the dock. I remember once seeing a huge automobile with a gleaming brass radiator drive up the unloading ramp, shift into a higher gear and rumble off toward town. It was a touring car and had the top up, and luggage was strapped onto the running boards. It had wooden-spoked wheels and white-walled tires. At North Deer Isle, my father-in-law Dr. Thomas Philip Haviland wrote about his childhood years waiting with the local boys all gathered on the North Deer Isle dock to see who was leaving or arriving, and there were teams awaiting passengers who would need rides to Deer Isle Village or to their summer cottages, and to provide cartage for their steamer trunks and smaller luggage.

My favorite was the *J. T. Morse*, which had huge paddlewheels, one on each side, of course, which were driven by a walking beam engine. I was fascinated watching the beam bobbing up and down, driven by a vertical single-cylinder steam engine rated at 600 horsepower. The *J. T. Morse*, 214 feet long overall and 199 feet long at the waterline and just 31 feet in beam, was launched in 1903 in East Boston, Massachusetts, and began carrying passengers during that season and was laid up over the winter in Camden, Maine.

The last steamship serving Stonington, until October in 1941, was the *W. S. White*. In the spring of 1942, all the remaining steamers were snapped up by the U.S. Government for World War II duties, and almost all freight for Deer Isle, Stonington, and Isle au Haut came across the bridge in trucks. Small freight and stores went out to Isle au Haut on a lobster boat owned and captained by Stanley Dodge. In my youth, it was used expressly for U.S. Mail, passenger and freight deliveries. At high tide, Stanley came directly into Frank Webb's dock beside his general store. At other stages of the tide he came into R. K. Barter's dock, I think. At any rate, he served Isle au Haut for many years in that capacity.

When Garland and I were older, we joined another lad and went on Kenneth Robbins's truck, delivering freight to grocery stores on the Island. Sometimes we went all the way to the store on Little Deer Isle, but most trips were to the store in Sunset, Bray's Store on the Long Cove Road, and stores in Deer Isle Village. We loved the rush of air in our faces as the flatbed truck roared along at possibly thirty miles an hour, considered high speed on Deer Isle's rough, mostly gravel-surfaced roadways in the late 1930s. Of course the *W. S. White*'s last trip to Stonington in 1941 was the end of that exciting time for us boys.

Freight deliveries to North Deer Isle by steamship ended before that era, and the beach near the old North Deer Isle steamship dock became the landing site of the Deer Isle-Sedgwick automobile and truck ferry. I don't think that my parents ever used the ferry, as it was easier to go to Rockland on a steamer. Dad took me over there to have my tonsils removed, and he took me to see a railroad passenger car that was sitting on the tracks all by itself. Rockland was the "big city" to my six-year-old eyes. The buildings were constructed of red bricks and had decorative granite windowsills and lintels, granite doorway frames sometimes, and beautiful dark-green, serpentine marble in the drugstore soda-fountain façade. Dad treated me to a vanilla ice cream after the operation!

Possibly the serpentine was quarried in the Reach Road quarry in North Deer Isle. From what I have seen, there was quite a lot of the material removed from the island's quarry; nothing remains of the quarry operation except the quarry hole with scars remaining on the vertical faces, where the stone was quarried with drills and channel bars.

I assume that serpentine has no cleavage lines, and the stone had to be quarried in all planes, vertical, horizontal, and crosswise by this method. Then a quarried block of serpentine had to be sawn with gang saws in order to get thin slabs to be used for countertops and facing pieces. One wonders if anyone now knows if the stone was processed on the island or if it was sent off-island to shops equipped to turn the rough blocks into finished and polished marble pieces. I also wonder if the stone was drilled by hand. On John L. Goss granite quarry, we had a steam drill that was used when a channel had to be drilled in order to start quarrying a new sheet of stone. We used late-model Ingersoll Rand pneumatic drills, which were quite fast, producing a three-inch-deep hole in three minutes. I remember talking to "Mel" Stinson years ago, and he had worked on one of the early stone quarries where all the holes were drilled by hand, long before the Spanish-American War. He told me that it was quite pleasant work, sitting on a sheet of stone drilling away by hand and scooping out the stone dust with a handmade long-handled spoon, to keep the drill bit from binding. For a lift line he stood to one side and drilled by holding the hand drill as nearly level as he cold judge by eye, and he pounded away with his quarry hammer, twisting the drill-bit a little after each stroke of the hammer. Nevertheless, polished serpentine marble is beautiful but very brittle material, used in building facing stone, mostly facing for inside surfaces of entrances these days.

37. WALDEN AMES BUILDS A GRANITE FOUNDATION

One day in the late 1930s, Walden Ames came up to an excavation that Lewis Sawyer had dug all by hand, as those kind of things were done in those days before backhoes and bulldozers. Walden arrived with his ox team, and on the wagon there was a long pole. I stopped walking to watch what he would do with it. He set a large block of stone down in the middle of the excavation and then lifted the spruce timber and carried it down into the excavation. He set the mast onto the stone foot block, and with the aid of the oxen he hoisted the mast to a nearly vertical position.

If I remember correctly, there were four rope guys, which he had

LAID-UP GRANITE FOUNDATION STONES OF 1939—THE HOUSE IN 2004.

already attached to the top of the post, and to crowbars that he drove into the ground with a long-handled wooden maul. They were spaced roughly equidistant and about ninety degrees from each other. He adjusted the lengths of line to make the mast stand as close to vertical as possible. The stone foot block served as a pivot point for the derrick, and the next day he brought up the derrick's boom and a single granite block. He attached the boom and the lines from the masthead fitting to the boom, which had a homemade winch attached to it, close to the mast end of the boom. Walden attached a set of chains with two hook-like objects that he called "dogs." The dogs had big iron rings on the inside ends, and a single chain ran through both rings, so that the sharply pointed dog-ends would not slip out of indentations called "dog holes," that were made by hand with a steel point and a quarry hammer in the opposite ends of the granite block. Once Walden had cranked the load off of the wagon, he swung it around and lowered it to the ground to position the granite block as a starting point in erecting the foundation walls. It seemed to take forever, but day by day the oxen hauled the single blocks of granite up from the Ames stone quarry, which was located south of the artificial pond and west of the farm house. Walden laid up the foundation walls stone by stone. He leveled the stones lengthwise and crosswise using a prybar, and he maintained their positions by wedging chips of granite between the stones below and the one he was positioning.

Then one day as I walked by, he had the derrick down and loaded onto the wagon. After he had loaded all his equipment onto the wagon he clucked his tongue and the team slowly hauled the wagon back to the saltwater farm, where possibly Walden rewarded each ox with an apple.

I was surprised to find that he actually liked children. Marm had always tried to keep us from bothering the Ames family by telling us that the brothers were going to chase us away. There was an apple tree by the end of the dam that had small apples that were red fleshed inside, and we craved them. So we would pick one every time we passed by, when the apples were ripe in late summer.

The Ames family are interred in the family cemetery down by the pond, inside a dressed stone-wall enclosure, and each grave is marked with a white marble stone. A historical marker of a way of life that no longer exists anywhere in Maine, or most likely, anywhere else in America.

In October of 2004, Pam and I drove down the Island to see if we could photograph the house where Walden had laid up the granite foundation. The new owner was very interested in my story of how "her" house was built. She invited us inside to see the kitchen and living room. There is a new ell on the east end of the small house, which rests upon a modern concrete foundation extension. The gaps between the granite blocks in the original foundation have been mortared to prevent water seeping in and heat loss from the furnace, which represents a new way of life dependent on heating oil—which will become ever more expensive as time marches on. Lewis Sawyer heated the house with wood. There aren't many houses left on the island that have dual or triple heating systems. Judith (Haskell) Hutchinson McGuire removed their auxiliary woodstove years ago and now laments that "I should have known better!"

38. HEATING WITH ANTHRACITE

I think it was in 1937 that Dad started to build a little workshop on that piece of land he bought from Arthur Carter. I learned something about keeping secrets from that episode. Dad had learned that a certain piece of land that bordered the main road from Stonington to Burnt Land Pond on the east side of the island was for sale for a very modest price. He told his brother, Elroy, who told Arthur Carter. Arthur "had th' money" and bought it. Time went on, and Dad managed to scrape together enough money to buy the tiny plot that we lived on for the price Arthur had paid for the entire forty acres!

We moved in 1938, into Dick's newly constructed "shop," which was merely a floor platform early in the year, when Marm famously declared, "We could live in this!" Leon was just 4, and he said to Donny McGuffey, "Daddy's building a shedhouse!" Donny laughed about it forever afterwards. Marm was worried that Charlie Cleveland wouldn't be able to get all our meager possessions onto his truck. To which he replied, "I could just as easily load this entire house onto my truck!"

Within a few days we were firmly entrenched. Dad had built a barn-type (gambrel) roof, which made it possible to stand up on the second floor without banging one's head. Garland and I were settled in on the east end in homemade bunks. A partition served as partial separation and a handy place to drill holes in the rafters, into which Dad forced several lengths of sawed-off old broom handles to serve as clothes poles.

There was a front door with a window in it; a used Home Clarion cast-iron woodstove equipped with coal grates, so that we could heat with anthracite; two homemade wall cupboards; a crude kitchen floor-cabinet with a shelf that held the drinking water in two ten-quart galvanized pails; and a cast-iron sink with a lead pipe drain that ran out onto the ground as greywater, "Arizona aquaculture."

Marm had what we thought were the best-looking rugosa roses on the Island, that she transplanted along the north side of the house. On the south side she planted dahlias and eventually yellow lilies that bloom even now, in June of 2008!

Dick worked on the house at night, using a pump-up, white-gasoline-fueled lantern, and he walked back to Clam City through the old paving motion quarry's tote road, through Great-Aunt Rhoda's tiny hayfields, past the red-spruce tree stumps where I had waited for the bear to "come out, so I could see it" when I was a tiny lad, finally to retire to bed after listening to his Sears and Roebucks battery-powered radio.

It was quite a radio; we could hear Winston Churchill on the shortwave feature of the set. Of course this radio went to the new house with us, and it lasted until Dick bought a large Philco radio from Ernest Snow's widow, Muriel, who was our neighbor and Edith (Knowlton) Smith's youngest sister. Muriel eventually moved to Massachusetts with her two sons. I only saw her once after that, when she came back to the Island for a visit with her family.

Construction went on almost every night until Dick had a roof on the tiny house, and a front door, which Fred Smith came over and hung for Dad.

Dick had an idea of using seal's oil to preserve the eastern-white-cedar shingles from decaying early. He climbed up onto the barn-type roof on a homemade ladder and painted the entire roof with seal's oil that he had "tried out" using an old galvanized washtub filled with seal's blubber and set over an old oil barrel used as a crude stove, down on the old Knowlton-Haskell homestead shore—where he and his twin brother, Elroy, had built a crude shallow-water dock, used by Uncle Elroy to dock his lobster boat at high water, to load or unload lobster traps and other heavy things.

The results of the seal's oil treatment were twofold: it definitely prolonged the life of wooden shingles; and secondly, it entertained folks walking by with the aroma of a seal's rookery. We endured that smell for years, and the shingles lasted!

Dad got an idea of heating the little house with hard coal. He ordered the set of coal grates for the Home Clarion woodstove and proceeded to learn how to use anthracite. It provided heat all night long, but the coal gas had to be burned off carefully before retiring for the night. We had a cat, and she woke Marm up with her yowling. Marm got up to let the cat outside and was promptly overcome by inhaling coal gas. Dad came in to get me to go fetch the doctor. I arose out of a sound sleep, and when I reached the head of the stairs I passed out and fell headlong into a case of evaporated milk at the foot of the stairs. By then Dick had opened the upstairs windows; he got everyone up and downstairs, then opened all the windows and the front door to bring in some fresh air. We three boys didn't go to school that morning, but we went after the noontime meal and told everyone about our escape from death.

We finished the winter with wood heat, and of course the house was not toasty warm all night. The bedrooms were unfinished, and shingle nails were sticking out of the pine boards with little rimes of frost around each nail in very cold weather.

We were soon acquainted with the neighbors next door, Fred and Edith Smith, who lived in an old New England-style house which had three structures all assembled into one length; the most distant from the living quarters was a cow shed, used as a garage by Fred from the early 1930s until they moved to a new house at the west end of Long Cove in Deer Isle. Uncle Elroy tuned up Fred Smith's old Whippet sedan so well that it went so fast that Fred crashed it. He replaced it with a 1929 Pontiac four-door sedan. They had one daughter and two dogs, Poo and Nookie;

they soon changed her name to Snookie! Upon our arrival below Tea Hill Corner, they had a large black Labrador and an even larger foxhound. Those two dogs seemed to bark all day long! They also had some gray geese. The gander would nip us "where we sit down," leaving a painful weal, and one did not want to walk around in their yard barefooted!

39. LIFE ON DEER ISLE JUST BEFORE WORLD WAR II

When we lived in Clam City, Marm would read to me *Keeper of the Bees*, *Girl of the Limberlost*, and *Freckles*, all books from grandmother Mary Jane Billings Knowlton Haskell's library. Somehow, *Girl of the Limberlost* has survived and is still with us; I liked *Keeper of the Bees* best.

My mother and I picked blueberries out in the "hardscrabble scrubbery" and rock-strewn land close to the little red-and-yellow house. One day, well before blueberries were ripe enough to pick, Dad was scouting along shore in his peapod rowing boat and saw that "Little Camp Island was just red with wild strawberries." The very next day we all straggled down through the Ames family's hayfield to their old quarry dock (which still stands intact today), and Dad pulled in the peapod, which was moored on an outhaul. We all climbed into the fifteen-foot craft and stowed a picnic lunch, some water, and little tin pails and empty lard cans to pick into. Dad rowed all of us out past the west end of Russ Island and landed us on the south side of Little Camp Island in one trip. He moored the boat by tying a length of line into the fluke end of a homemade grapnel and tied the painter to the ring end, balanced the device on the bow and shoved her off toward deep water. When the line had payed out to near the end, he fetched a yank on it, and the grapnel fell into the deep, and the boat tacked in the light breeze slowly back and forth on the painter. Garland and I played with empty mussel shells on the beach, while our parents "picked and picked" strawberries, and as the day progressed, it became quite warm in the direct sun. Our mother was busy for days making strawberry preserves on the kitchen woodstove.

Once in a while there seemed to be more blueberries on the other side of the fence, metaphorically speaking, and we would scout out likely spots in Great-Aunt Rhoda's hayfields along the fence lines, where the menfolks working with scythes would not likely destroy the berry bushes as they cut hay for winter fodder. Every once in a while, we would find a wonderfully productive little spot around the edges of a granite erratic, which would yield almost a quart of berries.

Our father was working in Pratt & Whitney during most of the war, but he must have been terribly lonely with our mother living at home and having only brief weekends to come home to be with the family. Some of the islanders moved to Connecticut and stayed there, returning home for the Fourth of July parade and celebration or possibly a week to visit with their parents, brothers and/or sisters and grandparents.

Sometimes our uncle Elroy would come to visit, and the twins would tell tales and sometimes verbally invent things. I remember Elroy telling about a particular Willys sedan that had stumped all the local mechanics. It would not run. It seemed that the intake passage from the up-draft carburetor was a steel sleeve that passed right through the exhaust manifold, and that acted as a vaporizer. The steel sleeve had rusted and was full of pinholes inside the section that passed up through the exhaust manifold. Elroy suspected that the trouble was in that sleeve—that looked perfectly sound to anyone examining the engine. He removed the entire assembly and shined a flashlight into the exhaust opening and upon close examination saw little pinpricks of light coming through the steel sleeve. So, he found a brass pipe that would just drive through the manifold, and with a little work with a hammer and a file he made the old car run as it should. He loved to tell that story.

Sometimes Dad would play a tune on his harmonica; he only played hymns, but we liked them anyway. Every once in a while, one of the local fishermen would come in, and there would be another story-telling session. One day one of our neighbors came in, and he was quite well into his cups; then he threw up on the floor, and Marm made him clean it all up by hitting him with the broom handle. She and we all laughed about that for years afterwards.

40. THE BRIDGE AND ELECTRICITY ARRIVE

"It was the best of times" in that clams were plentiful; "it was the worst of times" in that Hancock and Washington Counties, two of the poorest counties in all of the United States, were struggling to recover from the Great Depression. No matter what one thinks of Franklin D. Roosevelt's prewar years of the New Deal administration, life would be forever changed for the housewives and rural menfolk in the two counties and all over America, with FDR's Rural Electrification Act, which made electric lights and appliances possible, profits for the Republican manufacturers and businessmen, electric milking machines for the ten-cow farmers, electric water pumps, and many other things to lessen the labor of rural American family lives and routines.

In 1934 the WPA program began building bridges and causeways. By 1939 the new suspension bridge was opened connecting Little Deer Isle to the mainland, and in 1934 the rough cart-way from Deer Isle to Little Deer Isle was rebuilt following the natural course of the tidal sandbars to become a causeway usable at any stage of the tides.

It wasn't until 1948 that we had electricity put in! In 1948 Don Webb, Stonington Electric Company's "Iron Man," came up with the company's line truck and installed our electric service all by himself, installed the cable from the roadside utility pole to the house, all the hardware, and the little fuse box in the stairway that led upstairs. He also pulled in the armored cable that fed the first-floor central ceiling light. After he had installed all the inside wiring, he put on his hooks and climbed the utility pole at the end of our driveway and cut in the service wires to the house. Those wires lasted until 1991, when I had Tom McGuire put in a new three-conductor service cable, because Bangor Hydro didn't like our antique service wires and hookup. Now there is a stout conduit mast attached to the house and a "circus breaker box" inside the stairway.

Years later Dad converted all of our incandescent lights to fluorescents, way ahead of the latest plea from the save-the-world-from-global-warming folks! But even today we have emergency kerosene lamps at the Cabbage Patch cabin, against the ever-present chance that someone or something will knock down a Bangor Hydro electric pole and douse the lights for hours and hours.

As we grew older, Garland and I bypassed the Ames family's gravel-surfaced road to walk up through the woods from Clam City, making our own shortcut to Grammie Haskell's house, where our two orphan Hooper cousins and cousin Freda Haskell lived for a while. That household consisted of Grammie (Mary Jane Billings Knowlton Haskell) her unmarried daughter, Ethel Knowlton, Freda Haskell, Elston Hooper, and his sister, Marie, a couple cats, a cow and a pig, and a small flock of Rhode Island red hens and little chicks every once in a while. There was a small apple orchard with two pear trees and a damson plum tree. My favorite tree was a Red Astrachan, which produced a tart summer apple which we thought was delicious. The Havilands' summer cottage next door and the tiny subsistence farm that used to be Monty Small's on the North Deer Isle Road each have a Red Astrachan tree, which still produces these tart apples, possibly the seeds of the original immigrant trees brought to the New World from Sweden, in a similar fashion to the tough old-world farmers in Moberg's immigrant trilogy.*

As the Great Depression was about to arrive, Jenny Billings opened a bar at the intersection of the main road and the Clam City Road and Granite Avenue, directly across from the Catholic Church, where we could enjoy a bottle of soda pop. We didn't like the taste of Moxie, although Almond Dunham had a little glass almost every morning at Jewett Noyes's drugstore "down street." I think that he thought it was a tonic. It certainly tasted like medicine. Almond was a "scoop-along-shore" lobster fisherman; he had a few traps and hauled them alone. He had a tremendous bass voice and sang in the Reorganized Church of Jesus Christ of Latter Day Saints. The church building sat high above Main Street, and we trudged along the Clam City Road, past Reginald Greenlaw's Square Deal Garage, down Thurlow's Hill, to walk along the wooden sidewalk that covered the open sewer, which ran downhill from Babe Noyes's little house to exit into the harbor somewhere below. We continued along Main Street past the drug store, Ted Boyce's grocery store at the corner of what is now known as Pink Street, past the post office, Dr. Tewksbury's dental office, Town Hall, Ben Sturdee's grocery store, Dr. Noyes's Stonington Electric Power Company garages, and a large beautiful house high upon a granite formation, the Opera House, with a small branch of the Union Trust Company that was in a tiny building tucked in below, past Woodrow Cousins's, and then we climbed up the steep walkway to our church almost every Sunday.

After Joseph Smith, founder of the Mormon Church, was assassinated in 1841, his wife, Emma Hale Smith, founded the Reorganized Church, and its headquarters was in Independence, Missouri, for years. Emma did not condone multiple wives, and the new Church gained membership through missionary workers, two of which came to Stonington and stayed in Grammie Haskell's house, while they preached and founded the Stonington branch. There was another branch in Jonesport, and my father was particularly fond of hearing Newman Wilson preach at our church.

---

*Vilhelm Moberg, *The Emigrants; Unto a Good Land; The Last Letter Home*

41. LIFE IN THE 1940S

I was twelve years old on the first of January in 1940. We were living in our own little house on Route 15 north of Stonington's main cluster of houses and businesses. Leo Turley had a small farm with turkeys and hens running at large. I remember Mary Turley inviting us in to see the animals as we walked by on our way to town. Eventually the farm became "Will" Saunders's. He worked on Deer Isle Granite, known locally as "McGuire's." Pete Billings rented the north end of the main farm building; he married Helene Burns from Swans Island. Eventually they moved to the head of Webb's Cove to a house just off the Oceanville Road. Helene's brother Russell used to come over to Stonington on the mail boat, and he would walk up to visit his sister. Eventually, Russell and I met and became lifelong friends.

Edwin Thurlow had quit school in the sixth grade, and we drifted apart. He spent his life at sea in the Merchant Marine fleets. My first cousin Dennis Buckminster and his family moved to the old Fred P. Weed house in Stonington, directly across from John and Flossie Wallace's house. Harry Buckminster married my mother's sister Lunette, and they had two children, Marie and Dennis. Dennis used to ride his bicycle up to our house, and Garland, Dennis and I would romp through the woods and along the shore in Webb's Cove until way late in the day.

My cousin Carolyn Billings still lived with her grandparents in the old Barter homestead overlooking the Deer Isle Thoroughfare, Russ Island, and most of the Islands south toward Isle au Haut. My other cousin, Shirley Shepard, who also descended from John Jackson Billings, still lived with his mother, who had married George Donnelly. They lived in a new house that George built off the Green Head Road. Shirley was very smart in school, but we never became friends. He was a needler and always taunted me. But I would not be bullied and always fought back with my fists, retaining independence that way. Collis Jones and I dug clams together, and we were friends for all his life.

Thomas Warren lived in a nice house on Thurlow's Hill, and we were friends. He sold me a little ten-cent model airplane kit of a Piper cub, and it was the first one that I built that actually flew well. Everett Eaton was visiting, and I showed him how it would fly right off the floor. He almost cried; he wanted the little model so badly that I gave it to him, and he kept it for years and years.

Barbara Johnson and her sister Betty came up from Swans Island and attended school with us. Barbara was the first female that I paid any attention to. I was smitten, but she was playing the field, and eventually she married George Boyce and had several children. She became friends with my distant cousin Maxine Fifield, who married John Reid. That marriage failed, and Maxine married again. I haven't seen her for years.

Alvin Jones and I became friends, and he enlisted in the Air Force when World War II "came to Deer Isle." He married Barbara Bartlett, and eventually they had three sons. He used to come "flying" into our driveway and spin their 1932 Ford V8 around on the solid granite ledge, making the dust fly, and Dick would holler at him in a good-natured way. One day he came up to our little house bringing a little black pup, because his mother would not let him keep the little dog. By the time Dad came home from

AUTHOR STANDING IN DONALD McKAY'S YARD POSING FOR HIS COAST GUARD IDENTIFICATION PICTURE, WHICH WAS REQUIRED DIRECTLY AFTER THE PEARL HARBOR ATTACK IN 1941. NOTICE THE "RAGGEDY ANDY" JACKET SLEEVE HANGING IN RAGS.

work, the pup was firmly entrenched. We had eventually learned that my asthma was due to cat dander, and we had not had cats in quite a while.

I graduated from Stonington High School in 1945 but was drafted in the following spring; I went all the way down to Portland for the Army physical but was classified as 4F due to my asthma. I started working on John L. Goss Granite Quarry in the spring of 1947 and worked there until the last working day of November, 1950. I was drafted to serve in the U.S. Army during the "forgotten war" (in Korea).

Robert Carlton Hutchinson, "Hutch," and I were very close friends all his life. He lived a sort of floating existence between his mother's new marriage to Dr. Benjamin Lake Noyes and his sister Clemina (Sawyer) Knight at her mother's father's house, where their grandfather, Jack Reid, lived up the road (toward Deer Isle). Jack had a large farm, in our eyes: there were guinea hens, a cow, lots of ordinary hens, and I think there was also a pig or two. After Dr. Noyes died of cancer of the throat, Hutch lived in the doctor's house. Mrs. Estelle Noyes was very kind to Adrian Gray and me all her remaining years.

I bought my first car from Ralph Haskell. It was a 1925 Oakland six-cylinder; the engine looked very similar to the Pontiac six that came out in 1927 and quite possibly was the same engine. Truth in advertising had not been invented yet! I foolishly let Alan Dunham and Everett Billings talk me into going in on shares. But I learned from that ill-fated adventure. My next car was a 1929 Nash Advanced Six, a huge four-door sedan that had burned valves. I paid $200 for the eighteen-year-old antique. It was another learning experience. It had smooth truck tires all around. I bought two Sears and Roebucks 600X20 six-ply truck tires, and Dick and I mounted them on the spring-rimmed wire wheels using two tire irons and sandpaper, as the rims were rusty. The new front tires cured the front-end shimmy for quite a long time. We had tried replacing the king pins and bushings, but that didn't solve the shimmy. Years later I learned that it was mainly a wheel and tire balancing problem with cars that had straight front axles.

By 1950 the huge Nash Advanced Six engine needed to be completely rebuilt. I was earning $52 a week and paying Dad $20 a week for room and meals. With my extravagance at the gas pumps, there wasn't any money left to rebuild the engine properly. But I was told by my good friend "Gumper" Gray that a 1932 four-cylinder Plymouth was a good little car. "Budget" Eaton had one for sale for $40, so I bought it, and Gumper and I got it home somehow. The clutch was burned out. The valves were shot. It was a real schoolroom. Gumper and I worked on that thing off and on all summer. It wasn't much better on gas mileage than the Nash, but it was faster and had hydraulic brakes! Read "All's Fair in Love and War" (which was also published in the *International Haskell Families Society Newsletter*) for more details below.

42. FROM DAD'S JOURNALS, 1945

Jan. 1st: Earned $4,558.00 in 1942; $3,257.92 in 1943; $2,746.94 in 1944.

Jan. 5th: Cutting wood. Lots of snow, cold disagreeable month, some boat building going on at Moose Island Stonington-Deer Isle Yacht Basin Corp [Billings Marine in 2004]. Otis Shepard built a lobster boat. James "Casey" Robbins built a lobster boat. Bought car license, paid poll tax.

Feb. 3rd: Cold, loafing, that's still cutting a little wood.

Monday, Feb. 5th: Fair. $16.08. [Payment slip from L. G. Cortesi for chowder clams.]

Wednesday, Feb. 7th: Cold, overcast, N. E. winds. $8.64 clams.

Feb. 8th: Heavy snow storm.

Saturday Feb. 10th: Worked on the road, earned $9.90 . . . some rain in the night.

Feb. 17th: $4.80 [With payment slip from L. G. Cortesi for chowder clams].

Feb. 19: CLAMS $25.44.

Feb. 20th: Fair. Clams $17.76.

Feb. 21st: Fair. Clams $15.36.

Feb. 22nd: Fair. Clams $19.20.

Feb. 27th: $12.97; good weather continues warm and spring like.

March 3rd: $6.24 [With payment slip from L. G. Cortesi for 26 pounds of chowder clams @ 24 cents].

March 10th: 22 ½ pounds of chowder clams $5.40.

March 12th: 60 pounds of chowder clams @ 24 cents $14.40.

March 13th: Very good weather warm and spring like continues.

March 14th: 73 pounds of chowder clams $17.52.

March 16th: 31 pounds of chowder clams $7.44.

March 17th: 98 pounds of chowder clams $23.52.

March 21st: 50 pounds of chowder clams $12.00.

March 27th: 25 pounds @ 22 cents $5.50.

April 17th: 2 fish lines $2:00. 2 leads $5:00 [sinkers].

April 30th: Sold my car [1940 Nash Lafayette six-cylinder sedan] to George W. Gross this day $800. Hired with George Gross to go lobstering.

May 9th: Going lobstering with George Gross.

May 11th: Northeast winds snow and rain this day.

May 12th: Earned $10 this week.

May 14th: $10 today.

May 15th: Nothing.

May 16th: $10 today.

May 17th: Bought a suit of oil clothes $5.50 at R. K. Barter's.

43. Dick's Income, 1949

Dad's journals reveal that in 1949 he earned $2,564.13 for a whole year's work! (Form W2 U.S. Treasury Department, Internal Revenue Service.) Income tax? $10.50.

Dad was lobsterin' after work and on Saturdays. (Being a Latter Day Saint, he would not work on Sundays.) He kept a tally of his lobsterin' expenses but *naught* his earnings from fishing. He lost five traps (homemade) in 1952. "Lost" means that powerboats cut off the pot buoys and lines (pot warp). Dick built all his traps out of red-spruce bows and ordinary spruce laths. He knitted his own pot-heads and bait bags. He earned enough money so that it was worthwhile fishing!

He used Garland's old boat, which he and I put my old four-cylinder Plymouth engine into for power. He made a pot hauler out of a 1929

Chevrolet steering gear! He was very inventive. Early six-cylinder Buick steering gears would also work, as they were both worm-and-gearwheel type.

44. DICK'S STATIONARY-ENGINE SAWING MACHINE

In 1938 my father's fortunes had seemed to turn a corner. It had been ten years since he had been hit by that car, and his health and strength had improved. He had built a tiny house, eighteen feet long by twelve feet wide, and all five of us were jammed in there, happy to have our own little abode free from rent, but not from taxes.

Sometime in those years just before the United States became involved in the European war, Dick had acquired a Fairbanks and Morse stationary engine. It had been shoved back under the hayloft stairway of a distant Billings cousin and may have been used to hoist the sails on a huge four-masted schooner when it was fairly new. But as it was sliding down off a flatbed Ford truck on two stout wooden planks to rest beside the firewood pile, it resembled nothing more than an assembly of rusty metal parts adorned with two flywheels and a large rectangular iron casting that eventually came to be known as the cooling-water tank.

Dick took the cylinder head off the engine, and Lenny Judkins made a new exhaust valve in his lathe in Billings's Marine machine shop for the old Fairbanks and cleaned up the moving parts that separated inside the combustion chamber to create the spark "on time" of the make-and-break ignition system. The engine was so old it didn't have a sparkplug. Dick lapped in both valves with a "Jiffy" valve grinder and a liberal smear of Clover valve-grinding compound. He reassembled the engine with a homemade cylinder-head gasket, and attached ignition wires and a simple ignition coil to an old car battery. The addition of a gasoline tank (with gas in it) and some water in the cooling tank rendered the old Fairbanks ready to run! Garland and I gleefully jumped up and down as the Fairbanks and Morse finally barked into action.

Ralph Knowlton had a 1932 Chevrolet five-window coupe, which his little son had rendered dead in its tracks when he playfully poured dirt into the gas tank that was held onto the Chevy's rear frame irons with wide metal straps. Ralph was not a shade-tree mechanic, and Bob

McGuffie bought the car, so that he could put the six-cylinder engine in his lobster boat, a common practice in the lobster fisherman's world.

The old Chevy was dragged down to our place, and a stout tripod was erected using three red-spruce saplings, some pot warp and the ever-present wooden blocks. Dick reeved the blocks with used manila three-quarter-inch line, and a sling was made to hoist the Chevrolet six outta the chassis. Someone hauled the engine "ovah" to uncle Bob McGuffie's Sand Beach farm, and the engine was soon installed into Bob's wooden lobster boat.

Dick lined up the flange couplings with the aid of feeler gauges and thin oak shims under the homemade engine mounts, to make a smooth-running assembly. The engine was used without freshwater heat-transfer cooling equipment and lasted about eight years. The block rusted out, and the engine was replaced with a younger Chevrolet six.

Meanwhile, Dick had made a crosscut saw frame with two triangular supports for the cutoff saw's swinging table, and the front spring supports were used as hinge points for the table, which Dad had hammered out of the Chevy's stamped-steel dash panel. A running-board splash pan completed the table. The saw's mandrel was assembled from a sturdy inch-and-a-quarter shaft with adjustable plain bearings and a circular saw blade about twenty inches in diameter. Two short safety chains kept the table from falling onto the operator, as Dick sawed away with this contraption.

We usually sawed up five cords of green wood and heaved it onto a rough pile to be reassembled later into neat three-sided walls of "fitted firewood," if viewed from the open end. Several stacks of dry wood were stored inside Dick's shop to be used in really rainy weather. Five cords of softwood would heat the little house all winter. (With today's heating-oil prices, some Maine folks are reconverting to wood heat.)

The Fairbanks and Morse was fastened to two long spruce planks, and the saw frame was fastened to the far end of the wooden planks. The stationary engine had a flat-belt pulley on the left flywheel and a used fabric flat belt transferred the power to the cast-iron pulley on the mandrel of the saw frame. Belt dressing helped keep the belt from slipping, and Dick and I sawed "fitted" firewood from four-foot lengths of white birch, gray birch, red spruce, and a sometimes a fir tree, which we harvested on shares from "Les" Stinson's woodlot on the old colonial Stinson farmstead, which was located on Stinson's point in Webb's Cove, directly opposite the Settlement Quarry dock in the Oceanville section of Stonington. The old dock is now used as a lobster dealership and a kayak rental place, with daytrips in a small excursion boat, and most all of these things are advertised in the local paper, *Island Ad-Vantages*.

We used the sawing machine rig for several years, but Dick was unhappy with one of the loose flywheels, and he tried to tighten it on the crankshaft. Dad's methods were always, "don't use force, get a bigger hammer!" The tapered pin that secured the flywheel to the shaft had an early safety feature. The pin passed through the flywheel crankshaft boss and also through a partial bore through the crankshaft. This insured that the flywheel would not fly off the crankshaft when the engine was working, if the locking pin's retaining nut should work loose. Dad gave the flywheel a wicked rap with his quarry hammer, and the cast-iron flywheel broke in two right through the retaining hole in the boss. "Well o' course," that was the end of the sawing machine's usefulness.

Dick never found another inexpensive stationary engine that he could attach to the saw frame, and it sat there forlornly for quite some time. Eventually it went to the local dump or to an antique engine collector; I never enquired. It simply wasn't there after a while. So Dick used a huge Lombard chain saw that Wink brought up from Montauk Point, New York, where he worked for Perry B. Duryea & Son. It would whack up five cords of wood quite quickly, and the Lombard could be stored inside the saw sharpening shed, out of the weather.

Wallace "Bud" Carter made a firewood cutoff saw using a large Briggs & Stratton air-cooled engine mounted on an old Ford chassis. The whole works could be towed by a car or small pickup truck equipped with a tow bar and trailer ball. My brother-in-law keeps it at their new house on the Reach Road. I borrowed it once to saw up my firewood. It roars into action, and the large saw blade whirls around frighteningly, but it makes short work of reducing four-foot lengths of oak and ash into fitted lengths for our little Jøtul cast-iron camp stove.

45. HOME ON THE RANGE

After we moved to the new house below Tea Hill Corner, Dad built a henhouse some distance towards the back of the property and also up on a high spot of the granite ledge that underlies all of our little homestead, so that Marm could start keeping hens.

She began with two dozen Rhode Island Reds. I seem to remember they arrived one nice spring day, and they were immediately accepted as

HAROLD GREENLAW LOADING TRAPS AT THE CLAM CITY CO-OP. WIRE TRAPS ON THE STERN, RADAR DOME ON TOP OF HOUSE. Photo CMH.

pets. Eventually they came down with some ailment, and our mother, Mill, fed them medicine with an eyedropper. They all recovered, but some new hatchlings from her own broody hen did not. But that was later in the course of raising chickens. As the hatchlings matured, we began to feed them empty shucked-out clamshells, and the little broilers pecked away until the shells were almost surgically clean. Of course, once the pullets began laying; their eggshells seemed to be armor plated.

I would trudge down to Ben Sturdee's store in Stonington with a dozen eggs, and Ben would credit it toward something for our larder. Some days, as I walked downtown, "Aunt Ruth" (not really related to us at all, and not an endearment either) would call for me to bring back something from the store, where her husband worked as a clerk. I carried her groceries back, and she would give me a nickel.

When Charles Cleveland, the local trucker, brought a bag of chicken feed, I had to wheel it into Dad's shop on the wheelbarrow, as I couldn't lift a full bag at that time. I was merely ten years old. However, the time would come when I could carry a full bag!

Once in a while Marm would decide that a particular hen wasn't doing her job, not laying eggs, and she was "marked" for Sunday's dinner. I was the *matador de gallinas* (slaughterer of hens), and Mill would direct me to capture "that one." I chased the unlucky bird and grabbed her by both legs, gave her a lit' tap with the axe handle; then, while she was "commontoast," I put her head down on the sturdy maple chopping block, and with one whack of Dad's splitting axe, she was destined for the oven.

Say what you will, that old woodstove produced the most delicious roast "oven staffers" ever. After Garland became our "great white hunter," we had delicious rabbit stews cooked very slowly on the back firebox covers of the Home Clarion.

Trimmings were Marm's very own homegrown Katahdin potatoes, carrots, and beans. Oh! We might have been considered monetarily poor, but we ate well. In the summer and late fall, our table was graced with delicious Swiss chard, beet tops, or canned dandelion greens, and Marm's very own vine-ripened tomatoes. Sometimes she made Johnny cake, served with hard sauce. I haven't had any of that delicious dessert since 1974, some of the things that I really miss.

"Well o' course!" as Hez Robbins would shout while looking straight into the heavens, eventually keeping hens became more expensive than buying prepared chicken at the store. All the work became tiring as Mother aged and began having mysterious medical problems. The henhouse became an auxiliary woodshed and storage place for cast-off items.

SEA FLEA FROM BROOKSVILLE, AT CO-OP #2 DOCK, STONINGTON; WIRE TRAPS STORED ON THE DOCK. LOBSTAH FLEET IS IN TH' HABHAH. Photo Pam H. Haskell, 1999.

After Dad came home from working at Pratt & Whitney, he worked on the old John L. Goss granite quarry, but eventually it came under Deer Isle Granite management until the Kennedy Memorial job, after which the whole works seemed to collapse. Dad still sharpened saws for the fishermen and local carpenters or anyone else who might like to have a sharp handsaw. Sometimes he eked out $25 in a week by sharpening saws, and it might have worked out to ten cents an hour in time spent. Eventually, wire traps replaced the wooden "poverty crates" (to quote Skeet McDonald of Isle au Haut), and the fishermen didn't need to keep a hand saw on board their lobster boats. Fiberglass boats with marine diesel engine power replaced the wooden boats with automobile engines. But some of the older fishermen are having new wooden boats built, because they say the fiberglass "Clorox bottles" make their knees ache.

An aside: Dr. Thomas P. Haviland, my father-in-law, gave Dad some raspberry plants, and he planted them in the abandoned hen yard. All those residual droppings had leached into the poor soil and made it nitrogen-rich. The raspberry plants grew and produced delicious berries. Forty-seven years later, there may still have been one or two plants producing berries. However, in 2008 the plants had all succumbed to frost and neglect. I write about these times as if I missed them. But like an old Maine joke, "I couldn't stand another Maine wintah, deah!"

46. THE PERFECT HARLEQUIN

Before television became the center of family entertainment, some of the Stonington natives would come to visit and tell stories about their latest adventures, and that usually set the stage for an evening of tales, tall and short. When there were story-telling sessions, I enjoyed retelling the "Perfect Harlequin" tale for years and even today!

Beginning sometime after 1938, Dad wanted Garland and me to help him dig clams, which at that time earned 35 cents a bushel. Two men that Dad knew anchored their "buyer" boat in Webb's cove. We three descended onto the clam-flats (which is a misnomer, as the most productive areas were amidst the glacial erratic boulders scattered along the sloping shore). There were also flat areas of deep, sticky mud, but it was quite a while later that we discovered how to exploit them. I was just ten years old and Garland thirteen months younger than me. We scratched away, and each eventually accumulated a bushel of clams.

Dad was angered and frustrated when we sold our clams to the buyers. He wanted to keep our 35 cents. "I'd think you would want to help me out," he stormed, which only quenched what little enthusiasm we had for such brutal work.

As time went on and we grew older and stronger, we began to see clamming as a way to earn "spending money." During World War II, R. K. Barter's fish factory was buying clams "steamed out." Several clam diggers were working the flats "up in th' cove." One family had a rudimentary brush camp on the north side of Stinson's Point, and there they steamed their clams in a galvanized washtub and cut the heads (siphons) off with a pair of scissors, using a driftwood plank nailed to a white (skunk) spruce tree, with driftwood legs nailed on for supports, the whole assembly serving as a work table.

Our cousin Elston Hooper, Garland and I used a crevice in a granite ledge as our fireplace and steamed out our clams using driftwood and fallen spruce trees for fuel. We worked after school when the tides were favorable, and on weekends. We carried the cooked clams down to the fish factory in a ten-quart pail. The further we walked the heavier the load seemed to become.

We scratched away at this work for what seemed to be forever, and once in 1944, I earned $85 during the Thanksgiving week off from school. I had earned enough money to buy a Sears and Roebuck's suit, right out of the mail-order catalogue. It was brown, and I had some brand-new white shirts, shoes, and accessories for the class trip to Boston in the spring of 1945. I was quite proud of myself.

My friend Bobby Hutchinson lived at that time with his grandfather Jack Reid, one sister known as "Meanie," and her husband, known as "Bilgewater," in a square, two-story, hip-roofed house, just two houses north of our new abode located south of Tea Hill Corner. Jack had come from Scotland and in his old age made return trips in the summertime to visit friends and family.

Once and only once did Bobby get really mad at me. "Hutchie" and I walked over the Tea Hill Road, past the Knowlton cemetery where my grandmother is interred, dressed in our clamming gear, fisherman's hip-boots, the tops rolled down, raggedy clothes, and carrying our clam hoes and rollers. We passed through Ralph Knowlton's cow pasture gate, being careful to close and secure it, lest some cows got out. We continued down the slope past my grandmother's house to emerge at last on the sandy clam-flats in front of Dad's driftwood boathouse-cum-blacksmith's forge. We pulled the tops of the boots up and began digging clams out beyond the sandy area, which had recently been "dug over," in a patch of really soft and sticky mud. There was a trick to walking in the sticky mud. I had to break the mud's suction by twisting my foot and then slide it ahead, something like cross-country skiing, in order to move about in the "gumbo."

I had nearly filled one clam roller, and Hutch was struggling just to move about in the flats. Eventually, he pulled one boot partly off his foot, and while trying to retain his balance and restore the boot to his foot, holding his clam hoe in one hand and pulling on the boot top with the other, he overbalanced and fell face first, full length into the mud, with a tremendous splash. I began to laugh as he struggled to his feet, looking for all the world like a perfect harlequin. There was a vertical line of dark mud from the top of his head to the bottom of his hip boots, and I was standing there, doubled over, laughing. "Cabbage, you bastard, I'm gonna kill ya!" he roared. Elston and I had talked and talked about how much fun it would be to get "one of them city slickers" out in that soft mud and have him fall in face-first. But in retrospect, this was even funnier.

47. MORE TEA HILL MISCHIEF

Another mischief session seemed to occur at regular intervals, when the spring saltwater smelt-spawning run occurred. Elston, my cousin, and I went down to Webb's Brook to catch smelts on a rising tide well after dark, armed with empty clam rollers and flashlights. We made nightly excursions when the weather was fair. The "smelt brook" was known to us as Webb's Cove Brook, and the path down through the woods ran right past the Morrisons' privy. Elston, who had a wicked and destructive mindset, thought that pushing the outhouse over so it would lie flat on its side would be fun.

Almond "Zeke" Eaton was the caretaker, and he surmised that "we" were the culprits and read the riot act to us, not mincing any words!

I innocently told my friend Hutchie about Zeke's dressing us down, and he immediately came up with a new idea. Four of us strolled down along the spruce-tree-shaded driveway to the "Old Thompson Place" (Morrison's), pushed the privy over, lifted and carried it down to Little Webb's Cove, and pitched it into the water with a satisfying splash.

Zeke was outraged. He had to winch it back ashore with planks to serve as a ramp, and, aided by block and tackle, he and friends hove it up, high and somewhat more dry, on the high water. Apparently vexed, Mrs. Morrison invested in a modern indoor bathroom shortly after our last, not quite harmless, prank.

48. THE ICE-HOUSE RAID

Our first cousin Dennis Buckminster, son of Harry and Lunette (Torrey) Buckminster, moved to Stonington sometime during World War II, so that Harry could work in the Billings shipyard on Moose Island, which was reached by a narrow causeway that presently cuts through two lobster pounds. Dennis used to ride his bicycle up to our house through "Gray Town," past the Stonington High School, which contained at that time all twelve grades. There was no kindergarten, and "Head Start" was taught by diligent mothers at home. My mother taught me to read Beatrix Potter's *Peter Rabbit*, but I never became a mathematician.

When our cousin arrived, there were many adventures to keep us entertained all day, and we usually abandoned his bicycle in the yard and set out for Tea Hill right through the woods, as it was a challenge to navigate by the sun, which we could see once in a while as we plunged deeper into the spruce and gray birch forest. We usually reached the shore near Dad's old workshop-cum-forge, and from there we cruised the "old Indian trail" on Phoebe Thurston's Point as far as William and Emily Muir's house and studio, which sat on granite ledges overlooking the Deer Isle-Stonington thoroughfare, but we hardly ever actually walked past these buildings. The Thurston family settled in Green's Landing (now Stonington). Emily's parents bought the whole of Phoebe Thurston's Point and had local carpenters dismantle the old farmhouse and outbuildings; then they had a new summer home made out of the hand-hewn timbers. It used to sit upon a slight slope with a fieldstone wall at the beach line, with the house overlooking the Thoroughfare. The result was a handsome white cottage that was a landmark for fishermen and cruising sailboaters alike.

After Emily's parents passed away, she had the house demolished, and after her sculptor husband also passed away, she eventually began to sell off house lots on the point, where there are at least five summer cottages at the present time. She continued to paint in oil and make mosaics using seashells and beach pebbles. She also designed and had the local carpenters build summer homes on shore lots that she bought up after stricter federal regulations caused local dairy farms to close— the farmers being unable to buy the required equipment to make these tiny dairy farms profitable. Emily had at least six houses built on the old Charles Barbour property facing Crockett's Cove.

As we Tea Hill children grew older and married, we abandoned the old Indian trail. But several years ago, Pam and I ventured out along the north side of the point, and as we walked past the extensive Indian shell midden on the south side, we came upon a new house. We peeked over the top of a huge granite ledge and saw someone knitting in the sunny ocean-facing room. So we retreated, as we didn't want to alarm her.

Back to the 1940s: One morning Dennis arrived, and we left his bike leaning up against the shed and walked up to explore Burnt Land Pond for a change. At that time there was an abandoned ice house on the extreme east end of the pond. George Noyes had started an ice business, but refrigerators for America's kitchens were becoming almost common, and he gave up the business. A cart road provided access to the pond and the ice house that sat a little to the south of its graveled surface. Garland, Dennis, and I began to climb about amongst the beams and rafters, enjoying ourselves, when three youngsters from "Tarred Paper Avenue" ran in and began pitching rocks at us.

I ducked behind a vertical rafter brace, and the stones bounced off of the timber harmlessly! Unfortunately for the attackers, one stone hit Garland, who jumped down into the sawdust and grabbed up a heavy steel coal shovel, and screaming like a demon he began to whale about with the shovel. He knocked one down at once and then a second; the third had sense enough to abandon the attack and ran outside shouting to the others, "Git outta here!"

The first casualty got to his feet and was about to escape, when he realized that the third and largest one was in trouble: Garland was bashing him over and around his head with the shovel, and blood was running out of him. So he turned back and managed to drag the stunned attacker outside, while Garland stood ready to deliver more blows, as they staggered away, never, ever to bother us again. (In a 2008 telephone conversation with Garland, who lives in Texas, he said that his weapon was a logging peavy. Possibly he dropped the shovel and grabbed up the more formidable tool later in his outrage. Ironically, all three of our attackers have passed away.)

49. THE STEEL SKIFF

Dad had sold his fine carvel-planked peapod and a 1928 Chevrolet coach, as he needed money for expenses while he worked in Pratt & Whitney, until the first paycheck arrived, so we ranged around "the cove," from the old Knowlton-Haskell homestead shore, north and south without a boat. One day Dennis, Garland, and I walked up to the Oceanville storage yard, where the road commissioner kept assorted fifty-five-gallon drums of asphalt and other road repair items. We found one steel drum that was empty and rolled it down through the woods to the shore. We pushed and alternately towed it all the way back to Dad's shop, where we used one of his blacksmith's cut-off tools to open the drum like a clam shell by cutting right across both heads and down one side. A driftwood board made a makeshift seat, and like Huckleberry Finn we were ready for waterborne adventures. However, paddles were not satisfactory, as the craft whirled around like a Welsh coracle. So Garland fashioned wooden thole pins forced into drilled holes in a thick board, which was then fastened to the sides with nails driven through and clenched over. The three of us could swim well enough to get back to shore if the steel skiff sank, and we played with the thing for hours. Mooring it wasn't a problem: we simply sank it above the half-tide mark and retrieved it when we wanted to play.

Marm was worried about us drowning or something, and when Dad came home on one of his visits, he, Garland and I went down to O. B. & F. P. Weed's lumber yard on what is now called Atlantic Avenue and found two very wide and long white pine boards. These became the sides of a large skiff. Dad hacked out two driftwood frames and shaped a stem with his hewing axe. Garland and I enthusiastically helped bend the sides to meet the transom, using a doubled hunk of salvaged pot warp from Webb's Cove, found somewhere along its extensive shores. By twisting the lines with a long spruce sapling, Spanish-windlass fashion, we forced the ends to meet the transom, while Dad nailed the sides to the transom frames. We secured the cross-planked bottom with galvanized nails.

We two little boys hammered clumsily away, while Dad encouraged us. A stern seat was fashioned with a support brace, a midship thwart seat was constructed all out of white pine, and a triangular thwart seat filled the gap at the bow. A large hole bored crosswise through the stem provided a secure place to attach the salvaged pot-warp painter. With a set of oak thole pins and two spruce oars, we were ready to sail to Spain in our imaginations (from a wonderful "Newfie" folk song, "We're bound away, me boys").

Dad finished off the project with two coats of brindle gray paint. (He simply poured all his leftover paints into a one-gallon pail and stirred it all together, which amused the Webb's Cove lobster fishermen, Guy Eaton, Pete Knowlton, and Ken Jones immensely.) We explored all the nearby islands, fished for flounders in the cove, and Uncle Elroy tested his new Evinrude opposed-twin, 10-horsepower outboard by clamping it onto the skiff's transom sometime after the war had ended. He pronounced the skiff as being quite fast.

We had been on a clamming trip somewhere with Dad in the skiff and were rounding "the point" when we spied little Wink, our youngest brother, paddling across the cove in the steel skiff. He could not swim, so we quietly rowed up alongside of him and managed to get him aboard without mishap. The oil-drum boat only had an inch or so of freeboard, so we sank "her" right there in deep water, so that no other non-swimmer would drown playing in her. By then Wink was ten or eleven.

One day we were up in Little Webb's Cove, romping around. Dennis had left his bicycle lying in Ralph Knowlton's recently-harvested potato field, and I grabbed it up and climbed on board and started to pedal up the slope, shouting, "I'm going to town." Dennis let fly with a homemade arrow which had a nail embedded in the head to help it go straight. The arrow sliced neatly and rapidly through a fresh cow pie, which lubricated the shaft and changed its trajectory to lodge in my right temple. Down I went, kersmash, right into another fresh cow pie; blood was spurting out of my head. Collis Jones, Garland, and Dennis came running "to see if I was kilt." The bike seemed to be undamaged. I was nearly OK, so I walked home so that Marm could clean the wound and administer first aid. Marm was alarmed and worried about our bows and arrows. There was never another mishap with those toys.

We found a gravel pit on Great-Aunt Rhoda's land filled to overflowing with winter snowmelt and rainwater runoff, so we cleaned it out one dry summer day to use as a swimming hole the following spring. The water was nice and warm in late May, compared to the frigid ocean waters in Webb's Cove. So we merrily dove off the banks into the shallow pond, belly-whoppers being the preferred method. But by mid June the water had evaporated or leached away, so much that swimming wasn't possible. So we transferred our diving to the coal tipple mast on the old Noyes coal dock in Stonington, where Hutch held forth as champion noise-maker.

Several years later, Alan Dunham and I were going up to Deer Isle to swim in the lily pond, and we stopped to pick up Hutchie at R. K. Barter's lobster dock. He was quite wet up to above his knees from rousting lobster crates about, and he asked, "Is it OK if I come wet?" "Sure," said Alan. Hutch jumped off the dock, boots and all; then he rode on the right front fender all the way up to the Quaco Road, where the natives parked in someone's field while they went swimming.

50. THE FROG POND SWIMMING HOLE

Sometime during World War II, Dad came home from Connecticut and started working at Billings Marine on Moose Island, which was connected to Stonington by a narrow causeway. The yard had a contract to build air-sea rescue craft and a large wooden boat that eventually went to the Antarctic and was used for scientific exploration.

My mother's sister Lunette (Torrey) Buckminster and her family came down to Meeting House Hill and lived in Fred P. Weed's house, which was within walking distance of the shipyard. There were two children, Marie and her brother Dennis who was close to my age and Garland's. We were soon roaming the woods on Phoebe Thurston's Point in Webb's Cove, beachcombing, fishing for flounders, and digging clams for the larder.

One warm spring day, as we three boys walked out of the old woods road and coming upon the old gravel pit that was chock full of water, we thought that we could clean it out and use it as a swimming hole! Such excitement and energy—the gravel pit that was located about halfway between Clam City and our new yellow house on what is now called North Main Street. The three of us went down through the woods on the old tote road that was used to haul granite paving blocks from a small paving motion quarry out to North Main Street, back in the very early Green's Landing settlement days.

Considerable labor had been expended in building a very strong single-span granite bridge across the stream that wandered through the woods down to Ames Pond, near the end of the Clam City Road. The Ames family dammed the stream during the early granite-quarrying days, to sell water to the quarries on Green Island, Saint Helena Island, and possibly the larger quarries on Crotch Island, for use in the boilers. After John L. Goss quarrying operations had resulted in a huge reservoir on

Crotch Island, there was no longer a market for the Ames pond water. But the pond remains to this day, and in winter it may still serve as the local skating rink, where on sunny weekend days there might have been as many as twenty skaters enjoying the day skating, clowning around, and flirting with the local talent.

Once we were across the granite bridge, we shortly came to the old gravel pit, and we began to clean it out. It had been unused for quite some time, and there were old auto chassis and even sheet-metal parts of a Model T Ford coupe. Such industry! We worked and worked. I think that the planning stages were much better than the actual reward of being able to swim in the pond for a few weeks in early summer; by August there would be less than a foot of water in the pit. But in late May, the winter snowmelt and spring rains had filled the pit to make a nice swimming hole. We three jumped in and dogpaddled around noisily; the closest houses were quite well away from the pond. We swam there off and on, and it was almost a secret spot. In June the water was still high enough for a refreshing dip; by then bullfrogs were sounding off, and dragonflies and water spiders were active on the pond. We went up to Burnt Land Pond and caught some bluegills that we dumped into the pond, and for several years they survived in very shallow water conditions. Weather cycles changed, and eventually the gravel pit was just that, completely dry and without any signs of marine life.

One late February or early March day, my distant cousin, who lived in Clam City, enticed me to try out the spongy-looking ice on the old gravel pit. I walked out very carefully, while he stayed safely on the bank. Suddenly the ice gave way, and I plunged into the frigid water, feet first. I managed to smash my way ashore and rushed home up the old tote road. Dad wasn't the least bit sympathetic and lectured me about old pond ice. I never trusted my cousin again, and we never became friends, although his mother tried to mend the broken fences all her life.

51. ADVENTURES ON THE ICE AT BURNT LAND POND

On one of Dad's return trips from East Hartford, Connecticut, during World War II, he bought an old 1929 Chevrolet coach from Malcolm Williams for $40. General Motors made their bodies out of wood until 1937; these bodies were sheathed with thin panels of steel. The tops were covered with a rubberized fabric that leaked water after a few years. The "rain in Maine" leaked down through the structure and rapidly rotted the wooden doorposts and windshield supports.

Ralph Knowlton bought a used 1932 Chevrolet coupe. However, Garland and I removed the twenty-one-inch disc wheels from Dad's 1929 coach and installed the wheels from the coupe, which had decent tires, onto the old Chevy. The wood continued to decay, and one day the starboard door fell right out onto the ground as we turned left!

Eventually we had the doors tied on with pot warp, and near the end of being able to use the old car, the windshield fell out onto the hood and teetered there, while I stopped the vehicle at Tilden Knowlton's little store across from the old Stonington schoolhouse. I loaded the windshield onto the back seat and continued to the movies.

One very cold winter day in the late forties, after Dad had returned to Tea Hill for good, Hutch came down and we got the long hand crank and inserted it through the crank support hardware on the front of the Chevy to get it going. The '29 Chevys were the first model to have automatic spark advance and a fuel pump, but the gas gauge was still outside on the gas tank, which was slung between the rear frame spring supports. The car now had no windshield and had been left behind the saw sharpening workshop. We managed to get the six-cylinder engine going without breaking an arm. Sometimes an engine would kick back while being cranked by hand! I drove up to Burnt Land Pond and onto the ice-loading ramp on the east end of the pond, where George Noyes had the ice house. We drove out onto the ice, where we played at spinning it around on the slippery surface. Then we got an idea to ram a dead spruce tree, with nearly fatal results.

I got the ol' Chevy up to speed, and we shot off onto the frozen bog at the west end of the pond and rammed the tree, which promptly snapped off above the radiator height. The top portion then toppled in through the windshield opening and rammed directly between Hutch and me. The old car fetched up solid on the stump, and we then assessed the damage. Hutch had a bleeding scrape on his left shoulder, and I had some scratches on my right arm. We both had holes in our clothes and were quite surprised that the tree hadn't simply fallen over away from the car! We labored away trying to lever the old Chevy out over the spruce stump and eventually drove it back behind Dick's saw-sharpening shop, where it sat until Alfred Joyce bought the engine and transmission to put in his lobster boat. Dad, ever the Yankee trader, managed to recover more than his original expenditure.

Our adventures on ice were forever after limited to skating on Ames Pond, near the end of the Clam City Road. On nice winter weekend days, people would come from all over the Island to skate on the pond. Almost always somebody attempted to roast potatoes in the hot coals of a deadwood fire, which always seemed to be located in the spruce forest on the west side of the pond. Sometimes someone would cut some spruce and fir saplings and make a large, nearly comfortable tepee, the needle-covered boughs holding in some of the heat of the fire.

About the time that we were recovering from the jolt of knocking down the dead spruce tree, the Flying Santa Claus, Mr. Wincapaw, who was famous in Maine for dropping Christmas presents from his little airplane down to lighthouse keepers' families on Maine's offshore islands, started barnstormin' flights off of Burnt Land Pond. I heard the little Aeronca land upon the pond, so I pelted up the road to see what was goin' on! He took me up for a li'l flight over the town. It was one of those crystal-clear winter days, and I could see out over the bay to Isle au Haut and all the islands in between; I could see the extent of undersea ledges down through the deep green seawater from the air. Then he brought the red-colored light plane down as smooth as a smelt, and I was so thrilled that I paid for another flight right then and there. He let me fly the plane for a moment. I discovered that it's difficult to keep 'er level and straight. Pretty soon we landed again. His assistant stayed on the ice with their supply of gasoline. Every time that they shut 'er down to wait for another customer, it was his job was to restart the engine by pulling on the propeller. It was very, very cold and uncomfortable standing around on the pond ice, so I scuffed down the road to cuddle up with a good book, while they flew folks around for a few more flights.

52. My Cousin Melvin

Years later, I went down Tea Hill Road to what used to be our grandmother's house to interview my first cousin Melvin Haskell. It was early September. He was getting ready to take down the deer fence around his garden, clean it out, pull up all the plants and weeds and rototill it before the first frost. It was a crystal-clear day. The water in Webb's Cove was sparkling in the sunshine, crows were cawing in the woods, and always-hungry gulls were circling the lobster boats moving about on the water.

Melvin and his wife, Barbara, came to visit us during the 50th anniversary year of VJ Day, and he talked and talked about his experiences in World War II. I said, "Mel, you ought to write it all up!" But he didn't think so. One day I thought I might be able to write about his experiences. After several early morning visits, the following is Mel's story.

Melvin Fred Haskell, gunner's mate 1st class, United States Navy, was born in Stonington, Maine, on December 5th, 1922. He attended Stonington High School. He lived a short way from his father's twin brother Leroy E. Haskell's family on Clam City Road, which has been renamed Indian Point Road, but the natives stubbornly call it Clam City to this day. There is a view from his house out across the Deer Isle Thoroughfare to Russ Island, Harbor Island, and Green Island. You can see Isle au Haut over the treetops of Green Island.

Melvin joined the U.S. Navy on December 12th, 1940, and took basic training at Newport, Rhode Island. He was quartered in B Barracks, which somehow became infected with scarlet fever, so doctors thoroughly examined everyone who didn't have obvious signs of the ailment and transferred them to A Barracks. Eventually Melvin was assigned to the USS *Constitution* as seaman second class. "I was polishing brass and scrubbing decks to keep the old ship looking nice for the tourists," he said with a wry smile. "One day the battleship USS *Texas* came into Newport, and most of the trainees from A Barracks were assigned to duty on her. The new swabbies holystoned the teak decks, which was good occupational exercise."

Melvin wanted to become a seaman first class. First he tried for ship's electrician, but every request he submitted was passed over. There seemed to be endless lines applying for the most desirable ratings. Finally he tried for gunner's mate and was accepted.

The *Texas* had five gun turrets: two forward, two aft, and one amidships. He was assigned to the midship turret, which had two fourteen-inch naval rifles with barrels forty-five feet long. Each projectile weighed 1,600 pounds and was sent up to the turrets by a conveyor belt. The powder came on a separate conveyor, a single 100 lb. bag to each set of hooks.

A naval gun could be loaded in eleven seconds. The projectile was rammed into the breech with a mechanical rammer; then four bags of powder were pushed in; then a small capsule of fulminate of mercury was placed in the breech firing mechanism. The breech was closed, and it was ready to fire.

Sometime after 1940, the guns were sighted by radar, but originally with a range finder, and possibly the help of one of two spotter planes carried on top of the midship turret. A catapult powered by a black-powder charge launched the spotter plane. The turret was trained out; the pilot revved up the plane's big radial engine, and when the ship was rolling up to a favorable launching attitude, came a command from the bridge to fire! And the pilot had to get up to flying speed before the plane dropped into the sea! Once aloft, the pilot would observe where the projectiles were hitting and radio corrections to the ship.

"We were on the ball," Melvin said. "Everything was done by the book, and none of my men ever got hurt. The *Texas* was sent on convoy duty with the Atlantic fleet from Newport News to New York, traveling back and forth along the coast. Then she was sent to Newfoundland and docked at Argentia."

He reflected on that. "The wind blew somethin' wicked in that place! We made a few convoy trips to Reykjavik, Iceland, and Greenock, a small port on the west coast of Scotland. There wasn't much there, but the railroad tracks came right down to the pier, so we piled on board the train, and the steam locomotive hauled us off to Edinburgh to see the sights. "Once we went into Belfast, Northern Ireland, with a couple of cruisers, some destroyers, and about a dozen cargo ships carrying food, clothing and supplies for the war effort. We went to the Gold Coast of Africa a few times, escorting convoys of assorted types of cargo ships."

After December 7th, 1941, the *Texas* went to the Mediterranean. She bombarded French naval positions on the North African coast at Oran, Algiers, and Casablanca, Morocco. During her devastating bombardment of the French fleet at Casablanca, she punched huge holes above the waterline in the French battleship *Jean-Bart*. Afterwards she sailed to the Brooklyn Navy Yard for three months of refitting. Her guns were taken out and relined. The linings had worked out of the barrels about four inches, so they needed relining badly. "The ten barrels, weighing seventy tons each, were shipped to Dahlgren, Virginia, to be refurbished. While we were there, all the hydraulic systems of the five turrets were also cleaned and completely overhauled in preparation for the invasion of Normandy.

On June 6th, 1944, we went in with the invasion armada at 2:00 a.m. We worked slowly to a position to effectively bombard the German shore batteries and troop concentrations. Mine sweepers were crisscrossing our bows constantly, as we crept close enough to start shelling the Germans' concrete fortifications. At times we could see mines in the water very, very close to the sides of the ship. One or two actually scraped along the sides, but we were lucky and none of them went off!

At first the skipper anchored but soon decided that it wasn't a good idea. We kept under way all the time after that. If there were any German submarines in the vicinity, Allied destroyers and corvettes kept them down with depth charges. The Luftwaffe was so reduced in numbers that their planes were a mere nuisance by that time.

Sometime during the invasion, but after the beachhead was established, the *Texas* took a hit below the bridge. It buckled the deck plates and damaged the stairwell. There were some casualties. We retired to the Weymouth Naval Yard, England. We stayed there for about a week, while welders and other shipyard workers made repairs.

Next, the *Texas* was sent to bombard the Italian Riviera, as a diversion, while the main force invaded at Anzio. Before the Germans surrendered, we went through the Panama Canal and steamed to the Pacific. There we bombarded Iwo Jima and were attacked by kamikaze pilots. I was gunner's mate on the port side. The gunners were strapped in and straddling their anti-aircraft cannon mounts, when a pilot came diving in, waggling his wings from right to left in an attempt to make him harder to shoot down. When the command "Commence firing" came down from the bridge, we let him have it with the 20mm and 40mm cannons. His plane blew up in mid-air and the pilot fell out. There were aircraft pieces falling into the sea, and I think the pilot was dead before he hit the water. The Higgins boats were milling around and picked his body up. They took his remains to the hospital ship USS *Hope*, that was about four miles away. One of the kamikaze pilots was floating in the water. When one of the officers tried talking to him, he brandished a knife, so one of the Marines shot him. We shelled the Japanese shore positions, and after awhile the Marines went in and about a month later captured the island.

After Iwo Jima I flew to Frisco and went into hospital and from there to Boston, where I stayed with a friend, Madeline Goddis, who was like a sister to me. My mother, Christine (Terry) Haskell, had brought her up after she lost her parents. Madeline passed away about four years ago. Next I went back to the Newport, Rhode Island, Training Center for special training, and there were signs: DOGS AND SAILORS KEEP OFF THE GRASS!

When the Japanese surrendered, I went to Bremerhaven, Germany, on a troop ship with eighty sailors and five thousand relief troops. We navy personnel were quartered in Luftwaffe barracks with drop-down bunks supported by chains. I was in a room with three other men, and we began to learn how to run the German heavy cruiser *Prinz Eugen*. Eventually, we moved onto the ship and were told to find a place to sleep, so another feller and I scouted around and found the admiral's cabin below the bridge. We were there, nice and cozy, for about two weeks before the ship's officers discovered we were in there and routed us out.

The ship had two captains, one American and one German. We took her out on a shakedown cruise, and they worked her up to twenty-seven knots, as fast as they dared to, I suppose! She had two main diesel engines and two propeller shafts and was very maneuverable. She could turn on a dime by going ahead on one engine and reversing the other one. The gun turrets had metric-sized cannons. They were about nine- or ten-inch bores, I would say. Her turrets were more automated than the *Texas*, which was an old World War I battleship with three-legged masts. Tips for the projectiles, which were stainless steel, were kept in a wooden box. There were eight to ten fuses in a row and four or five rows of these tips in the box. They could be set to explode in midair or to penetrate heavy armor plating and explode inside the target ship. The detonator charges were fulminate of mercury and had to be handled very carefully, as it was an unstable explosive. We took the *Prinz Eugen* across the Atlantic and into Boston, then sailed down the coast and tied up in the Philadelphia Naval Shipyard. A team of metallurgists came aboard, and I was with them for about three days while they tested the hardness of the ship's guns and other metal parts.

Sometime later we went through the Panama Canal and cruised to Bikini Atoll as part of the atomic tests, A. H. Graubart, USN, commanding. We were there four or five months, benchmarking sections of the ships. There were three blasts, A, B, and C. The target ships were arranged in a circle, with the old *Nevada* painted a bright orange—so the bomber pilot and bombardier could easily spot her—anchored in the center. After the first blast, the *Nevada* was gone! Blast C was underwater. I went down into the ships after the blasts and took radioactive readings, wearing special breathing apparatus. I had to take this gear off in order to get down into the ships' magazines to take samples of the black powder and the explosive charges inside the ships' projectiles. There was very little radioactivity inside the *Prinz Eugen*.

After awhile I received notice of my terminal leave, while I was ashore on Kwajalein, and I asked a WAVE in the headquarters building, "How do I get back to the States?" She said, "Walk over to the Army Air Force Base and get onto one of the transport planes. They fly out twice a day." So, I took my sea bag and climbed aboard a big four-engine plane. It had pipe racks running the length of the cargo area. I loaded my gear up onto those and tried to get comfortable. I wasn't, but it beat rowing home. We landed at Wake Island, and eventually I arrived at the Fargo Building Separation Center in San Francisco. I was honorably discharged on December 10th, 1946. My discharge paper lists my ratings held as: AS, S2C, SIC, GM3C, GM2C, GM1C.

I married Barbara Sorel in June of 1949, and there are four children: Susan, Sandra, Vivian, and Donald. Susan has three daughters and one son. Sandra has one daughter and two sons. Vivian has one of each, and Donald has two daughters.

Melvin and Barbara live in the house where his father Elroy and twin Leroy grew up with their mother Mary Jane Billings Knowlton Haskell, three half-brothers, Albert, Raymond, and Cecil, two half-sisters, Ethel and Florence, and one sister, Christie Mae Haskell. Mel has made many renovations to the old house, reinforcing floor joists, replacing the drafty windows with Thermopane, but like Maine folks of olden times, he uses wood for "back-up" winter heat.

There is a narrow view through a gap in the spruce forest out over Webb's Cove. The house is built high on the side of a sloping granite ledge, as are most of the houses in Stonington. The foundation is made of interlocking granite blocks without mortar and has a dirt floor, a common practice at that time.

Webb's Cove is busy with the comings and goings of lobster boats and mussel draggers. They sell their catches to the lobster dealer on what used to be the old Settlement Granite Quarry dock. Melvin has a "victory"-type vegetable garden, a small orchard, and a grape arbor. They have a little dog, Sparky, who barks furiously but is very friendly and affectionate. Barbara works part-time in the variety store in Burnt Cove. Mel does most of the cooking. He was watching television when I arrived, and Sparky barked in greeting but was soon hushed, comfortable and content.

BURNT COVE LOBSTERMAN'S DOCK AND OLD-STYLE TRAPS, 2004. Photo Pam H. Haskell.

53. ADVENTURES WITH ZEKE

Almond "Zeke" Eaton lived with his mother, who had been cast off by her husband in favor of another woman (which was not unusual on Deer Isle, or anywhere else for that matter). Their house was a small, square, one-storied, hip-roofed building located on the south side of the Tea Hill Road—the first house on the south side at that time, east of the main road, Maine State Route 15. Out behind, there was a little privy and a cow barn, which housed a 1924 Star touring car. One bright sunny day Zeke got the old engine running and himself lubricated as well, with a few Colt 45s (canned beer). He proceeded to drive on the Tea Hill Road and wandered off the asphalt and hit something immovable, resulting in bent dumb irons, and broke the timing-gear casting of the little four-cylinder engine: the crankcase oil seeped out all the while that the motor was running. We antique car nuts were distraught. The car was ruined, we thought. This was long before the nearly magic works of old car restorers were known to us. But bear with me: Zeke and his Colt 45s had further adventures, to our cost!

One Christmas Eve event was memorable. I had been up to Webb's Cove digging clams for the kitchen larder, and when I emerged from the shortcut down through the woods past Ernest Snow's chicken farm, there was Zeke, well into his cups, holding a gallon jug of milk in each hand. He saw me and started to cuss me out. He swung one of the glass containers at me, which crashed into the other glass jug, and the milk spilled into the deep snow as the glass shattered. I continued toward our little yellow house quite unperturbed. Later that night my brother Garland and our buddy Bobby Hutch found Zeke sticking out of a snowdrift on the hill that begins the Tea Hill Road. The two of them bundled Zeke into the back seat of the old Hudson sedan and carted Zeke home, as he was in very bad shape from the cold and would have died from hypothermia. His mother must have thawed him out somehow, because in a few days he was up and around, good as new!

Years later our father, "Dick," let Zeke use the old peapod for clamming expeditions to the islands nearby. Dad had bought a little single-cylinder outboard motor, and he made a crude wooden saddle affair, which hung out over the stem, upon which he mounted the little motor. Income from the sale of clams and sharpening saws supplemented Dad's Social Security check income.

Dad decided to turn the old boathouse-shop-cum-forge ninety degrees, so that he could sit in there and watch the diving ducks on nice sunny warm autumn days. He worked for days jacking the old driftwood building up, placing newer driftwood joists under the structure to reinforce its tender parts, and once ready he pulled it around to face east using a set of blocks, three-quarter-inch manila line, and muscle.

My mother had gone up to the old Knowlton-Haskell homestead to help and was amazed that he could move the building all by himself. After it had been swiveled around ninety degrees, Dick scavenged two large windows from somewhere and installed them on the east side, so that he could sit inside and watch the waterfowl that swam and dove for mussels and other food right in front of the old boathouse. (Back in the Great Depression days he would have shot the ducks, and we would have eaten them!) Dick built in a rudimentary kitchen with a cast-iron sink, a driftwood counter, and our ancient Morris chair (ancestor to modern recliners?), as well as a couple of old wooden chairs. Zeke installed an army-type wooden folding cot and sometimes slept there.

"Well o' course," one day Zeke got into his supply of Colt 45 and started to build a fire in the pot-bellied woodstove in the boathouse. Somehow he caught the building on fire, and he panicked and ran away. Someone saw the smoke rising up from the shore and called the fire department, but by the time that they got there all they could do was roast hot dogs and marshmallows on the smoldering remains.

Late in this September 2009, I called Barbara Haskell to volunteer to drive down to the old Knowlton-Haskell homestead and cut up a spruce tree that had fallen across the old boat ramp that was making access to the shore a little difficult. Barbara said that her children were coming there shortly to build a new boathouse, because the one that cousin Melvin had built to replace Dick's driftwood boatshed-cum-forge had succumbed to neglect and rainwater leaking down through the roof. My first cousin Melvin is now very frail and a little bit out of this world, to put it politely.

54. Marm's Well
and Deaths in the Family

When we moved from Clam City to the Tea Hill Corners section of Stonington, we used our neighbor's well, and to show their appreciation they very considerately put their pigpen up against their southwest property line—but not quite under our west-facing bedroom window, so that we could enjoy the aromas issuing forth on hot, nearly windless nights. We didn't mind the piggery music and soft squishing sounds, but with the wind out of the westerly quadrants, the ammonia-laced vapors were "somethin' wicked."

Fall rolled around, and our neighbor wanted to slaughter the hog. So he asked Dick to strike the happy old pig a fatal blow with a sledgehammer. But Dad chose a quarry drilling hammer, and while the neighbor diverted the porker with some cut-up slices of apple Dick gave the beast a tremendous blow with the weapon of choice; when the sow fell into his outstretched hand, he slit her throat with his homemade hunting knife. They had considered shooting the animal but thought that the bullet might ricochet off of a rock with tragic results.

Even with these shared domestic works, my mother chafed about being reminded that we were using their well. Marm didn't like the neighbor's wife, not one little bit. Garland was lobstering out of Webb's Cove with Dick's old peapod, and Dad and I were working on "John L. Goss"; we never mentioned that it was a quarry, as we assumed that anyone that asked "Whataya driving at?" would know what we were talking about.

The summer was nearly over, and one Friday after work, Dad and I came rumbling up from downtown in my big old 1929 Nash Advanced Six. It had 600 x 20-inch tires on spider wire wheels and snap rims like trucks of that vintage. There were two spare wheels in fender wells, and the sedan was six feet tall. We climbed out of the ancient relic and found Marm digging a hole in the woods near the southwest property line. "Whatcha doin', Marm, diggin' a well?"

She answered in a tirade against our neighbor's wife. Dad and I were highly amused, but she was very determined to have her own well. Saturday morning after breakfast we rigged up a crude tripod out of three spruce saplings and some rope, and with a single-sheave pulley, a "hunka manila line," and an old ten-quart pail, we began to dig a well for Marm.

The glaciers were not very kind or tidy, and there were several erratic rough granite stones below the surface, which required more engineering and some rigging, more hemp lines and lotsa grunt work to hoist these big chunks of granite up out of the hole. We slipped driftwood planks under the rocks and lowered them onto these planks, and from there they were rolled over to the property line to serve as a rough stone wall.

We slaved away on the project "but never on Sunday!" until at last we struck water, and Dick managed to secure some sections of round terra cotta well tiles, and we lowered them one at a time into the excavation, where they nestled snugly into the rims nicely vertical and nearly plumb. It took several days for the mud and silt to settle out of the water, and for a while it was nice to lug two ten-quart pails of water up from the well to Marm's tidy little kitchen.

Then, as aforementioned, Marm decided that we needed a bigger house, so she dug and dug to make a cellar hole. She went all around the neighborhood with Dad's homemade wheelbarrow and gathered up stones to make the three foundation walls. The fourth wall was formed by the sloping granite ledge upon which the house rested. She mortared and set the stones quite plumb and straight, all by eye. I was going as cook on the *Lynn* at the time, but between trips I worked on the addition with Dick.

Then, sometime after the new construction was completed, Dad bought the combination stove, which used wood on one end and propane on the other. This feature was very convenient, as breakfast could be started using propane, while the woodstove end was warming up. While I was yachting (1953-1957), my youngest brother dug a trench to the well, and a water line was installed. Dad rigged up a Jabsco marine water pump, and it worked quite well but very noisily until much later, when he bought a shallow-well jet pump.

Sometime after Pam and I were married, we arrived one day to find a well-drilling rig noisily drilling right down through the granite ledge upon which the little house sits. The bore is only sixty-five feet deep, and they must have hit a seam between the sheets (layers) of granite, as there is sufficient water flow to allow using a clothes-washing machine. The resulting water supply is very clear and tastes of granite, and I suspect it has radon leaching into the water.

Wink also designed and built the kitchen cabinets in the new extension. The jet pump sat under the counter-top ell, where there are shelves under two shallow pull-out drawers that contain the kitchen tableware. Everything worked in a cozy and tidy arrangement and may be used again someday soon. Marm used to make quilts, and the neighbors came over and sewed away for hours gossiping, drinking tea or coffee, and nibbling on Marm's very good cakes and cookies.

Herb Jones had an Aeronca light plane. His uncle, Tilden Knowlton, bought a strip of land on the Burnt Cove crossroad, and after a bulldozer had scraped out a gravel-surfaced flight strip 1,500 feet long, Herb began teaching folks to fly. Garland took lessons, and after seventy hours earned his private-pilot's license. Then he and "Fudd" earned their aircraft and engines licenses. Garland went to Miami, Florida, where he took courses at the Embry Riddle Aircraft and Engines School of Aeronautics on the GI Bill. He worked in the aircraft industries until he retired. Garland lives in Allen, Texas, with his wife, Betty, and they have a very pretty housecat for a pet. He has one son, Leroy "Dickie" Haskell, by his first wife, Kathryn. Dickie lives in Arvada, Colorado, and is an electrician. Wink was working for Duryea in Montauk, and I was yachting, so the "auld house" was an empty nest.

Marm became ill in the fifties with an abdominal tumor and succumbed to that in April of 1986. Leroy called up just as I was attempting to replace the radiator in the 1980 Pontiac midsized wagon. I managed to start one of the threaded unions cross-threaded and abandoned that task. We borrowed Pam's mother's little Chevette, and jammed in like sardines we drove all night, as Dick was there alone without anyone to console him. Garland and Betty flew up from Dallas, and Wink was jammed into the tiny car with us. We came upon a crash scene in Meriden, Connecticut, and had to wait until an eighteen-wheeler pulled to the left about eight inches, allowing us to climb up over the curb and pass all the wreckage on the right-hand sidewalk. Even so, it took almost twelve hours from door to door. After the funeral, Dad continued living in the little yellow house, alone.

In March of 1989 Melinda, Wink, and I drove to the Island and "camped" in the cabin to attend the twins' ninetieth birthday party in Rockland. We didn't hook up the water and flushed the toilet by filling the tank from a five-gallon bucket carried over from Pam's brother Bill's spring. I slept on a futon on the floor next to the little Jøtul woodstove and was just able to keep the heat up to 60°F by stoking the stove every two hours through the night. We had planned to return to the cabin and spend another night, but we decided to continue from Rockland to Philly after the party was over, as we had three drivers. On March 18th we awoke to freezing rain! After breakfast we turned off the bottled gas, loaded our luggage, and drove to Rockland to attend the party. There we met cousin Melvin's daughter Sandra and her children, her brother Donald, and other relatives. About three in the afternoon we set out for the Maine Turnpike, but the roads to the 'pike were coated with ice, and we slithered and slid around a lot, but once we were on the 'pike, which was sanded, we were able to buzz along with traffic until we were south of the ice. It was still a long trip, time-wise.

In 1989, we arrived for our vacation in the North Deer Isle log cabin and drove down to Stonington to visit Dick, where we found him up on the roof of his shop shingling, all by himself, at 90 years of age. So I sent Pam back to the cabin, while I helped Dad finish the roof. He had plenty of hammers in the shop, and we managed to finish in the early afternoon, after taking a run to Baiter's Lumber Co. in his old Dodge Coronet wagon for another bundle of asphalt shingles. I called Pam, and she came down to retrieve me.

That fall my cousin Erma (Howard) Weed called to tell me that Dick was not able to take care of himself. So I flew to Bangor, Maine, rented a car from Budget Rent-a-Car, and drove down to Stonington. Dad had a bag all packed, and in the morning we drove back to Bangor and caught a flight to Philly. We installed him on the second floor in the back bedroom, away from the traffic noises, not that noise was a problem, as he was very hard of hearing by then. Eventually he wanted to go home again, and Wink took him back. I tried to get him into the Island Nursing Home by phone but was not successful. However, cousin Melvin F. Haskell took the task in hand and had Dad in there in no time at all. Dick was quite happy there, as he knew most of the attendants and elderly folks.

Doctors here in Philadelphia and there in Maine had not told him that he had prostate cancer, but he figured it out all by himself, and on Nov.

30th, 1990, he passed away. For his funeral our daughter Melinda and her husband, Edward Adams, and I drove up to Maine in the daytime in our '89 Ford Taurus wagon, and Wink drove up in his big Dodge delivery van. Garland and Betty flew up from Dallas again, and we all attended the funeral service in Stonington on a rainy afternoon.

55. Ford Bray's Story of the Rockefeller Granite Fountain Bowl

We quarrymen were sitting around in the hoisting house down in the quarry hole eating our lunches and drinking coffee or tea out of thermos bottles, and Forrest "Ford" Bray was telling us about the massive block of stone that had to be quarried and transported down to the cutting shed. It was so large a block of granite that only Number One Derrick could lift it out of the place where it was quarried. Old Numbah One lifted 'er right out of the spot where she was broken outta the sheet of stone, boys. Ol' man Bill McKinley (the superintendent) just had to climb up onto the crudely-made flat car and ride down to the scales. (His ego overcame his common sense.) The flat car was lowered down to th' low spot, and boss quarryman Cleveland switched the wickwire cable to the gang saw derrick's hoisting house, so that the operatin' engineer could haul the flat car up over the rise and ease 'er down onto the Fairbanks and Morse scales.

The usual next step was to haul the flat car up into the cuttin' shed. But as the car crept over the high point, something went wrong, and the flat car tipped over; the huge block of stone slid down onto the ground, and McKinley went down with the load. Fortunately he was thrown clear, but he landed poorly and broke his leg. The quarry's ferryboat took him over to Stonington, and Dr. Benjamin Lake Noyes set his leg. However, something went sour, and it healed in a bow shape, and forever after he walked with a limp.

The huge block of stone had to be cut right where it fell, as there wasn't a derrick large enough or near enough to the site to lift it again. There is a photograph in the *Deer Isle and Stonington* postcard history series booklet published by Arcadia for the Deer Isle-Stonington Historical Society that shows the John D. Rockefeller fountain bowl all nicely shored up with timbers and nicely leveled, so that the stone-cutters could cut it to shape. The John L. Goss stiff-leg dock derrick is partly shown behind the

JOHN L. GOSS HOISTING HOUSE IN FOREGROUND; NOTE FLYWHEEL OF STEAM HOISTER AND EXHAUST STACK RUNNING STRAIGHT UP; THE STIFF-LEG DERRICK IS ON THE DOCK WITH THE GROUT PILE SLOPING INTO THE HARBOR; BEYOND IS THE BLACKSMITH SHOP ON THE LEFT AND GANG-SAW BUILDING TO ITS RIGHT; THE CUTTING SHED IS BEHIND THE BLACKSMITH'S SHOP. Photo William Haviland, after the John F. Kennedy Memorial granite job.

workmen, and a ladder is shown leaning against the bowl. The finished bowl was shipped by barge or sailing schooner and eventually arrived at the Rockefeller estate. On page 70 of the booklet there is a photo of the finished fountain at the Rockefeller Estate in Tarrytown-on-Hudson. One wonders if it still exists.

56. SANTA'S UNEXPECTED VISIT

I used to pop into Dr. Noyes's house unannounced. Estelle (Reid) Sawyer Hutchinson Noyes seemed to enjoy my friendship with her youngest, Robert Carlton Hutchinson, also known as Hutchie. We would raid her refrigerator for prime examples of Washington state "delicious" apples and then run off to find or make some mischief.

But one evening, close to Christmas, she asked me to dress up as Santa Claus and drop off a bagful of presents to a family who needed some financial help. So we attacked the problem of costume. Mrs. Noyes had scrounged up a Santa's suit, but she didn't have the little black boots, and the red cap with the white pompom had been misplaced.

So, with her live-in daughter Meanie at the controls, we drove up to our little house, and I brought out my battered clam-digging boots, and the two ladies pronounced them, "good enough!" The best substitute for a red cap we could find was a green helmet affair that was used for shoveling snow or something of that nature. Dressed in this attire and disguised with a nearly-white imitation beard held on with an elastic band, and loaded down with a "crocus sack" (burlap bag) full of mysterious packages all wrapped with fancy paper, ribbons, and bows, we were prepared for our Rudolph the Red-Nosed arrival.

Meanie dropped me off at the roadside, and she and Estelle waited, while I purposely avoided the long driveway and negotiated a shortcut path through a swampy wooded area, then up over a huge granite ledge, and finally down the other side to a snug little house nestled in a grove of red-spruce trees, which tend to be taller and straighter than the ever-present skunk-spruce variety. I managed a poor imitation of my friend Kelp Dunham's voice in a nervous ho-ho-ho! and pounded on the door, which was soon opened by the father of the numerous family. I presented him with the bag of goodies, and he tried to guess who I might be. He put the bag on the floor and stepped outside and asked me who the presents were from in a low voice, but I just shook my head, backed away, turned, and "made my escape," as Dad would say.

Meanie had the big Buick Roadmaster straight eight running, and once I was in and closed the door, she made a rapid departure, just in case the parent had run after me to get a clue as to who had presented them with presents. It was an exciting adventure, and I was very nervous until we had returned to Stonington's Main Street.

The last time I saw Estelle must have been in 1955. I had quit my waiter's job on a company yacht, the *Addonway*, an eighty-two-footer built at New York Ship and Light on the Hudson River on Upper Manhattan Island. I climbed up her granite steps to pay a quick visit and to say hello, and to my surprise, my 1945 high school graduation classmate, Adrian Gray, was right behind me. Estelle saw us and said, "Here are my boys!" in a most sincere welcoming manner. Her son Robert C. Hutchinson had married Judith Haskell, one of our distant cousins, descended from Ignatius Haskell, and was living in Deer Isle across from my mother's sister, Geneva (Torrey) Howard. We chatted a bit, and I left, never to see her again.

57. A FALL CLAM TIDE

On a cold November morning in 1946, at "half past daylight," Dad and I drove our ancient 1929 Chevrolet six-cylinder coach up to the Knowlton-Haskell homestead and left it while we set out for the day's adventures. We walked downhill through Ralph Knowlton's woodlot, on down across his cow pasture, which in the late 1700's had been a Colonial subsistence farm. All that was left in the mid 1940's was a sunken outline of the house foundation and several sadly neglected apple trees, one of which was a russet, which had a distinctly different flavor and kept well all winter. I climbed up high enough to capture a few to gnaw on during the day. We were slightly startled by the furious roar of the wings of a ruffed grouse, as it flew up out of ground cover in the orchard, and Dad wished that he had brought his shotgun along. There were chickadees with their cheerful songs flitting about in the trees and alders as we straggled along the wooded path that wound around close to the glacial debris beach toward the end of Cyrus's point, where we kept the family workboat, a thirteen-foot carvel-planked peapod.*

Lewis Eaton built this one to his own design in the Sunshine section of Deer Isle over a hundred years ago; recent repairs by Paul Sewall and some fiberglass keep it in use today. We pulled the "pod" in on the outhaul, untied the painter, and loaded our six homemade wire-mesh clam rollers, hoes and equipment.

We clambered in and shoved off with an oar; I rowed out past Ken Jones's herring weir and close inshore along Phoebe Thurston's Point to shape a course to the west end of Camp Island, across the Deer Isle-Stonington Thoroughfare, into a good stiff breeze.

Once there we unloaded the clammin' gear and moored the peapod by tying the painter onto the homemade anchor's ring, then resting the anchor on the breast hook with a length of anchor rode tied onto the fluke end yoke; we shoved 'er off with a following wind. After she had drifted out far enough to keep from grounding out, Dad gave a yank

*Howard Chapelle, *Boat Building*, (W. W. Norton Co., 1941, p. 402).

on the line, which snapped the anchor overboard and the peapod rode nicely to her tether all through the clam tide.

We proceeded to dig for clams; by scouting around a bit, we found a very large colony of clams, and we chased the tide down till it turned—and then kept just barely ahead of the inflowing seawater until we were above the productive level of sandy clam-flats.

Fish crows kept us company from a safe distance, two blue jays scolded us from the alders close to the beach, and herring gulls glided past from time to time, hoping for happy scavenging, and mewling what sounded like, "Mine! mine!"

By the time the tide had driven us out of the clam-flats, we had nine bushels of clams bagged up in crocus sacks. Once they were loaded into the little peapod, she would have just about four inches of freeboard with the two of us in there with the cargo. Meanwhile, the wind had picked up outta th' sou'west, and the seas looked to be overwhelming.

Dad decided to put up our little bit of triangular homemade sail, and raised the nicely-shaved spruce sapling mast and inserted it into the for'ard thwart seat mast hole and into the mast step below. He placed the slender spruce boom fork against the mast and threaded the sheet line down through the gunwale's inwale and let the whole works trail out into the wind as we got under way. "You steer and I'll trim 'er," he instructed, as I shoved off, wading with my boots pulled all the way up, and clambered aboard stiff-legged to perch on the stern thwart seat, with our stout ash oar out over the side to act as a rudder, Viking-style.

We were soon out into the wind, and Dad pulled the sheet line in, and the sail promptly filled, and "she gathered up her skirts and raced along, the starboard rail just skimming the watah." Dad would lean forward as the little boat rose on the backside of the swells and then lean aft as she raced down the face of each following sea, something like surfboarding. I held a steady course with the oar, our sail was crudely simple, but we surged along, and by the time we had Humpkin's Ledge bearing amidship off to the starboard, I knew that we were more than halfway to Phoebe Thurston's Point.

I was quite excited by the danger of the moment, but Dad seemed to have done it all before many, many times. I thought that we were in an extremely dangerous situation: one loss of balance or the boat broaching would surely swamp the boat, with death by hypothermia or drowning the result. I doggedly kept paying very close attention to our course as we continued to skim along; I bailed and bailed with an old battered kitchen aluminum pot as some seawater came in over the rail from time to time.

We flushed a small flock of eider ducks; some dove to safety, and the rest flapped furiously as they tried to get airborne in the heavy seas; once aloft they skimmed along rapidly and wheeled around to fly into the wind, then splashed down to continue feeding on mussels on the bottom of the Thoroughfare. Whistlers* (golden-eyed diving ducks), very beautiful with their iridescent head feathers, sped past at nearly sixty miles per hour, very high in the sky; they tended out behind Kai's Island up in the north end of Webb's Cove.

Eventually, we sailed past the red-spruce-wooded east end of the point and lost our wind. With relief we shipped our sail and rowed in to the homemade Haskell dock and unloaded our treasure. Then we rowed over to Cyrus's Point to the outhaul; tied the boat on and pulled her out to where she would lie afloat at any stage of the tide.

Out to the cottages east of us, a huge raft of oldsquaws were yodeling to us as we walked back along the shore to carry the bags of clams up the steep hill, Dad clutching one corner of the bags and I the other, to load them into the old Chevy. It wasn't wise to try to drive down to the shore; the cart-way was soft and muddy, and the old skinny-tired car would most likely sink, especially with nine bushels of clams inside and one driver.

After several trips up and down the slope, we were loaded and ready for home. The old car was reliable but was hard to start. Once fired up, it ran well, and we rumbled up the graveled gradient without missing a beat, past Captain George Knowlton's house on the starboard hand. Ralph Knowlton, his son, lived in the west-end, added-on structure that included a cow barn, all part of the main house. Ralph had a small herd of black-and-white cows, and he delivered milk to his customers, including us, using a 1939 Pontiac sedan. He managed to put two children through college with the proceeds from the dairy farm. This was before government regulations forbade the sale of raw milk. After a very few years these small dairy farms ceased to exist. The gated fences fell down, and the Island folks forgot about subsistence farming.

We continued past the house where I was born. There were four more houses on the north side of the Tea Hill Road and only three on the south side; Grammie Haskell's house sat way down the slope on the south side, and way beyond that there was a distant cousin living alone; she was called Aunt Net Knowlton. The Colonial wagon road went downhill past the Knowlton–Haskell homestead and through a

Peterson Field Guides, Eastern Birds, p. 60.

boggy area, then slightly uphill past the abandoned Phoebe Thurston farmstead, and still more uphill past Aunt Net Knowlton's, then down a very rough wagon track to the Ames family's saltwater farm. A right-angled right turn by their front door started the nicely-graveled road that was maintained by Walden Ames with his ox team to the top of the hill west of their farm, where it met the less well-maintained Clam City Road to Stonington, which was also gravel-surfaced in my youth.

Once we arrived at our house, we had "suppah," and then we cleared away the table and chairs and began the long process of shucking out and cleaning clams for sale at R. K. Barter's fish factory on Sea Breeze Avenue. My younger brother Garland and Marm joined in this tedious chore, and sometimes it was one in the morning before we could get to bed. The next day we loaded the washtub full of clams into the Chevy and took them down to the factory, where the Island ladies that worked there passed the word that "Dick Haskell and his son are here with some ol' beautiful clams! Bettah git yourself some, deah!" And they came rushing down the concrete stairs with some kind of container to bail out the clams, which were all sold right there, never reaching the market. We were well known amongst the factory workers.

Our days were regulated by the tides; each digging day began an hour later than the previous day, the cycles continuing until the morning tide could begin a new early-morning cycle. We dug clams even after the saltwater ice formed along the shores. Marm had knitted two pairs of heavy woolen mittens for each of us, so that we could put on a dry pair after we had finished digging.

I earned enough money to buy our very first, brand-new refrigerator with my earnings. Our children were often bemused by my telling stories of how "I dug that refrigerator out of the clam-flats!" It didn't seem possible to their little minds that a new refrigerator would just be there waiting to be dug out!

One day I was cleaning our Remington automatic shotgun and managed to cut a nice little round hole through the linoleum carpet. (One of the Island colloquial expressions is that linoleum floor covering is called "carpet.") Marm scolded me, and I said, "Don't worry, Marm, I'll buy ya a bran' new one." It took a lot more digging clams, but the new one was inlaid linoleum, and it's still there, quite the worse for wear! Even in the dead of winter I would walk up to Webb's Cove and flip ice cakes to open a tiny spot amongst the glacial erratic boulders, where I could get enough clams for a nice chowder, sometimes even enough for a large mess of steamers.

Sometime after Thanksgiving, but not just before Christmas, we gave up clamming for "th' wintah" and cut firewood on shares on Bill Stinson's Point," which belonged to Les Stinson at that time.

58. Appendicitis Operation at Castine's Hospital in 1947

In the winter of 1947, I developed a pain in my lower abdomen. Dick went down and got Dr. Arnold Brown, who wasn't sure what was wrong with me, so Dick and Dr. Brown drove me over to Castine in the doctor's brand-new Chevy sedan. It was snowing when we left the Island, and by the time we got to the dreadful twisting roller-coaster hills in Penobscot, the Chevy was laboring and bucking through the drifts. The rear wheels shuddered and jumped up and down at times, but we struggled along and finally pulled up at the front door of the hospital. Dr Babcock was very businesslike, and he poked and probed and suddenly called out, "Beulah, get the operatin' room ready!"

Dr. Brown became the anesthetist and knocked me out with old-fashioned ether, while Dr. Babcock and nurse Beulah performed the operation. My appendix had ruptured, and we had arrived just in time! I awoke feeling very sore and not too well with strange bubble-like sensations rising inside my head.

In a day or so, George Fifield came in to the other bed in the same room. We got along famously; my comments amused him so much that he laughed until his side ached. After a few days of laughing and giggling with George, someone—Bob McGuffie, I think—came and drove me back to the little yellow house below Tea Hill Corner. I was annoyed that I couldn't skate on the frozen Stonington Harbor ice with the other boys from town. I don't think that the harbor ever froze over with thick enough saltwater ice to be skated on again.

Spring arrived; the ice in Webb's Cove had all melted or drifted out to sea, although there were little rims of ice here and there anchored in the saltwater marsh grasses. My first cousin Elston Hooper and I grunted and lifted in unison to get the heavy white-pine skiff turned over and down off the bank to row around looking for flounders still hibernating in the mud. We speared a few for the larder and rigged up an outhaul so that we could moor the skiff. It would soon be time to go smelting in the brook that ran down into little Webb's Cove. During the winter there had been a couple of smelt shacks out on the ice in Webb's Cove, and fishermen would sit inside, out of the wind, fishing through a hole in the ice for smelts. I never tried it myself, but for a few winters several tiny smelt houses were used during the worst of the Great Depression years, and there were two remaining on into the late 1940s.

59. A Near-Tragedy

In 1947 I started working in the John L. Goss granite quarry on Crotch Island, a short boat ride from Stonington. The workmen all arrived at the Eastern Steamship dock, where we all clambered aboard the quarry boat *J. Douglas*, operated by Captain Ed Knowlton. Once all the workers were aboard, he started the Palmer marine engine, someone cast off the lines, and we were under way. The course was southwest past Two Bush Island and then southwest-by-west straight for the loading dock, where we climbed up the wooden triple-width ladders to the stone storage yard. From there the men separated to go to their work locations.

We quarrymen walked up the train tracks to the lowest of three hoisting houses, where the derrick operator built a scrap-wood fire in the stove made out of an empty drum. We sat around waiting for the starting signal. There was always a story-telling session, but it had to be short in the morning, as there was little time before the work began. The hoisting engineer worked alone, as soon the whistle blew and we had all climbed up the ladders to the top of the sheet of stone we were working on at the time.

The week commenced with the boss quarryman laying out chalk lines, which we youngsters scored along with sharp chisels called tracers. By the time we finished, compressed air in the line was high enough to operate pneumatic plug drills, and we began to drill holes along the line about three inches deep and spaced about six inches apart. Then we inserted two half-rounds and a steel wedge into each hole, and the breaker began to pound on wedges, moving along the line to maintain some sort of even pressure on the quoins. As the breaker pounded away, the frequency or ping worked up the scale of this anvil chorus until finally the stone broke away with a pop. If the stone broke clean without a wind, concavity, or bulge, the breaker would say, "Good breakin'!" But if the stone were less than perfect he would say, "Poor drillin'!"

At eleven o'clock, the steam whistle on the power house down at the shore blew, and we rattled down the ladders to the hoisting house where

Jim, the hoisting engineer, had hung our lunch pails up close to the stove, and my two corned-beef sandwiches were pleasantly warm.

Ford, the tale spinner, would hold forth with some story of his fishing days with his brother Smokey. The entertainment continued until the whistle blew again, and we filed out through the door, back up the ladders to continue breathing stone dust, loading quarried stone onto random piles or onto the flatbed railroad car and similar work, until quitting time, when we grabbed our lunch buckets and straggled down the tracks to the shore for the return trip to Stonington.

Dad and I walked back and forth from home at that time, but I wanted to have a car, and Wyman Haskell, who lived in Oceanville, had a huge old Nash Ambassador Advanced Six that I thought was just wonderful. My automotive education was about to begin. Soon Carlisle Webb had the old monster for sale at $200. Wyman had traded it in on a 1936 Oldsmobile six-cylinder sedan. I managed to scrape together just enough money, and equipped with temporary plates I ventured forth.

I soon learned that the speed had to be kept down to less than thirty miles per hour or it would begin to shimmy violently. After a while I saved up enough money to buy two new Sears and Roebuck's 600 x 20-inch truck tires, and Dad and I mounted them on the front wheels, which had demountable rims like a truck. With new tires the shimmying stopped, and the old Nash could be driven at speeds up to fifty-five miles per hour, but the fuel consumption was a dismal eight miles per gallon at that speed. So we usually churned along at thirty, which was still at an uneconomical twelve miles per gallon, and it seemed to use a quart of oil a week, whether it was driven or not.

I hadn't had the Ambassador more than a month or two, when duck-hunting season opened, and I was supposed to pick up Digger and Hutch (everyone had a nickname in Stonington!) who were out hunting eider ducks. I invited Carmie to ride up to the Pressey Village Road with me to the rendezvous with our two friends, who were out in the bay at the end of a long sandbar in a skiff, with decoys deployed and equipped with twelve-gauge shotguns. When we arrived at the top of the driveway that ran downhill to the shore, we could see one of them jumping up and waving from the boat. So I flicked the lights on and off and started down the long gravel-surfaced drive. After I turned the motor off, we sat around talking and eventually saw the skiff approaching the beach. Shortly the boat was out of sight below the rough surf and wild bushes and weeds along the bank. Soon my very close friend Hutch came up from the shore, brandishing our old Meridian double-barreled shotgun and bellowing, "I'm gonna kill ya', you simpleton, you have just shot Digger!" A traumatic announcement, at least!

"I don't have a gun, Hutch! It has to be someone else." I was now thoroughly alarmed and worried about Digger's survival. I left Carmie there, while Hutch went charging off into the woods with the shotgun.

Digger eased painfully into the Nash, and I started the ancient motor in preparation to take him to Doctor Kaufman's. I started off at full throttle, but my passenger asked me to slow down as the lurching and pitching was painful to the wounded area, and he pulled up his clothes to show me where the bullet had gone completely through his body. The bullet hole didn't bleed much, but it looked swollen and inflamed, which was quite frightening.

Once we were up onto the asphalt-surfaced Pressey Village Road and headed toward Deer Isle, the ride was smoother and we rolled rapidly along to the doctor's office. Since Dr. Kaufman was not in the house, I left Digger there and started back to pick up Hutch and Carmie. As I turned right to pass through Deer Isle Village, I saw the doctor coming toward me, so stuck my arm out the window, and he stopped. I said, "There's a feller up in your office that has just been shot!" He immediately drove toward his office at top speed, and I returned to the dirt road to pick up my friends.

Fortunately, Hutch had not seen anyone in his search for the sniper. Years later we found out who had taken the pot shot at them. People talk, and eventually word got back to us. It was much too late for legal action, but saddening and sobering nonetheless to find out that it was someone who should have had more sense and who, for us, was always distrusted from that time on. The shooting victim was very lucky, in the sense that it could have been fatal. The bullet just missed his vital organs, and after a while he was as active as ever. He is now a lobster fisherman, mooring his lobster boat in the little cove at Green Head, where he can keep an eye on it from his house.

60. GARLAND'S SIX-LOBSTER-TRAP EPISODE, AND OTHERS

Sometime around 1947 my brother Garland, thirteen months younger than me, started lobsterin'. Dad had a few old wooden traps, and after the two of them had refurbished all the existing equipment with new pot heads, bridle lines, and warps, repainted all the wooden buoys, and "Garlie" was issued a brand-new lobster license, he started learning the bottom with Dad teaching him the fine points of lobsterin' as our grandfather knew it.

There was a small half-tide ledge right in the cove that produced a "counter" now and then, and sometimes there would be a "keeper" just off Phoebe Thurston's point. A small-boat fisherman could tend his traps inside Merchants' Row, because the inner islands provided some protection from the winds that usually blew up after two in the afternoon. There were several "scoop-along-shore" fishermen working a few traps Saturdays, and after the normal workday at either Billings Marine or the two stone quarries that were operating at that time. But most of them had some kind of powerboat. Nowadays they almost all have outboard motors for power and a single-cylinder Briggs & Stratton to power their pot haulers. "I doubt that there are any serious young fishermen starting out by using oars as we did!" noted Garland Leroy Haskell on March 26, 2005.

Fifty traps were about all a man could handle working from a rowboat. Garland had traps nestled into sunken boulder fields that he and Dad had located over a long period of time searching on the low water, using a lead sounding line. They simply lowered the line with the sounding lead fastened on the end to the approximate depth shown on the chart and rowed around slowly until one of them felt a solid "tunk" on the line. If they found several rocks in this manner, one of them would mark the chart with tiny crosses, indicating a grouping of stones where lobsters would most likely try to hide. Of course, the modern fishermen have electronic instruments that show these bottom structures very nicely. But that is the way my grandfather and my father worked. There was no other way to find bottom features in the early lobster fishing years.

Garland fished amongst the glacial erratics littering the bottom of the granite shores as far out as Devil's Island and as far east as Bold Island. There was a particular spot on the east end of Grog Island Ledge where Garlie managed to catch a "counter" every day he hauled his traps. Eventually he and Dad built a lobster car, which was about six feet by six feet and about five feet deep, where Garland kept his catches until he sold them at one of the dealerships in Stonington. He had to dump crushed crabs and dead sculpins into the lobster car to feed the captured "bugs." He moored the lobster car in deeper water south of Cyrus's Point.

While all this was going on, I was working on John L. Goss Granite Quarry, and Albert Nevells worked with me when there was a load of stone being shipped by barge to one of the big coastal cities. Dad would be the stevedore, while Al and I put slings on the boxed, cut stone, and Jimmy Gray ran the steam-powered, stiff-leg derrick on the dock. One day, after the fall duck-hunting season began, Al said he would sell me his 1865 Springfield single-shot 45-70 rifle for "Two dollars and a couple sea ducks." Garland and I were going over to Sheep Island to try our luck anyway, and I managed to knock three of the big eider ducks down as they flew by our blind. I think between the two of us we shot the bag limit for one hunter that day but never wanted to shoot eiders again.

The next day, a Saturday, I took three ducks and two dollars down to Albert, who seemed pleased to have them. I took the heavy rifle home and got a box of ammunition in Bangor at Dakin's. Then Dad, Garland, and I went out into the woods behind the house to test-fire the Springfield. With the very first shot I drilled a large red-spruce tree dead center and the bullet passed right through. It was not a tiny sapling but a substantial tough tree over ten inches in diameter. Aunt Ruth walked all the way over to the house to complain about us firing the gun so close to her house (about 2,000 yards away). We were highly amused. She was always trying to put something over on us, and that's why we called her Aunt Ruth. It was not an endearment.

Garland had six traps along the west side of Grog Island Ledge—but let's have Garland's version of the event.

My six traps were new, made from oak bows purchased with the proceeds of my daily catch, from Colwell Bros. The rest I made and knit the potheads at night at home. I set them on the west side of Grog Island ledges to soak; they won't fish when bubbles are still rising.

"They never caught anything!" Dad said. "Someone's haulin' them before you do!"

I landed the peapod in the very small cove on the southeast side of Grog Island and walked across the island and out on that long ledge to the nor'west and hid behind a big rock covered with seaweed; it was dead low "watah." Then, at barely daybreak came . . . The rest you know.

Garland heard a single-cylinder marine engine "a-poundin' away," as the particularly ungainly little lobster boat came into view. The part-time fisherman shut down the engine, as it had no reverse gear, and pulled the first of Garland's traps. Once he had taken the lobsters out, he coiled the line and dropped the trap into the coil so that the whole works sank to the bottom. He repeated this activity with all six traps.

Garland had taken my 1865 Springfield rifle and was thoroughly enraged as he ran out onto the ledge waving the heavy firearm and shouting at the thief, who slowly pounded away with impunity in his ugly craft. Perhaps seeing he had been caught in action was enough to deter a repeat performance. I asked Garland, "Why didn't ya take a shot at 'im? That ol' cannon would knock the bow right offa that ol' scow!" I guess Garlie thought it was too much a risk of killing the scoundrel, even though he would earn a sharpshooter's medal when he joined the Marine Corps sometime after that.

Dad made a copper-tined grapnel out of very heavy-gauge copper wire, bound the six tines and shafts together with cod line, and using a new length of nine-thread line to tow it with, they rowed out to the scene of the crime and dragged and dragged for days and days, eventually retrieving all six traps. The copper tines would straighten out if the grapnel lodged between two granite boulders and could eventually be retrieved, whereas a steel grapnel would lodge securely. Dad had a trick for that problem also. He fastened the line to the grapnel end and led it back to the bail ring, where he tied the towing line to the bail with rotten twine so he could part it off if it became lodged. Then the grapnel would lift clear by the tines end. Sometimes even that didn't work!

Garland wrote down another three adventures that go like this.

I shot something in Bold Island Channel four times the size of a seal; the sun was coming up, and this thing was swimming fast to my left, toward deeper water. I fired a shot from your 45-70 with a Peters high-velocity cartridge, and hit it at the water line, leaving a huge pool of blood. Watch the *History Channel*. They say rogue bull walrus have been seen as far south as Long Island, N.Y. Now I know, maybe, what it was. It sank right away, and I couldn't harpoon it.

Another time: A porpoise, or I should say a school of 'em, came up behind me. I was using the stand-up Dickies, rowing along, and as I pushed the oars into the water, a very large porpoise hit my starboard oar and bent it like a bow. It came out of my hand. I didn't know what happened. It hit me in the chest and I did a flip, landing on my back, head-first, into the stern of the peapod; the oars cut my hand, and knocked the wind outta me. I staggered to a sitting position just in time to see a very stunned porpoise spiraling away. He stove me up pretty good. I've been in a few fisticuffs, but I never took a right like that before!

Later: I sold a bushel of lobsters to Rockefeller, or rather to the cap'n of his converted sub-chaser. Looked like Cousteau's *Calypso*. They had cruised over to Shingle Island, which Rockefeller owned at the time, and a bunch o' landlubbers were going to have a picnic. The skipper ran me down, chasing after me for some lobstahs!

Garland and Dad had restored, sort of, an old sloop boat that had been converted to power. Garland fished part of 1949 and until October 1950 with the old *Scullpoogin*. When the Korean War broke out on June 27th, 1950, he decided to beat the draft and enlist in the Marine Corps, so that when he was discharged, he'd be free to do something without risk of being recalled. That October he had to rush to get his little lobster boat hauled up out of water onto the homemade ramp by Dad's shop and stack all his traps. They sat for three years behind Dad's old boathouse-cum-forge. We hauled his lobster car up onto the beach.

When he came home after the war, Garland wrote regarding his boat:

> There wasn't much left after three years in the USMC and my getting out in mid October of 1953. I went up to the cove and looked at the old boat. She needed more repairs. A couple planks had started off of her. So I went stern-man with George Gross several times. We got six lobsters one day! Another time I was seasick. Can you imagine that, after making a twenty-four-thousand-mile cruise with the navy and with NATO all over?

Garland started working at Billings Marine on Moose Island, while they had a contract to build air-sea rescue craft for the military. These were scaled down PT boats, sixty-three feet long and powered by two Hall Scott marine engines with an auxiliary diesel for emergency power.

61. MY BROTHER AND THE *SCULLPOOGIN*

Garland used the old *Scullpoogin* to tend his traps, and with a new lobster car moored out in Webb's Cove, he could hold his lobsters for sale at a higher price per pound than at the time when lobsters were the most plentiful and at the lowest price. He had to feed them with used lobster bait and crabs that he mooched before he dropped them into the lobster car. Eventually Garland saved enough money to buy a new single-cylinder Universal marine engine with a reversing gear. It was a modern four-cycle engine. The exhaust was just as noisy as that of the old Mianus, but I think he rigged up an automobile muffler on it.

One day he was tending his traps down by Eastern Mark Island and somehow ran over his warp, which then wound around and jammed into the propeller, stalling the engine. He was in a pickle, "blowing down onto a lee shore," as the sailboat people would call his situation! Eastern Mark Island rises vertically from the sea, and although he was almost close enough to leap ashore, it was impossible, because the strata rose vertically from below the water level! He dragged Dad's homemade grapnel out from under the fantail and tied on a piece of line, whirled the anchor around in the air like David's sling and cast it as far ahead as it would go. Fortunately one of the four tines jammed into a crack in the rocks below and the boat held fast. He tied his fish knife onto the gaff, and by sticking his head down under the steamboat stern he managed to cut a lot of the warp out of the propeller. His luck held, and the Universal fired right up, and he clawed off the dangerously close ledges. He hauled the grapnel straight up as he passed over it. He was one lucky feller! Some lobster fishermen come to grief working close to the rocks and ledges where *Homarus americanus* likes to hide. We mourn the unlucky ones who sometimes get caught in the same sort of predicament.

He steered for home "very slowly," he told me over the phone. He beached the *Scullpoogin* and jammed some deck boards under each side to keep the boat from flopping over as the tide went out. He then cut the rest of the line out of the propeller. He said the whirling mass of rope had unscrewed the outside packing nut assembly, so he refastened it with the crude and rusty tools on board. Sometime later he sold the Universal to Newell Hutchinson and joined the Marines in October 1950.

What happened to the *Scullpoogin*? Dad developed a stomach ulcer and eventually had surgery. After he recovered, he began to feel much better, and he repaired the boat. Then he removed the engine from my 1932 Plymouth sedan and installed it in the *Scullpoogin* with a little help from me. Dad fished for lobsters with the old boat for several seasons after that, tending his traps after working hours on the stone quarry and on Saturdays. Then she developed an incurable leak, most likely up through one of the iron keel bolt fastenings. He finally became so frustrated with the leaky old craft that he sawed her into manageable pieces with a big

Lombard chainsaw and burned the pieces all to ashes down on the gravel beach below the high-tide line.

62. Captain Ed's Practical Joke

Ralph K. Barter was severely wounded in World War I, and he came home with only one arm. He was determined to succeed in life and worked very hard and made some very successful business deals to become quite wealthy in his own right. He bought the old sardine factory in Stonington and during World War II canned mussels, clams, and ground fish, which included cod, hake, pollock, and haddock. He had a marine equipment store and a lobster dealership on Atlantic Avenue. He also had a fleet of working boats. The oldest was the *Christopher*, which had a huge Fairbanks and Morse two-cylinder crude-oil engine. Our father went as engineer on the old sardine carrier. He developed a technique for starting the ancient diesel. He would pump up a blowtorch and get it heated up and blowing out a hot flame, to heat the glow plugs on the sides of the diesel cylinder heads. Once the glow plugs were red-hot he would turn off the blowtorch and then turn it right back on, which produced a fine fog of hot fuel. Then he would open the compressed-air starting valve, while directing this fine blowtorch mist into the crankcase intake valves, and the Fairbanks would start right up!

The *Christopher* was out of the harbor with our father, and Fred Smith, our next-door neighbor, was going along as deck hand. They were off on a trip to bring herring in to R. K. Barter's canning factory on Sea Breeze Avenue. Garland and I were exploring along the Stonington waterfront when we came upon a gaggle of old-timers sitting on a wooden bench that was part of R. K. Barter's hardware store and lobster dealership dock. The old soaks were enjoying the sun and were fibbing away with local gossip. Captain Ed Knowlton was sitting there, and he spoke right up, "Boys, do you know that the *Christopher* has gone down with all hands?"

I believed him, and we pelted up the road to tell Marm, and she told Edith Smith, Fred's wife. However, the Smith family had a telephone, and Edith called Muriel Fifield, the day-shift operator on the switchboard above Frank Webb's store at that time. Muriel was a very smart lady and she said, "Oh! don't believe anything that Cap'n Ed says! Now you just hold on the line a minute or two an' I'll find out what's goin' on!"

Very shortly Muriel came back on the line and said, "Now that's some of Cap'n Ed's teasin', an' I think I'll just tell him a thing or two! Lan' sakes, we have enough to worry about without him makin' somethin' up!"

Sometime later in the week, Dick came home with Fred in his dark-red 1929 Pontiac sedan. We were happily all together again, and once burned we were forever afterwards shy of anything Cap'n Ed had to say. After a while we got to know Captain Ed Knowlton as a kindly person, who liked to tease Charles Grant and other old-timers who would gather on R. K. Barter's dockside benches and gossip while soaking up the warm sunshine and gentle southwest breezes.

Lobster fishermen were always trying to sneak a pailful of short lobsters home for supper. Once Herman Hutchinson had a ten-quart pailful of snappers on board, and he came into Barter's to sell his legal catch. There up above the lobster car was the fish warden, and Herman sneaked the ten-quart pail over the side to dump the contents. However a snapper grabbed the bail and did not let go. Herman just left the pail upside down drifting beside his lobster boat. The little lobster kept a steady grip on the bail, and the pail continued to bob alongside the old wooden boat. Meanwhile, Cap'n Ed had noticed that Herman was acting strangely and diverted the warden's attention with a tale. Herman rescued his ten-quart pail, and the snapper was set free to flip its tail and rapidly disappear below. Herman started his boat engine and ran over to his mooring in Green Head Cove. He loved to tell my brother Garland that story for years afterward.

Jason Gross was a kindly old salt who had gone to sea on the large four-masted schooners, and he liked to tell me things. I used to mow Father Poliquin's lawn at the rectory, where he lived alone, of course. He was a strange person, actually. Sometimes he would take me with him as he collected money from the Catholic families on the island. He liked to wade in the warmer waters along the Deer Isle bar. I would sit quietly in his big Packard sedan, while he splashed about. Recently my brother Garland mentioned that Father Poliquin had fondled "my little twinkie" in a letter to me which firmly convinced me that the priest was a pervert. I was a sophomore in high school by then, and sometimes I had to wait for my money, which the not-so-good father owed me for mowing the lawn with a crude push mower. Jason quietly assured me that Father Poliquin was "slow to divvy up."

During my senior year at Stonington High School, I worked Saturdays at Reginald Greenlaw's Plymouth-Dodge dealership. I wanted to be a mechanic, but Reggie was sarcastic and arrogant, which did not please me at all, at all. So after I had graduated I went down to work in R. K. Barter's fish factory, to work with other Island kids, Wiley Knowlton, Colby Weed, Henry Bray, Jr., and Warren Gray, who was older than us. Chester Eaton was a boss of some sort, and he stepped on Garland's heels, kidding around. Garland did not like that one little bit and went home right then and there. Chester was so surprised that he walked up to our house trying to make amends, but Garland was not the least bit pliable. Carl Burgess was another foreman, and he had the unenviable job of keeping the high-school boys in line. In moments of inactivity, we entertained ourselves with throwing herring up into the air to see if a gull could catch it before it hit the water. Wiley thought it would be fun to put a fireworks into a large herring and light the fuse. Of course a herring gull caught the fish and swallowed it. The firecracker exploded, and the gull was blown to pieces. Not a nice trick at all. Several of the old-timers admonished Wiley immediately.

63. COOTIE-DOG

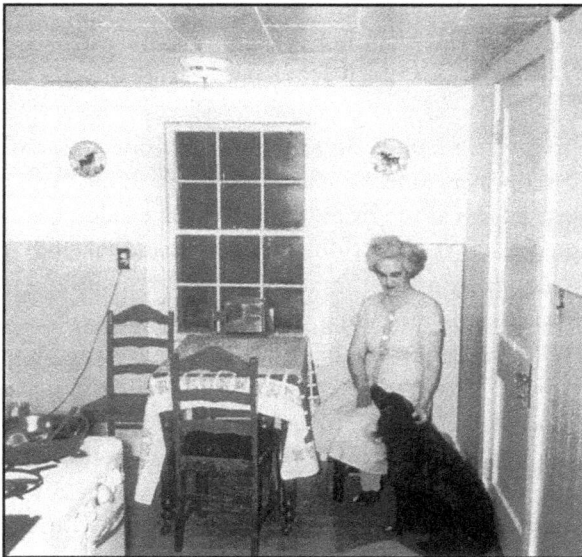

MARM WITH COOTIE-DOG IN THE KITCHEN, 1956.

Sometime after I had passed my Maine driver's test, we were sitting around after breakfast when Digger Jones came flying into the dooryard in the family Ford, which was a 1932 V8 Victoria, a two-door sedan of sorts. He always arrived in a swirl of dust as he spun the V8 around on top of the granite ledge. He leaped out with a huge grin on his face and came into the house with a dark little bundle of energy that turned out to be a wiggling, mostly-black pup. She promptly peed on the linoleum carpet, but quick work with a mop cleaned that up, and we proceeded to learn to live with a dog. Digger had been firmly refused permission to keep the pup by his mother, Biney, and she could be formidable. By the time that Dad came home from work, driving our ancient 1929 Chevrolet coach, the pup was firmly entrenched.

Garland trained Cootie to be a hunting dog. She would swim out in the cold waters of the local ponds and bring back the solitary black duck that had succumbed to our ancient Meridian double-barreled shotgun. The only way to get the duck away from Cootie was to shoot another one. She never learned any other tricks and was always barking at strangers walking past on the main road. I am quite sure that she annoyed Alvin Jenkins's mother, as she shied away from Cootie to the other side of the road. There was a lot of foot traffic in those days, because there wasn't a car for every family as late as 1947. Georgie Stinson drove a "cracker box" Model T Ford coupe until 1950, I think. He was so familiar with Model T's that he replaced a timing gear in the Stonington schoolyard in the night with hand tools and a flashlight. But he got home again driving the "high-rise" coupe.

Cootie-dog loved to hunt, and Garland took her everywhere in his Model A coach. Collis Jones came down one day with the Ford and wanted to sell it to Garland for $75. Dad went outside and lifted the hood on the passenger side. He took one look at the engine and closed the hood. Right then and there we dug into our Levis and produced $75, and Garland had himself a reliable little car. After Collis left on foot, Dad went out and opened the hood again, got a couple wrenches out of the saw-sharpening shop and turned the gasoline line from the cowl-mounted gas tank down flat. Collis had it in a vertical loop, and the Ford would get vapor lock when heat built up under the hood.

Garlie and Cootie-dog went off hunting and almost always came home with some game. There were several ponds on the Island where black ducks gathered to feed in the shallows. Of course, driving off the main roads in a Ford could provide some unexpected entertainment. There was a pond on the west side of the island that could be reached by driving into the woods on a logging road. The nearest house was Shirley Stinson's farm, near the town line. In 1947 the pond was very remote. As Garland slowly crawled into the woods in low gear, he came upon a local couple, coupled as it were! There was an immediate thrashing about inside the big Pontiac as the young folks tried to cover themselves up with clothes. Garland merely waved as he surged past, driving right out into the alders! Cootie-dog swam out and brought back a nice black duck. When Garland returned along the woods road, the Pontiac and passengers were gone.

64. THE GUNNING ROCK INCIDENT

One Saturday in the fall of 1949 my cousin Elston Hooper and I decided to go hunting for saltwater diving ducks that my father called "coots" but were probably white-winged scoters. Since we lived in a depressed area, we hunted ducks for food, not sport. The tide was just right, so we pulled in and untied the rowboat, put our shotguns on board, and clambered in. We kept the decoys in the boat all the time during hunting season. We rowed out past the herring weir, continued beyond Phoebe Thurston's Point, and soon approached the half-tide ledge that we called the Gunning Rock, which lies just east of Channel Rock, a very prominent landmark at the mouth of Webb's Cove. It got its name because that's where the ducks still like to dive for sustenance. Dad had painted the old peapod brindle, the muddy, grayish brown, because he thought ducks could see in color, and the dun color would camouflage the boat to appear as a rock mixed in with seaweed. We set out our tollers and hauled the peapod up on the backside of the ledge, secured the painter to a rock and scrooched down in the crevice that sloped down toward the ocean and the decoys.

As daylight brightened the waters south and east of us, ducks began to fly about. It was too early in the fall for the oldsquaws and common goldeneyes. They migrated a bit later, almost too late for the hunting season. Just as a flock of scoters came flying toward us, Elston, who was behind and slightly above me, pushed his Ithaca double-barreled 12-gauge out to bring it to bear on the ducks. He was wearing a heavy woolen Pendleton shirt with flap pockets. The two outside hammers on the Ithaca caught just enough on one of those flaps to fire the left barrel first. The blast of birdshot passed by my left ear and scoured all the barnacles and marine growth off the ledge, just missing my head. The recoil was enough to make the barrels jump far enough to the right that, when the other barrel fired, the charge whizzed by my right ear, again scouring the ledge completely clean of marine life! My head had been in between both blasts, and I was stone deaf for the rest of the day, considerably disoriented and most likely shaking like an aspen leaf. But right then and there, while I was still alive, I decided to take up the decoys and go ashore. I told "Cowflapper": "We're goin' ashore, an' I'm not goin' gunnin' with you agin until you get rid of that Ithaca!"

As our family history worked out, I never did go hunting again with Elston Webster Hooper. He was born August 9, 1925, and passed away on May 9th, 1953, while I was returning from Montauk, N.Y., serving as cook on the *Lynn*, a sixty-foot, wet-welled lobster smack. His sister, Beatrice Marie Hooper, was born on July 19th, 1927, and died on May 22nd, 1960, of cancer. Both were interred beside our grandfather Freeman Charles Haskell in the Stonington Cemetery or "the heater," as the natives call it.

65. Our Six-Cylinder Chevy and Other Car Memories

Author (left) and Duck Davis with the 1928 Chevrolet four-cylinder.

Dad bought a 1929 Chevrolet coach on one of his rare trips home during the last good war, known in our school's history books as World War II. General Motors had brought Chevrolet sales to the number-one spot in 1929, and the new Chevys had automatic spark advance, a fuel pump, and four-wheel mechanical brakes carried over from the 1928 model year. The little black coach was fifteen years old at that time, and Garland and I were allowed to drive it up and down the driveway, but not on the roads.

Russell Burns came up from Swans Island, and we became lifelong friends. One day we ventured forth on a li'l cruise around the Island. Russell is a year older than I and was already a competent driver at that time. We managed to uneventfully circumnavigate the Island and return the car to its resting place beside Dad's workshop. Gasoline was a rip-roaring 20 cents a gallon at that time, and no longer rationed.

Alan Dunham and I went down to Boston for a few days, and since the fish factory was closed for the winter, I applied for a job at Raytheon in Waltham, Mass. I spent the winter in Boston working in the plant as inter-office "mail person," to use the politically-correct title of today.

Raytheon was manufacturing radar sets for small ships and experimenting with a radar range. It didn't sell well on the market, and after the patents had run out there were suddenly microwave ovens and ranges all over the place! I lived with my mother's sister and her family, and I realize at this time in my life that it was an awful imposition. However, I "bombed out" and returned to the Island, where Dad managed to get me hired on at what is now Billings Marine.

Well o' course, it didn't last. Dad got into a rhubarb with a self-appointed expert and was fired on the spot. At the end of the week, I was pink-slipped. Then Dad got me hired on at John L. Goss Granite Quarry as a seasoned quarryman, skipping the "lumper" title. We walked to the quarry boat wharf every morning and back again in the evening. There were several hours of daylight during the summer months, and if the tide was right I would walk up to Tea Hill and dig clams for the larder.

By 1950 our front yard was usually filled with cars on weekends, as I had become quite an accomplished shade-tree mechanic. Nag Robbins had bought a 1939 Pontiac straight-eight, two-door sedan from Everett Billings's cousin, and it hadn't been tuned up in ages. I took the sparkplugs out to discover that the gaps were averaging eighty thousandths of an inch. I was simply amazed that the old thing would even start. We made a li'l trip to the local garage in my really junky '32 Plymouth sedan and bought new sparkplugs, ignition wires, a distributor cap, ignition points, and a rotor button. After I had assembled all these items in the correct order and adjusted the point gap, the Pontiac would perform quite briskly. "Clamhead" (Donald) Billings had captured a 1932 Oldsmobile six-cylinder sedan, which had a high-compression cylinder head but surely would run on the regular gasoline of 1950. He drove that car for several years; then his uncle gave him a 1939 Buick Century sedan, which was really fast, compared to Garland's 1929 Ford and my huge '29 Nash Advanced Six.

After I had started as cook on the *Lynn*, a lobster smack carrying live lobsters from Maine and Clark's Harbour, Nova Scotia, I was solvent enough to buy a 1947 Ford flathead six, and Fudd and I drove it to Yonkers and back once, between trips on the *Lynn*. It would cruise at seventy, and the gas mileage worked out to seventeen miles to the gallon, not much by today's standards, but much better than the Nash, which would get twelve if driven slower than forty miles per hour!

I used to go down to Swans Island to visit Russell Burns. He had a 1928 Model A Ford at first, and Mike Dow and I slept in the Ford. Mike did not make a return trip. On one of my later trips Russell had a 1930 Willys-Knight; it was a small six-cylinder car, and the engine ran so quietly that we could hear the sparkplugs snap as ignition occurred. The gas line from the tank slung between the frame rails in the rear had become plugged, and we poured gasoline into the vacuum tank after that tiny supply ran out. We were driving around in alders in what used to be a farmer's field when the engine stopped. When I opened the hood to put in some more gas I almost fell into an old house foundation. That's how close we were to having a serious crash down into the excavation, car and all!

Russell married Alice Joyce, and I didn't see him very often after that. He used to come up to Stonington and stay with his sister, Helene (Burns) Billings, who lives on the Oceanville Road, then and now. In this new century, Russell lives in Ellsworth, Maine, and he has remarried Margaret (Weed). Alice passed away several years ago. Nag Robbins has passed away, and also Donny Billings. Only Duck Davis and Digger Jones remain of the friends who visited our dooryard all those years ago.

66. More About the *Scullpoogin*

After my father passed away, November 30th, 1990, my brothers and I went down to the old house and sorted out things that we each wanted to keep. Neither Garland nor Leon wanted Dad's old journals, so I captured all of them and lately I have been reading through some, which brought to mind the adventures that follow.

In the late 1940s, the John L. Goss granite quarry was staggering along with small orders for curbstones, bridge facings, polished veneer for buildings, and random stone blocks to be used on other projects by stoneworks far away from Stonington. The technology was definitely 19th-century, with coal-fired boilers that powered three air compressors and a steam turbine that generated direct-current electricity to operate the huge stone saws, the overhead electric crane, and other electric motors. The steam-powered air compressors maintained compressed air, which powered the stonecutters' tools. All the hoisting engines operated on compressed air, except those near the powerhouse. The stiff-leg loading derrick on the shipping dock and a rig to unload the coal barges that came with soft coal ran on steam, and the hoists were within a few feet of the boilers. I started working "up on the hill," as we quarrymen called it, from sometime in 1947 to the last working day of November, 1950.

Meanwhile, my brother Garland decided to try "lobsterin'." He used Dick's peapod to tend his traps and managed to earn enough money to keep him solvent all winter, when his traps were all ashore. He never took to clamming and eventually gave up fishing forever. However, he did earn enough money to buy a powerboat, an old Muscongus Bay sloop that had been converted to gasoline-engine power by someone, long before I ever saw her. Gene Robbins had rigged her up with a mast and boom, a hoist of some kind, and a drag, and he went around the Island dragging for flounders. He was so successful that we haven't caught any flounders in Webb's Cove since then.

I remember one day, possibly in 1945, when I saw Gene coming in past the Eastern Steamship dock with a fifty-five-gallon drum perched on the port washboard. He was holding the barrel with one hand, when all of a sudden he "found" the top of a submerged ledge. The old boat bounced over the obstruction, and Gene went down on his soft tissue. The steel drum went over the side and promptly sank to the bottom, contents and all. Gene looked and looked, but whatever he had lost remained on the bottom and out of sight.

The little boat may have been Donny McGuffey's starter boat. He and Carroll Joyce built his present craft in a shed at the Sand Beach farm. It has the classic lines of the older gasoline-powered fishing boats, and he keeps it moored just outside the granite ledges, a beautiful scene that appeared in several issues of *National Geographic* magazine as a Ford Motor Company advertisement in 2002.

At any rate, he had pulled her "outta watah," and she was laid up on the bank at the Sand Beach farm. Quite some time after that, Garland and my father went over to inspect the old hulk. The Durant four-cylinder engine had been removed. Garland paid Donny Mc Guffey something for the "remains," and the three of them worked her down onto the beach in her cradle to await a favorable tide on a Saturday.

Donny McGuffey towed her as far as Green Head in Stonington. (Donny is our half-first cousin: his mother was Florence Knowlton, Dad's half-sister.) From that point, they towed her, rowing the peapod in turns, with the coamings and stem cap just showing out of water, all the way to Webb's Cove.

I was sort of exempt from this endeavor, although I hadn't even been asked to help. I bet I could have gotten someone to tow it the rest of the way over to the cove under power. I had a huge 1929 Nash Ambassador six-cylinder sedan at that time, and I did take a curiosity run down to Stonington's harbor to have a look at them laboring away at the oars in the peapod, the old sloop just barely showing above the water. I don't remember exactly when they got home that day, but I think it was well after dark.

They made another cradle out of two spruce driftwood fish-weir stakes and anything else that came to hand, and when I saw it next, they had managed to haul it high and dry onto Cyrus's Point with a set of falls, some pot-warp slings, and muscle.

There was never any surplus money floating about in our house, so all repairs and paintwork were done with whatever could be salvaged or made from something else. Garland told me that he had rowed over to the abandoned Settlement quarry, climbed up into the structure, and sawn through a timber with a handsaw. The great length of western fir eventually fell to the cutting-shed floor, and he dragged it down to the shore, dumped it overboard, and by tying the painter onto it towed it over to the improvised building site, rowing the peapod, stern-first all the way across the cove. The timber was sawn, hewn, and shaped into a replacement keel. Several other pieces of the Settlement quarry timber were used to make the king post and attendant deadwood, and a shaft log for the propeller shaft. I kept well away from interfering with all that industry.

Eventually they were ready to steam some new ribs into the *Scullpoogin*, as it was being called about this stage of the restoration. Sometime in early summer, the project was nearing completion. They had made new garboard planks and replaced several others that were in very poor condition. I think that it was painted white, but my memory fails. Usually Dad painted his marine equipment brindle, but possibly they painted it white to show some class.

Dick, my dad, assembled a usable marine engine by taking parts from two that were given to him by Mel Stinson, who lived on what is now called the Indian Point Road—but was Clam City to all of us—just for old times' sake. Dad took the two Mianus engines apart, and one crankshaft was scored too badly to be safe to use. The other one he took to Billings Marine, and Jerry Eaton arc-welded the scored shaft, so Len Judkins, their shop machinist, could turn it out round and smooth on his lathe to make useable journals. Dick found an old Schebler carburetor in his boxes of salvaged marine equipment. The bore of the instrument was too large, so he made a funnel-shaped venturi out of sheet metal, and the old Mianus eventually barked into action. Of course, there were other things that had to be done to it before it would work reliably.

Dad took the "make-and-break" ignition parts out of the cylinder head and cleaned them up, so the moving part would rotate through an arc freely in its sleeve. Then there was the matter of what was called the "firing pin." Lenny made one out of steel that held up as long as "we" used the ancient two-cycle engine. The cooling-water pump was a simple plunger, operating vertically in a brass sleeve. The plunger was driven by a tiny brass connecting rod that followed an eccentric on the crankshaft. A small brass ball served as a check valve.

Dad was so skilled at operating the Mianus that he could get it to stop turning by lifting the firing pin; at the last possible moment he would drop the pin, and it would start running backwards! Direct reverse! Which reminds me of one Dick's favorite stories. It seems that one of the tugboats close by, but not in Stonington, had a huge Fairbanks and Morse diesel, and it had direct reversing. One day Casey, the captain, came into the dock at a good clip and rang down on the engine room telegraph for reverse. The engineer's timing was a just a teeny mite off, and the Fairbanks failed to start in reverse. The tug promptly rammed the dock and knocked it overboard, stonework and all. Dad would clap his hands and laugh, which was as funny as the story.

67. Haskell Genealogy and Rebuilding a Derrick

As a youth, our father fell down while running with a scythe and cut his hand almost to the bone. His mother, Mary Jane (Billings) Knowlton Haskell, bandaged his hand, and the resulting scar was positive identification for us forever after. The two twins were little Haskell rascals and always scheming up pranks. Being human, they often quarreled. But they were very loyal to each other.

They were followed in birth by a sister, Christie Mae Haskell, who was the mother of Elston Hooper and Beatrice Marie Hooper. Christie's husband, Charles Hooper, promptly disappeared and left the family to their fate. Mary Jane and her new husband, Freeman Charles Haskell, folded them all into the little Knowlton-Haskell Household. Freeman sent Albert Knowlton and his older brother Raymond to an accounting school in Rockland, Maine. Albert became an accountant in the U.S. Navy during World War I, and Raymond went to Los Angeles on the cross-country railroad, where he became an accountant for the Union Pacific Railroad. He managed to cross the country using railroad passes for a week or so of vacation all his life.

Florence Knowlton married Robert McGuffie, and they had two children, Evangeline and Donald. "Vangie" married Percival "Bud" Knowlton, but there were no children in their marriage. Donald married Norma Eaton, and they had two daughters, Donna and Jean. Ethel Knowlton never married, and Cecil Knowlton married Mae Blair; there were three children.

Leroy E. Haskell was very close to his half-brother Cecil, and they worked together very amicably. Dick, my father, often told about a clam tide adventure in Marsh Cove on Kimball's Island, where they dug nine bushels of clams in one clam tide. There were so many clams that Cecil dug while Dick washed and bagged the clams, and Dick couldn't keep up with the digger, who simply tossed the clams out ahead of his trench onto the beach.

Cecil was working on John L. Goss granite quarry repairing the powerhouse roof, which was slick with skim ice. He slipped on the ice and fell onto a granite ledge, killing himself instantly. Mae Blair Knowlton moved away from Stonington, and her three sons grew up in the southlands.

At John L. Goss granite quarry, Number Five Derrick was on top of the original granite monolith, where the stone was truly pink from the abundant feldspar crystals in the matrix. As each sheet of stone was quarried away, the color of the newly exposed granite proved to be a darker shade. Only the southwest corner of the original top sheets of stone retained their distinct red tint. I haven't visited the old quarry in years but passed by on the Isle au Haut mail boat *Mink*, on the crystal-clear 23rd of August, 2008. After looking intently at the quarry, I think that the top sheet on th' sou'west corner has finally been quarried away, from what I could see from the deck as we cruised by. The working granite face of the new top sheet of stone seems to have been channeled like the workings of Barre, Vermont, where each layer of granite is quarried by drilling and connecting the drill holes with a channel bar; a much slower method, but it results in more useable stone blocks with considerably less wasted stone (grout).

In the fall of 1948, my dad and I removed five feet of the main mast on the Number Five Derrick. The adventure began with a search for a suitable Oregon fir mast timber. My dad found one on what used to be Ryan & Parker, a defunct quarry also located on Crotch Island. Someone had thoughtfully left it supported on some railroad ties. In spite of its age, the wood was still sound. Cap'n Ed Knowlton brought the *J. Douglas* around to the remains of the Ryan Parker loading dock, where Gumper Gray, the other lads and I used to swim at lunchtime. Dick tied a large hawser onto the fir masthead with a timber hitch. The hawser was paid out over the dockside, and Cap'n Ed ran off a little distance calculated to be safe. The hawser was left quite slack, and once all the things that might fetch up the mast were cleared away, Dick gave Cap'n Ed a hand signal: "Let 'er rip!"

He opened the throttle on the huge Palmer marine engine, and the old boat surged ahead. Dick and I stood well clear of the mast as it snaked noisily over the side of the dock. Like a very huge torpedo, it dove under the surface as the *J. Douglas* gathered momentum, and Cap'n Ed kept running until the timber resurfaced; then he proceeded more slowly to the John L. Goss quarry dock. I don't remember who went down over the side of the dock to arrange a sling on the mast at its midpoint, but I remember Jimmy Gray hoisting the timber up out of the water and Dick guiding the old mast onto the flatcar for its trip up to the quarry hole.

Howard Hutchinson operated the hoister that towed the mast up past the first hump on its way to Number Five Derrick, which was used to hoist the fir timber up onto the top sheet of stone. There was a lot of walking and climbing ladders involved in this project. The hoisting-engineer, Jimmy Gray, had to climb down from the dock's stiff-leg derrick hoisting house, then walk all the way from the dock up to the hoisting house on top of the southwest corner of the huge granite monolith, climbing several wooden ladders on his way up there, while Dick and I trailed along behind.

With another timber hitch on the used fir masthead Jimmy hoisted it up alongside of Number Five Derrick, where it was temporarily secured with a manila sling. The new timber was to serve as our stiff leg for the major project that was slowly getting started. Four hefty manila lines were run from the stiff-leg's mast cap to huge steel staples that were left in place from previous derrick locations; one staple was found down on the bottom sheet of stone, but the other three were up nearer the top. We hoisted a huge steel block up to the stiff-leg's masthead and secured it with a new piece of wickwire and several grabs. Finally we were able to run a length of wickwire through the block and down to the old Number Five Derrick's mast in such a secure fashion that the steel wickwire cut into the punky old fir. Jimmy lifted the old mast out of its foot-block casting. Dick and I kept well clear of the hoisting operation until Jimmy dogged the hoister. Then we cut off five feet of bad wood with a common two-man wood saw, being careful to keep the blade running square to the mast's length. Dad made a nice adze in his forge and sharpened it by hand, and we proceeded to hew away at the huge fir timber to make a newly-tapered butt end to fit into the gray iron foot-block casting.

Of course, it all took time, and winter had arrived. We retreated to the hoisting house from time to time to warm up by Jimmy's oil-barrel fire. Eventually, we lowered the old mast for a trial fit. It was still too tight, and Jimmy hoisted it up again. On the third try, many days later, the timber squeezed into the footing, and Dick pronounced it "Good enough!" Oh! But we were not finished yet! We commandeered all the quarrymen to re-tension all of the Number Five Derrick's masthead guy wires. We trooped around the quarry for nearly a week carrying a set of falls, huge metal grabs, Stillson wrenches, and our own brute strength. The hook on one end of the block and tackle was hooked into the steel staple in the sheet of stone, and the other block was hooked onto the cable grab (which worked like a Chinese finger, securely fastening itself to the galvanized steel cable guy wire). We shortened each of the guy wires about five feet, allowing some slack because the wires expanced and contracted in concert with the season's temperatures. All these tightenings and loosenings were accompanied with a long straight stick, which Merrill or Dick used to sight onto the Number Five mast, to assure that it was truly plumb. At one point in this tedious operation, a well-used Stillson wrench slipped off the nut of the cable grab and took a bite out of Dick's hand. He cursed and threw the wrench out into Ryan and Parker's quarry hole, that was full of rainwater. The wrench sailed gracefully in a parabola arc something like a boomerang, except that the circles kept getting closer and closer to the water as it fell in with a splash. Beanie scolded Dick for wasting the wrench, but Dad said, "It's all wore out! Time to get a new one!" Gumper seconded the motion. We all laughed except Beanie!

The newly repaired Number Five Derrick served to hoist tons and tons of granite blocks all through 1949 and 1950 without trouble. I think that Dick and Jimmy replaced all the wickwire cables on it, but by then I was back drilling little three-inch-deep holes with Carson Hutchinson, Gumper Gray, Jr., and Joyce and Wiley Knowlton.

68. Dick's Quarry Work

My dad had erected a wooden derrick on the newer of the two Eastern Steamship docks, to be used by the Deer Isle Granite Company to load saw blocks onto flatbed trucks, to be hauled off of Deer Isle by these trucks. Dick and his helpers erected the mast and boom on the south side of the Eastern Steamship freight storage building in a position to lift the granite blocks up out of a small war-surplus landing craft. The recycled landing craft was towed to Stonington from the Crotch Island, Deer Isle Granite Quarry dock by the *Sunbeam*, the all-purpose passenger and ferry boat.

The hoisting-engine shed was tucked onto the dock outside the freight handling building. A Chrysler marine engine had been rigged up by Dick and his helpers. One very cold winter day, a Sterling chain-driven tractor truck came down, towing a big flatbed trailer. It had arrived late in the day. Dick hoisted the large granite blocks up out of the landing craft and swung them around, then lowered them one at a time—also one to a landing-craft load, which kept the *Sunbeam* busy shuttling back and forth from the stone quarry's dock to the old Eastern Steamship dock for quite some time. The flatbed trailer could hold perhaps three granite blocks, which were then chained securely onto the big flatbed trailer. The Sterling's driver stayed overnight.

In the morning, the Sterling's diesel would not start. Dick hauled the oil-drip-catching pan out from under the Chrysler marine hoisting engine and slid it under the Sterling. He dumped nearly two bags of charcoal into the pan and set it all afire with gasoline from the Chrysler hoisting engine's fuel tank. After a while, the charcoal glowed red, and the oil in the big diesel began to bubble, and the starter cranked the diesel right up!

Dick hauled the red-hot drip pan right out from under the Sterling with a hastily-made hook on the end of an old Ford brake rod that had been found on a 1932 Ford chassis left on the east side of the freight storage building by Prentis Shepard for some reason or other. Possibly the chassis had come up from the Turner family's saltwater farm, which was located on the east side of Isle au Haut, overlooking York Island's harbor, where Dick spent some time, as related in his autobiography, which is included in the beginning stories of this book. I had been down to Isle au Haut with Elmer "Fudd" Gross and saw a 1932 Ford's sheet-metal body all scattered around in pieces. Perhaps it was the chassis from the same vehicle and was destined to be used for a homemade garden tractor. Anyway, it was there in the following winter of 1954-55 at just at the right time. I am quite sure that the date that I saw the remains of the 1932 Ford at the Turners' Isle au Haut home was in the early summer of 1954, when I had a week's vacation and had driven back to Deer Isle in my Sunbeam Talbot model 90 sport sedan. Fudd invited me to go down to Head Harbor with his parents in Virgil Gross's lobster boat. That was the trip where Fudd and I salvaged the Model A Ford transmission that was in Bert Nevell's wrecked car.

69. More Quarry Stories, Cars, and the Red Barn Dances

I went down to Boston with Alan Dunham in 1946 as an adventure: two Island lads in the Big City. His father was Eugene "Gene" Dunham, who married Bessie Fifield; they had one son, Alan, who was nearly my age, and we played together at the Sand Beach farm when Garland, my brother, was born. At one time in our youth, Alan Dunham and Alan

STIFF-LEG DERRICK IN JOHN L. GOSS QUARRY DOCK; STONE READY TO SHIP BY BARGE; SCOTT ISLAND, GREEN ISLAND, AND SAND ISLAND, LEFT TO RIGHT IN BACKGROUND.

Gott used to congregate at Bessie's house and play Spike Jones records on an old wind-up Victrola. Alan Gott was in my class at school, and he was the son of Freda (Haskell) and Carl Gott, who was the rural letter carrier in Stonington.

I remember that Alan Dunham and I got a tremendous kick out of ice-cold Pepsi Cola in East Boston at a little mom-and-pop store. We stayed with a Fifield cousin of Alan's, and we met my half-Irish cousins, Janet and Renee, and Natalie, who is the sole survivor in 2008. Alan and I went to Revere Beach with Janet O'Leary, my oldest cousin, a year older than me. She brought along a friend of hers as my date. The water on the beach was as warm as bath water, and we had a wonderful time. Eventually Alan and Janet were married, and they had two sons, Alan and Brian.

It was sometime later that I decided to go to Boston and get a job. I lived with Aunt Franscene and her family, a very audacious thing to do, to say the least. However, as aforementioned, fame and fortune eluded me as I worked in the company mailroom at Raytheon in Waltham, Mass. Eventually, I returned to the Island to find that my dad had been fired— again. His first cousins seemed to fire Dick every once in a while at "the shipyard," just to keep in practice! He always got into a squabble over there with his Billings family cousins. So he managed to get hired at John L. Goss granite quarry, and pretty soon I was hired also. I worked in the boiler room as coal passer with Howard Haskell, who was the fireman. I kept the coal bunkers full of soft coal and wheeled the ashes uphill to the ash heap.

My uncle, Elroy Freeman Haskell, identical twin to my father, was also known as Dick to the Islanders. The premise being that if one called out, "Hello, Dick!" that would not be an embarrassing mistaken identity. Uncle Elroy was the night fireman, who scooted across the Thoroughfare in his homemade sixteen-foot wooden skiff powered by a 10-horse, opposed-twin Evinrude outboard motor. He had to have the boilers up to 150 pounds of steam pressure by the time that we workers clambered up the slippery wooden dock ladders onto the dock adjacent to the coal piles, the dock's stiff-leg derrick and the powerhouse engine room, where the steam compressors were resting, until Keith Eaton came in and started them up every workday morning. Compressed air and electricity ran almost everything on the quarry, the hoisting-engines and the stonecutters' tools and the quarrymen's plug drills and jackhammers. All the electric tools and machines were driven by a small steam-turbine-driven direct-current generator set that was also in the powerhouse.

Howard (Haskell) lived in Deer Isle, just south of the old Settlers' Cemetery, on the west side of the main road to Stonington, that ran

TWO ABANDONED STEAM-POWERED COMPRESSORS; KEITH EATON'S DOMAIN FROM 1948 TO 1950.

down the east side of the Island. Most of the quarry workers lived far enough away that they drove to the quarry boat landing, but Dick and I walked down from Tea Hill Corners. Neither of us smoked, so we stayed out on deck or crowded into the pilothouse of the *J. Douglas*. She was a homely boat, but we were very fond of her. She was powered by a large four-cylinder Palmer marine engine. Dick and I jammed into the pilothouse with Cap'n Ed Knowlton when it was very cold or raining. Almost all the others were smokers, and they went aft into the main house, which had bench seats along both sides of the deck house. The men smoked pipes or cigarettes as they faced each other and told stories, while we had a short boat ride every workday morning and evening, as we crossed the Thoroughfare to Crotch Island, where both working quarries were located during my youth.

Deer Isle Granite was the other quarry, and we simply called it "McGuire's," for the folks who owned and ran it. Almost everything on Deer Isle Granite was powered by diesel engines. Their compressed-air line ran alongside their railroad tracks up to the quarry hole. There was a small steam-powered switching locomotive that hauled flatcars around Deer Isle Granite's yard and up to the quarry's derrick, where quarried blocks of granite were loaded onto the flatcar to be towed down to the yard. Alex McGuffey was boss quarryman over there, and we knew some of their quarrymen: Clayton Haskell, who worked down in the cutting shed yard; Ernest Coombs was boss quarryman there. I knew Will Saunders, who boxed up the cut stone for shipment, James Gray, Alec Larrabee, and especially "Moon" Dunham, who would walk out to the edge of the sheet of stone and shout over to us, "I hear thy voice!" Another well-known character was Clyde Brown, derrick maintenance man on Deer Isle Granite. He greased the sheaves (grooved wheels that kept the wire ropes in line and parallel to each other as the two sets of blocks worked in tandem to make the hoisting action.) The top set of sheaves also controlled the angle of the steel boom; a woven-steel pennant ran on two fixed sheaves and was fastened to the bottom block, which rode up and down the vertical wooden mast, bearing the load on the derrick for every hoist. Clyde would ride up to the top of the derrick and climb up onto the masthead cap and stand there, admiring the view. He must have had very, very good balance.

Back at John L. Goss, Neville Eaton sometimes fired the boilers when Howard was off for any reason. I never had any interest in learning how to fire the boilers. The boiler room was hot, of course, and on good days Howard and I would sit on the dock eating our lunch and dangling our

"Down in the hole," from left: Gordon "Gumper" Gray, Carson Hutchinson, Eugene "Junior" Joyce, Henry "Hemp" Bray, Sr., Merrill "Beany" Knowlton (boss quarryman), Forrest "Ford" Bray; the main hoisting derrick is in the background, masthead guy wires shown in upper left corner, three running down, anchored to huge staples in stone. "Gumper has his quarryman's hammer in his right hand. Carson always had a cigarette hanging out of his mouth. Only Gumper and I are alive now! The other six all poundin' stone in the hereafter." —CMH

feet over the side, enjoying the cool weather, the beautiful view of Green Island and Rock Island and others that were within our field of vision, and the marine activity that was always going on in the Stonington waters.

Eventually, Merrill Knowlton, the boss quarryman, asked John Wallace to have me sent up to work in the quarry. Dick called him Beany, as he was tall and slender as a beanpole. My father had fallen overboard in Webb's Cove when they were little boys growing up together; Merrill hauled my father out of the water because he couldn't swim a stroke at that time. It was many years later, in 1990 specifically, that my father told the good folks at the Island Nursing Home while they were all at their evening meal that Merrill had saved his life.

Up in the quarry, I ran an Ingersoll Rand plug drill and sometimes a bigger jackhammer that was actually a larger and faster drill. The drill bits were sharpened in the blacksmith's shop that was situated across from the quarry's timekeeper's office, where Harold Small was the timekeeper and John Wallace was the superintendent. John had been a "hard boss" up in the quarry in my dad's youth, and one day as the Number One Derrick was pulling a stone down onto dunnage (piles of wood to soften the fall of the heavy stone), the dog hole broke out, and the huge steel dogs and chains sprang loose and flailed and slatted around in the work space. Dad and some others dropped to the stone surface, but one of the dogs hit John in the head, and he was hospitalized for quite some time. After he recovered and came back to work, he was a different man, almost avuncular.

There were about four drillers, and we wore cotton gloves to turn the plug-drill wrenches back and forth to make the plug-drill bits drill cleaner and faster. There were no kneeling pads, so we would use the left-hand glove to cushion one knee while the right-hand glove took the beating, the wear and tear of the plug drill wrench.

Most of the time we were making dimension stock for specific orders, and these huge blocks of granite were shipped to other states on wooden barges. The *Eugenie Spofford* tugboat had been long gone by the time I came to work on the quarry, but our father, Dick, used to help tow barges down to Boston, New York, or other places with the little steam-powered tugboat, when I was a tiny lad. Cap'n George Knowlton was skipper in my youth, and Hezekiah Robbins was cook, Roy Cook was engineer, and Dick was the deckhand. I remember Garland and myself going on board one time, and Hez gave a doughnut to each of us two little shavers; we were awed! The tug gleamed in our eyes, the steam engine seemed to be huge, and Roy kept the boiler fired as he worked down in the engine room by himself.

The quarry, in my early youth, also owned a lighter, the *Annie Ruben*. I think that she was also powered by a steam engine. The newer Eastern Steamship dock's west end collapsed at some time in the 1930s, and Garland and I walked over the Clam City Road and along a shoreside pathway to watch Mr. Ferguson, the diver, send bubbles up as he worked underwater resetting the granite blocks. The *Annie Ruben* had a steam-driven pile driver working to drive wooden pilings into the mud to help contain the granite blocks in their proper facing alignment. That repair went on for quite some time, and of course we found new entertainment.

Our dad was the derrick maintenance man on John L. Goss, and he always asked for Jimmy Gray to run the hoisting-engine, as the other hoisting-engineer was a wild man in comparison. Jim was very cautious and gentle with the control levers and friction brakes. It would be easy to squash the workman between the huge hoisting blocks if the engineer was not very very careful, as Dick or Clyde rode up standing inside the wire ropes as the bottom block ran up the mast toward the top block. Dad never climbed up onto the top plate. He greased the pins and sheaves and masthead pivot pin while standing on the top of the bottom block.

Once in a while, we would have to quarry a roof stone for a mausoleum. First, we had to drill and break a very deep block of granite, before drilling and splitting it using very long half-rounds and long thin tapered wedges. Ford Bray usually ran the Ingersoll Rand jackhammer drill, sighting on a stick held by Beanie to achieve a truly vertical drill hole. We carried the extra-long drill bits back and forth on a flatcar to the blacksmith's shop. Charles Dorety was the boss blacksmith, and Alva Hutchinson was the apprentice. Alva was not in my class at school, but we were thick as thieves when we were in school. I walked over to his house on the back side of Green Head sometimes. He had an older brother, Vernal, who wrote two books. One was *A Maine Town in The Civil War*, and the other was *When Revolution Came*. Their mother was very sick and usually lying on a cot in the living room. It made me feel very sad that she was not well. She was a very nice, sweet lady, and I didn't like to go there at all after a while.

I would gladly hike down to the blacksmith shop to get a hod full of newly sharpened plug drills and climb back up the slope and ladders to get up onto the work area. Charlie would sharpen the plug drills while I waited. He never drank alcohol and took a very dim view of anyone who did. He always commented on his ability to keep warm in the wintertime without anything to drink but coffee or tea. Alva was usually hung over on Monday mornings and was not very friendly. Sometime around Wednesday, he was his usual jovial self, but as the years passed away he became more sour and cross. I hardly ever saw him after I left John L. Goss on the last working day of November of 1950.

Up in the quarry there were several young lads my age or close to it. Wiley Knowlton, Beanie's son; Eugene Joyce, who married my distant cousin, Betty Haskell; Carson Hutchinson; Gordon "Gumper" Gray, who has been a close friend all these years. He lives in New Hampshire now, after years working on natural-gas drilling rigs. We had both found something better than working on the stone quarry. He is 85, five years older than me. Forrest "Ford" Bray was an old hand on the quarry; he could operate the derricks, drill the roof stones, and operate the steam drill. Henry "Hemp" Bray was another old-timer, and George "Buck" Pickering was the breaker. However, Ford usually broke the roof stone blocks.

Near the end of summer of 1947, I found out that Wyman Haskell in Oceanville was trading his 1929 Nash Ambassador long-wheelbased sedan in on a 1936 Oldsmobile at Carlisle Webb's (his son-in-law). I loved the looks of that large car. It had fender wells with a spare tire on each side. It was a gas-and-oil hog; those old long-stroke motors all seemed to wear out the cylinder bores early. It would churn along at fifty miles an hour effortlessly but gobbled gas at eight miles to the gallon.

During that same summer on John L. Goss's we ran out of easily-quarried stone, so we began to make a channel, which consisted of drilling holes in a straight line with the jackhammer, spaced about eighteen inches apart and nearly down through the virgin sheet of stone. Donald "Duck" Davis was hired to become the tool boy. So he carried the dulled drill bits to the blacksmith's shop and brought back the newly sharpened ones.

After it seemed like an entire summer of drilling these channel holes, Beanie blew the stone dust out of every one of them and began loading the holes with dynamite. Each hole was topped off with a blasting cap stuffed inside the top stick. The blasting caps were wired in series, and just like a John Wayne movie, the wires were fastened to a magneto's terminals. We all crawled into our bomb-proof shelter, and Beanie walked out to the edge of the sheet and shouted, "Fire in the hole!" three times, spacing each call so that anyone walking up the tracks could get behind or into some kind of shelter. Then Merrill crawled into our shelter, and Ford Bray pushed the plunger down. There was an immediate blast. All the dynamite went off at once; dishes jumped and rattled in the kitchens and pantries of the houses over in Stonington. There was a shower of flying bits of granite against the piled-up stones of our bomb-proof shelter. After the blasting was over and the stone dust settled, we had to shovel all the pulverized stone into grout boxes and send it down the south side of the hill to be dumped onto the grout pile. It took what seemed to be an entire hot dusty summer working down in the channel. There wasn't a breath of wind to ease our miseries of shoveling the very heavy, wet, sticky slurry that the stone dust became after a rainy day or two. We really, really enjoyed a little swim off a nearby abandoned quarry dock at lunchtime during that chore. Eventually, we had a nice wide channel, and we traced a chalk line, pounding away with our quarry hammers while sitting on the granite and hitching along as we pounded away upon our tracers (merely crude chisels, sharpened by Charlie in his forge.)

Merrill laid out a new quarrying line with his blue chalk and cotton twine. One day Gumper Gray greased his chalk line, and Merrill was not the least bit pleased with that. I never knew who did it till Gumper sent me an e-mail recently. (We both got a chuckle out of that bit of news!)

We youngsters drilled along this new line running roughly east to create a new work area. This time, Ford Bray operated the steam drill, which had been sitting around unused for a long time. In between steam-drill holes, we drilled knox holes with the Ingersoll Rand jackhammer drill about two feet deep. After we had drilled all the holes, Beanie cleaned them out again with his galvanized iron pipe and compressed air. (I never understood why the boss quarrymen didn't use a copper pipe, as copper would not create a spark.) Hollis Gray blew himself up years ago cleaning out a drill hole that had an unexploded charge of black powder. His face was pockmarked with powder burns for the rest of his life. It didn't do much for his mentality, either.

We loaded each of the drilled holes with black powder and one blasting cap, and stuffed newspaper into the holes, then poured stone dust in on top of that, pounded it down to contain the charge. Once again we retreated to our bomb-proof, while Merrill shouted out the safety warnings. Black powder has a more gentle blast, and after three loadings and blastings there appeared a tiny crack following the chiseled line to the edge of the older channel. Once the crack was evident, Merrill changed to fine powder. We lads went down to the powder house and brought up several cans of DuPont fine powder. The powder house was a small shed lined with matched-board paneling on the inside in an attempt to control moisture. It looked for all the world like a large, three-hole privy. It sat far away from the cutting shed and the other buildings in case of an accidental explosion.

Years ago, when dynamite had been a new invention, the boss quarryman was blasting a channel, and a case of ninety-proof dynamite had been left outside on the very top sheet, well away from the work area. When the magneto was pushed down, the extra case of dynamite blew up in a sympathetic explosion, sending pieces of stone flying across the quarry hole and as far as the ocean quite some distance below. "My crimes!" Dick, exclaimed, "There were holes all through the hoisting house, where chunks of stone blew right through th' sides, up on top of th' hill!"

Of course, it wasn't all work, stone dust and grime. We youngsters would play "shoulders." If one of us was off his guard, another would paste him right in the shoulder and nearly knock him down. It was not wise to run down the tracks at quitting time, as someone would try to trip anyone who wasn't fully alert. Wiley had played a trick on me earlier in the day, and I caught his flying feet just right, so he went headlong into the railroad ties. His lunchbox went sailing, hit a stone and broke his thermos. Beanie, who was out of the play, suddenly asked, "What the hell is going on?" Wiley said to me later, on our *J. Douglas* ride to the Stonington dock, that he had it coming. Ford caught me one day as I was drilling near a newly-formed rain puddle. He threw a huge hunk of grout into the "lake" and drenched me! Someone was always crimping the hose line so that the plug drill wouldn't work. Then they would laugh as we looked up to see what was going on.

Every once in a while, the soft-coal pile began to need replenishing, and a tugboat would bring an old wooden barge loaded with 1,500 tons of soft coal alongside of the boiler-room dock, which ran east and west into the Crotch Island cove. There was enough depth of water there at low tide to keep the old barges afloat at any stage of the tide. We quarrymen came over each morning to shovel coal into old donkey boiler shells that had been crudely converted to huge coal buckets. The buckets were lifted and carried to and from the coal barge to the growing soft-coal pile on the John L. Goss dock. There was a crude Blondin rig that worked like the high-line devices the Pacific-coast logging companies used to carry the huge firs across streams, and it required a very deft steam-hoisting engineer to keep the buckets traveling smoothly to or away from the barge and dumping them onto the coal pile. We all got in under the edge of the hatches when these contraptions were lifting or lowering the crude buckets. Most of the time, there would be day workers helping shovel out the loads of coal; one the workers was George Dunham, who was Linnie Dunham's father. Linnie was in my 1945 graduating class at Stonington High School. George was very strong and could keep up with us young pups hour after hour! Harvest Nevills and several other men from Stonington came over every day that we were unloading coal. We flailed away with wide coal shovels, and at quitting time we would all be as black as the coal.

Sometimes we would drive to Deer Isle's Lily Pond for a cleansing swim after working all day shoveling coal. I can't imagine that all that coal dust did anything good to the water supply for Deer Isle village. It took several days for us to unload the barge, and it sat empty at the dockside waiting to be towed away for several more days. The barge skipper must have been lonesome, tucked away in the mouth of the cove without any means of getting into town. We lads were almost glad to return to quarrying stone after a week or so of very actively shoveling coal. Howard Haskell and Neville Eaton were keepers of the boiler room, while we were up on the hill breathing in stone dust all day long.

We all climbed down the ladders to sit in the lower hoisting house to eat our lunch, and in cold weather Charlie Bye or Jimmie Gray, the hoisting engineer of the day, had a fire going in the fifty-five-gallon-oil-drum stove with our dinner pails hung on wires over the rising heat, so that the contents would be toasty warm.

Marm had made two corned-beef sandwiches and tucked in two homemade doughnuts for my lunch, loaded with cholesterol, but delicious! Ford Bray would tell stories about fishing or the old quarry days. One of his favorite stories was about his brother Smoky, who had bought a Reo engine out of a wrecked car somewhere and installed it in his scallop-fishing-rigged workboat. The very first day while working the engine hard, it began to smoke and lose power. When they limped in to the mooring that day, Smoky simply unbolted the Reo from its engine mounts and hoisted it up out of the engine bed, swung it over onto the top of the boat's washboard railing, unhooked his sling, and pushed the Reo over the side with a satisfying splash. He replaced that wimpy engine with a big straight-eight Buick, and that held up to the strain.

Ford bragged about the old quarrying days when John L. Goss was working three gangs up on the hill. "We quarried six hundred tons of stone a day, boys! We would have it down on the dock all ready to ship. Sometimes there were up to four schooners waiting out in th' habbah, deah! Waitin' to load with stone, even four-masted schooners! Those were some ol' wicked days ol' son!"

During the sticky, hot summer days up in the hole, we would walk down to the abandoned stone quarry dock and jump overboard, "skinny dipping." Gumper and I rigged a driftwood plank to serve as a diving board, and several of us cannon-balled into the very cool ocean water below. Lunch hour never lasted long enough, but it was a refreshing interlude just the same.

Shortly after we had pushed the new work-area stone away from the rest of sheet of stone with the fine blasting powder by as much as a quarter of an inch that time (1949, I think), we began to quarry it into blocks five feet deep by five or six feet wide by up to ten feet long. Bud Hutchinson was up on the very top, giving hand signals to Jimmy Gray, who operated the bull-gear pulling engine up in the hoisting house on the top of the hill. This crude equipment towed the quarried blocks to the edge of the channel, and the Number Five Derrick lifted the blocks and swung them out over the edge and down onto a flatcar on the track way below, and it was sent down the slope on rails to be towed up over a slight rise and then lowered by the towing and restraining cable down to the scales, where Harold Small would record the weight. One of the hoisting engineers would be up in the dock's stiff-leg derrick's hoisting house, where the hoisting engine and the swinging engine were run by steam directly from the boiler room below. He would lift a block of stone and swing it away from the flatcar to be piled on the dock, ready to be loaded onto the next barge that came in.

Dick was usually the stevedore, and I would be his helper. We would stow the blocks in the hold of the old wooden barges and shim them in place with scrap lumber, so that the uneven blocks would not teeter, either from side to side or fore and aft. One day, long before I worked there, one of the dogs slipped and a huge block of stone fell into the hold. Dick was in under the edge of the hatch opening and was not hurt. There were always close calls, and sometimes workers were badly or fatally hurt.

We never liked having our lunch in the hoisting house up on the top of the hill. It was exposed to the winter's fierce winds and was drafty. We preferred to climb down the ladders to eat in the more cozy hoisting house down in the quarry hole out of the wind, where a brave little red squirrel would come in and spin one of Marm's doughnuts on a nail until it had succeeded in gnawing through the doughnut, allowing it to fall on to the ground below. We were easily amused all the while we were being entertained.

Some days it poured rain all day, and the rules were that we would stay two hours. And if the weather remained soaking wet, we would go back to Stonington on the *J. Douglas*. But if it cleared off a little, we would work in the rain. But a steady downpour made working a miserable experience. In snowy weather, we usually cleared off the area that we were working in with shovels and a beat-up old broom and proceeded to drill and break as usual. Dog holes would be drilled with a stubby dog-drill bit inserted into the plug drill's tool opening, and the huge dogs would be dragged out to each end of the stone, chains and all, and the hoisting engineer would take a strain on the chains, guided by hand signals from Merrill or Ford. Everyone stood quite clear when this activity took place! If a dog was not hooked well, the dog could fly off with terrific force! The derrick would dance, quiver and shake, the guy wires hopping up and down, threatening to bring the whole works down upon our heads. Fortunately, most of the time the stone pulled out and was lifted onto the stone pile or flatcar, and we began to trace and drill for another stone, day after stone-dust-filled day! I remember one time that Merrill was in a hurry and wanted us to start on a lift line right away, so I grabbed my Ingersoll Rand plug drill and hose and jumped down onto the staging, which wasn't all that well braced up, and the entire staging went down onto the dunnage. Beanie growled at me like a stern schoolmaster; he didn't like my quick response! I rode the staging boards down like in a rodeo and didn't even fall over into the stone pile.

Just about this time in the fall or early winter, we were hauling quarried stone on the bull gear, Bud Hutchinson was up on the hill giving signs to Jimmy Gray in the hoisting house, and everything was just right. Nothing broke; every haul-out was easily performed; there were no snarls; the chains did not fetch up, and we labored away all day. The flatcar rolled up and down the track without a hitch or derailment, and at quitting time Harold Small told me, "Best day in a long time: six hundred tons today, ol' son." Ford Bray never talked about the good old six-hundred-ton day again. But we never quarried that much stone in one day again, either!

One very cold 1949 night, there was a freezing rain, and in the morning Dick slipped and fell on his ass right off the front-door step. He came back into the house cursing and lifted the ash pan out of the woodstove and sprinkled ashes all the way to the main road. We took our lunch pails and slithered and slid all the way to the top of the first hill. We simply sat down and slid down to the bottom, then carefully continued on to the steep hill that leads down to Granite Street, where we sat down and slid again, right down to the nearly level street that runs to the Eastern Steamship dock, where the *J. Douglas* was waiting for us. Some of the workers crashed their cars trying to get to Stonington, and some simply stayed home until the ice melted off. After we slipped and slid up to the quarry hole, we emptied the fifty-five-gallon-oil-drum stove's ashes onto the places where we had to walk. We then built a fire in the air compressor's inch-and-a-half coil line to vaporize the moisture, so that the plug drills would work. For several days, the temperature was ten below zero or colder, and we could not put more than one wedge and two half rounds into a drilled hole before our hands became too cold to work! So we retired to the hoisting house, where Ford held court, as it were, with stories of the good old days.

Sometimes I would stop in at the blacksmith's shop to chat with Alva Hutchinson, who was getting grouchier and grouchier, and after a while I stopped trying to kid around with him. Charlie remained his constant taciturn self.

I had run off the road in a snowstorm in my huge Nash and bent the front axle. I bought another Nash from Lyman Haskell, who had saved it for spare parts. Dad helped me straighten the frame and the axle, but the Nash was never right after that. So I sold it for $50. Gumper Gray had been telling me how good a 1932 Plymouth four-cylinder was, and one of the Little Deer Isle lads had one. He got the ancient Plymouth stuck in the mud somewhere and burned out the clutch racing the engine. So I bought it for $40 from Budget Eaton, who had acquired it. He ran an automobile general repair garage, where Heanssler's Gulf station is located in Deer Isle today. Gumper and I worked on that old wreck for days, getting it to run again. Almost on the very first test trip the pot-metal carburetor's sliding venturi choke assembly crystallized and broke off, and I limped home with black smoke pouring out of the exhaust. Gumper managed to fit a Model A Ford carburetor onto the Plymouth intake manifold flange by grinding off the heads of two bolts so that the bolts would squeeze down into the threaded Ford flange mounting holes.

The flywheel was scoured gunmetal blue where the Little Deer Islander had burned out the clutch. Norman Robbins, Dennis Robbins's son, who lived on the Wheat Field Road at that time, had a flywheel from a 1930 Plymouth and a rusty pressure plate. So I bought them and cleaned off their rusty faces with fine sandpaper. Carlisle Webb had a clutch disk for a 1934 Plymouth, so I installed these parts into the '32 Plymouth, and it worked so well that the floating-power engine twisted the radiator hose nipple right off the radiator. Dick was a whiz with solder and its usages. He soldered the nipple right back on for me. The original floating-power control spring and its hardware had either fallen off or had been removed long before I bought the car. So I bolted a stamped steel brace to the top rear cylinder head bolt, and that controlled the flopping motor, but the vibration was very severe! So I slid two

AUTHOR'S 1927 MODEL T TOURING CAR IN 1956, DUCK DAVIS AT THE WHEEL.

rubber shock absorbers from an old Ford onto a very long bolt, which I passed up through a hole in the frame rail, and with two more rubber shock absorbers on top of the frame rail the motor behaved, and the vibration was tolerable.

Soon after that, Duck Davis and I were riding around in his 1925 Model T Ford touring car, and we picked up a young lad who wanted a ride to Blue Hill, and he told us where we could get another touring car just like the one we were riding in, so we drove over to Blue Hill and found that the Ford was a 1927, the last year for the Model T. It had an earlier rear end than the '27s, equipped with thirty-inch wooden-spoked wheels, clincher rims and tires. Eventually we returned in my Nash carrying a five-gallon can of gas, jumper wires and a hand-operated tire pump. We pumped up the tires, took out the sparkplugs, poured in some 30-weight oil and put the plugs back in, hooked up the jumper wires and cranked and cranked the Ford's motor with the hand crank. We were almost getting blisters before the engine fired once!

Out came the plugs again, and we dribbled a little gasoline into each hole, refastened the sparkplugs and cranked some more. The engine had been building up compression, as the oil worked in around the piston rings and began to seal the gas-and-air mixture into the combustion chamber. Suddenly it started up, and Duck switched the engine onto the magneto. The radiator leaked like a sieve, but it began to seal itself as we kept bailing water into it. Duck drove it back to Deer Isle without license plates, and we left it by my father's saw-sharpening shop.

The Model T was to occupy our spare time for the rest of the summer. Driving it home without a battery burned out the generator, and I had a hard time finding one on the island. Not that they were scarce, but anyone who had one was not willing to sell it. "Ya never know when ya might need it!" was the most familiar story. Eventually I procured one, and with a new vaporizer plate in the intake manifold, it started much easier. In 1926 the Ford Motor Company put the gas tank up on the cowl. The gas simply ran down to the carburetor by gravity. However, it was not a safe location if one had a head-on crash, and folks were soon to discover this unsafe location when the much faster Model A came out in late 1927, and there were some crashes, and possibly one of the crashed cars caught on fire. It only takes one for litigation to force changes. By 1932, Fords had a fuel pump, and the gas tank was relocated to the rear between the dumb irons, like Chevrolet and the others.

One day the boss stonecutter, Ernest Poitras, came up and wanted someone to drill lewis holes down in the yard. One always finds out who the boss thinks the least of, as I was picked to go down and work for Ernest. So I learned how to drill the tiny triangle-shaped lewis holes. Did you ever wonder how those heavy granite stones were lifted into place without any dog holes showing? The lewis holes were drilled to make rectangular holes about one-half inch wide and wider at the bottom than at the top, so that special wedge-shaped pieces of steel were pushed down into the holes; then two half-round wedges were pushed in, and the triangle-shaped piece was locked in solidly as the hoist lifted the stone with a chain looped through a ring on each of the two wedge-shaped lewises. "Crude but it worked," our son Nathan would say. Therefore, bridge and polished building facing stones show a smooth face, as the stones were lifted into their places with these devices.

Everytime someone was off sick down in the cutting-shed yard, I was sent to work there. I learned how to set up the stone gang-saw carriages. Spruce or pine boards had to be fastened in place to direct the steel shot down into the trough where the long steel blades ran back and forth, as a direct-current electric motor moved the flat-belt-driven saw frames back and forth noisily all day and sometimes all night. When Deer Isle Granite and John L. Goss were busy with orders, there were four gang saws rasping away round the clock. And when the wind was outta th' sou'west, we could hear them nearly two miles away, a-rish a-rash a-rish a-rash sounds, as the steel blades wore thin slots down through the granite saw blocks. Once in a while, two saws would synchronize their movements together, changing the rhythms. I was always aware of the noise, but it didn't disturb my sleep.

A load of steel shot came in on the *J. Douglas*, and we quarrymen lads had to go down and load these burlap bags full of shot onto a flatcar, so it could be towed up the slope to the gang-saw building. It was exhausting work; the bags were all floppy, of course, and heavy as sin, and when the last bag was stored away, we were saggin'.

One day I was working with Raymond Poitras, washing the rust off the newly-sawn slabs of granite with sulfuric acid, and Raymond let his swab and stick fall into my face. I quickly grabbed up the hose and jammed it into my face to dilute the acid that might have burned me blind. I kept my eyes wide open for several minutes. Fortunately, I didn't work with him again.

Sometime later, the yard boss stonecutter, Ernest Poitras, sent up one of the yard workers up to summon me down to work in the high-speed-electric-saw shed. Just about the time I was climbing down the ladders, the steam whistle blew four blasts. Merrill shouted for everyone to gather their belongings (lunch boxes and jackets) and go down to the dock. We straggled down there and were told that the stonecutter who had been running the high-speed saw had been electrocuted somehow. I was instantly shocked to think that it could have been me! The *J. Douglas* returned to the quarry's dock, and we all went home. Uncle Elroy came over in his outboard-powered skiff and tended the boilers all night, starting just a little earlier than usual.

After the June 25th North Korean surprise attack crossing the 38th parallel, the South Koreans and American troops were retreating southward. I received a draft notice in the mail with instructions to report to the draft board in Ellsworth, Maine. I had been rated 4F in World War II, so I was a bit surprised. As it turned out, anyone of draft age in Hancock County who had a heartbeat was called up.

The Stonington lobster fishermen had been having a poor season. They were still using homemade wooden traps. Hydraulic pot haulers were just beginning to be adopted by the high liners (fishermen who were fierce to catch the most lobsters in a season). Wire traps had not been invented at that time. These two inventions and depth finders would change the lobster fishing industry forever. One quiet, sunny day, lobster fisherman Pearl Haskell came over to the quarry looking for a job. I asked him if he was going to take my place; he was a little surprised but recovered nicely when I told him that I had been drafted for the "Korean Caper." I took my quarry hammer and lunch pail home on my last day at John L. Goss, never to return.

Before I leave the stone quarry years behind, let me tell you how my father leveled the mausoleum roof stones, so that Al Stinson could operate the surfacing machine. Dick simply sighted on the high-tide line of Green Island to get the stone level in the north and south plane, and then turned himself ninety degrees to sight on the high-tide line of George's Head Island to establish the east and west plane. He shimmed the large roof stones securely so that the hammering of the surfacing machine did not disturb the level position! Dick never told the other yard men how he did it so easily and quickly—job security from skills that the others did not have!

1950 rolled around, and what a year it was. There was a wife-swap club in Deer Isle, but Stonington's Saturday night dances at the Red Barn ran a close second in extracurricular sexual activities. One of the heating-oil delivery truck drivers was delivering more than heating oil. Some of the gals working at the fish factory could be seen sneaking off with someone for a tryst amongst the empty barrels on the second floor of the old Eastern Steamship dock building. But it wouldn't do to write out the participants' names, even now. I enjoyed going to the Red Barn dances on Saturday nights. The barn was used as the temporary Stonington High School basketball court and as a dance hall. It was located behind the Stonington Post Office on Pink Street. One Saturday night when I walked in, a complete stranger hollered at me, "Hey! Pa Kettle!" So I joined her in a Lady of the Lake contra dance, and after the dance I drove her back to Goose Cove Lodge. I thought that she was just dandy. Shirley Evans was from Slippery Rock, Pennsylvania, and every Saturday night I took her back to the Goose Cove Lodge, where she worked as a waitress all during that long, wonderful summer. I was soon to find out that Shirley was engaged to be married!

However, there was another Pennsy gal at the dances, Pamela Haviland, from the Germantown section of Philadelphia. She was a great friend of my distant cousin Cornelia Billings, and she danced a Jitterbug with Icky Austin. There was a John Paul Jones dance, and I danced a tiny bit with Pamela and several other girls, when the music stopped and each dancer continued with whoever was holding one's right hand. About this time, we planned to have a beach party on the Sunshine bar (a causeway). I asked Pamela to come to the party as Phil Raymond's date. That's about as audacious as one can get! Dick Solon and Phil Raymond grabbed each other's ankles and rolled along the beach like a cartwheel until Phil bashed his head onto a granite erratic and almost knocked himself out.

Uncle Sam had plans for me that none of us knew about. The North Koreans had invaded South Korea, but in midsummer we were having too much fun to be concerned with a war more than half the world away from Deer Isle! The very last day before Pamela went back to Philadelphia for the winter, I asked her to go to the movies in Stonington, and we were just beginning a relationship that has survived 52 years so far!

70. The Army, Pam, and My Homecoming

Just as we quarrymen were enjoying jumping off the Ryan and Parker Granite Quarry's remaining dock into the frigid Crotch Island water at noontime near June 25th, North Korea invaded South Korea, and before fall they almost pushed the American and South Korean armed forces off the peninsula. Dick, remembering his great-grandfather Peter H. Haskell, Jr.'s treatment by General Sedgwick and the U.S. Government in the Civil War, would not let me enlist. But I was drafted, scooped up amidst 108 Maine youths from all over the state.

I don't remember exactly now, but I think that uncle Bob McGuffey took me to Ellsworth for my physical examination on December 1st, 1950, in his 1938 Dodge business coupe, his go-to-work car, all rusty and trusty. Neville Eaton was coal passer on the same quarry with me, but he never worked in the quarry itself. He and I were the only lads from Stonington, and Reggie Sewall was from Little Deer Isle. We were soon climbing the stairs to the draft board on the second floor of a building on Main Street in Ellsworth. It was organized chaos, people talking, officials ordering us into lines in alphabetical order as we were called by our last names. We all had rudimentary examinations by some doctors. I remember a recruit named McPherson from upstate Maine somewhere, who had taken a pot shot at a game warden. He was interviewed by the State Police in a room off from the rest of us.

After a while, we climbed down the stairs to board a little Ford-powered bus. It had an automatic two-speed transmission, and the Ford V8 motor was either straining away or screaming in the lower ratio, and each shift was accompanied with by a sharp metallic bang. After belting roughly up old Route 1A to Bangor, we transferred to a train that was hauled along by a huge Baldwin steam locomotive. Away we went, to arrive eventually in Ft. Devens, Massachusetts, in U.S. Army school buses painted olive drab. We were separated into groups, and that evening we had a "G.I. party," which consisted of cleaning the barracks with push brooms and a lot of water and scouring with strong cleaning fluids. Over the next day or so, we were tested with physical exams and multiple-choice written exams. I was told that I had qualified for officer training school. But of course, nothing ever came of that.

Eventually, we "fell out and fell in" to a rough formation, and as one's name was called out that person was told to "fall out and fall in over here" or "over there." Soon, there were groups going to Ft. Benning, Georgia, to train as paratroopers. Suddenly Reggie Sewall was shouting and jumping up and down, "Hi! Hi! Hi! I didn't sign up for that." He was waving his arms frantically. Very soon, Reggie was standing all alone, while Neville and I were loaded into another olive-drab painted school bus and carted off to the train station. Reggie was on KP for days and days until he was sent to Ft. Wood, Washington, overlooking the Pacific Ocean. Neville and I didn't see Reggie again until we were all back on Deer Isle. He told me years afterwards that one day he went on sick call, and the doctor who examined him asked him if he could see out of his cat's eye, a genetic defect that seemed to be quite common on Deer Isle. Reggie replied, "I can see daylight!" After a while, Reggie was discharged and sent back to Little Deer Isle. I think that Ft. Wood is now a park. It was the only military installation with disappearing guns, if my memory has not failed me altogether.

I don't remember if Hutch enlisted or was drafted, but he was operating a Baldwin locomotive hauling aviation gasoline up to the front lines, when a Russian MiG fighter came sweeping down, strafing the train. Hutch pushed the Korean fireman out of the cab, and he jumped out himself, and the whole trainload of gasoline went up in a spectacular explosion. He and the fireman escaped alive but were scraped, bruised and bleeding from their contact with the railroad embankment at high speed, as they rolled down to safety into the roadbed ditch.

Meanwhile, fighting General Joe Walker was defending South Korea with any soldiers, cooks and motor-pool mechanics and other normally non-combatants that could shoot a rifle. The North Koreans and Chinese (who had joined the battle) were relentless. General Douglas McArthur made an exciting invasion behind the North Korean lines at Pusan and surprised the enemy.

It seemed to take forever and ever as we were rattling and banging south to Alabama's Camp Rucker—which I later learned had been a prisoner-of-war camp for captured Germans in World War I—and sometimes the passenger train was left standing on a side track, while more important freight trains rumbled past. On one of these pauses, we saw a black man who, proudly grinning, held up a very large catfish for us to admire. He was standing on a large, squared timber, that seemed to be some kind of brace for the railroad bridge that crossed the little river at that point.

Eventually, we arrived in Camp Rucker and were met by the same kind of olive-drab school buses, our cadre for the near future. One sergeant was from Utah and was a Mormon; another was a career U.S. Army sergeant, who had been in Indochina and spoke several dialects in singsong Chinese, when he felt like showing off. We liked them both and got along well with most of them. One warrant officer was a bully, and we didn't get to like him very much, and there was an ex-paratrooper sergeant who was a terror, but one day he got bitten by a rattlesnake, and he was much nicer after he recovered. The army at that time was not integrated, and the Afro-American troops were always seen marching somewhere. I met one of them when we were out on a training hike, and he seemed to be very, very smart.

We started basic training and special ammunition classes, mixed with calisthenics and eventually unloading ammunition that arrived in eighteen-wheelers. I didn't see Neville Eaton very often, as he was in another barracks. There were some southern lads in our barracks and two or three New York City wise guys, who naturally held the farm boys and Maineiacs in contempt as being too dumb to walk even, except Marty Feldman—he was a talker and knew more jokes than Bob Hope! He was slightly splay-footed and walked with a swagger. He carried a switchblade tucked into his waistband, and I suppose he knew how to use it. But he wasn't half as dangerous as Louie Guertin, who was a fighter with a terrifically fast punch. Louie could not read nor write, so I wrote letters home for him and Herbie Howe, who was from Washburn, Maine. I could not understand how they got along in the world so poorly prepared. I made sure to be friends with Louie and a couple other tough guys. Hollywood doesn't have all the actors! There was a recruit in one of the barracks who was of Portuguese descent, and he played a mandolin and sang in his native tongue. He never associated with us Anglos, but there were some other Portuguese lads in the outfit, and they got together with the mandolin player and had little sing-a-longs. However, one of them was friendly with me, and we got along very well. Neville chummed around with Johnnie Hoffses, from upstate Maine, and I joined Marty Feldman in the PX, drinking beer and telling bad jokes. We always had an audience gathered around the table.

There was also Stanley "Lightning" Burkes from Estill Springs, Tennessee, who invited me to go home with him. What an experience that was! We took a bus from the nearest large town to Chattanooga. The bus wound around a huge strip-mined area, where there were huge, treeless, lumpy mounds of blackened earth. It didn't look as if there would ever be anything growing upon the tortured landscape again! We hitchhiked to Estill Springs from the bus station and eventually arrived at a rough woods road that led to his parents' home.

There was a 1936 Chevrolet sinking slowly into the ground. His father was sitting barefooted in a homemade rocking chair on the front porch. We walked through the house to his bedroom, where a full-grown hen was walking on his bed. Lightning swept the hen out through the open window. We deposited our luggage and went into the kitchen to meet his mother, who was a tiny southern gal. She was making southern fried chicken. After the evening meal, Lightning borrowed his brother's flatbed lumber truck (the family business was a "peckerwood sawmill"; Stanley Burkes said it was a Tennessee local name for any small sawmill operation), and we drove to a tiny house perched upon a hillside, where

Lightning bought some white lightning, which he brought out in a pint Mason jar. I tried a tiny sip: powerful stuff! I'm sure that a few sips of that would put me right on my backside! Then we drove through a shallow, sandy-bottomed riverbed to a long, low, gray, weathered house, where Lightning went in to "see a girl" that he knew. I sat alone in the old truck's cab quite a while; eventually Lightning emerged from the house, and we drove back through the river, and that night we took two girls to a movie in a larger town, still riding in the flatbed truck. My date was named Ophelia Floyd; she seemed to be a slender little thing, but after we returned to duty, I wrote to her several times, and she sent me photos of a big brawny gal who looked as if she could swing an axe as easily as Paul Bunyan, the legendary Maine lumberjack.

Our three-day pass was nearly over, and Lightning's uncle took us to the bus station in Chattanooga in a faded green 1939 Ford sedan. It was a very fast ride, and I suspect that the Ford was a moonshiner's vehicle. When we got back to Camp Rucker, I was rewarded with guard duty. We had recruits supposedly standing guard in cotton fields, as if someone would steal a field!

Letters from Marm at home in Stonington informed me that Mike Dow and Thomas Warren were also in Camp Rucker, so I walked over to see them. It was a long hike in the very hot Alabama weather. They were both homesick and didn't want to talk very much. I have a photo of another recruit from their barracks standing with Mike and me by a signpost. Mike was a handsome soldier. I didn't bother to hike over to see Mike and Tom again. It seemed to be unsatisfactory, and telling jokes with Marty Feldman was more fun. Sometimes, Herbie Howe from Washburn, Maine, would seek me out to write to his parents, or to read a letter from them to him. Louie Guertin wasn't as homesick as Herbie, but once in a while he would come over, and I would read his letters from home or write one for him.

Then there were military maneuvers. We would be a red team and would be loading and unloading simulated ammo onto or off of the GM six-bys (GM six-wheel-drive trucks). One night, we were told to load up our gear, and with everything shoved into backpacks, we rested in a grassy ditch by the tote road until some tanks came along, and we climbed up onto these and "rode out to freedom." Louie Guertin and I were left in Squad 10 to count the unused blank cartridges used in the simulated battles. Eventually, we were brought back to our barracks, and through all this camping and tramping through the southern pine plantations, I managed to write letters home and to Ophelia Floyd and Pamela Haviland.

The 481st Ordnance Ammo was essentially a labor unit, and we practiced marching and loading ammunition. The storage and handling consisted of wooden ammunition boxes filled with sand to simulate real ammunition. We were attending classes when every once in a while we were told, "Fall out and fall in over here." Then we would be loaded onto six-bys and hauled off to the ammo shelters to unload real ammunition, "one-oh-five howitzer shells." The first time that happened, Herbie jumped up into the trailer and kicked the wooden retaining cleat out from under the first projectile, which rolled off the trailer's bed and crashed down onto the concrete apron, sending little concrete chips flying in all directions and almost all the recruits running for their lives. I realized that the TNT explosive was so new that it would take a lot of rough handling and not explode. However, the older shells inside the shelter were apt to explode if they were carelessly tossed around.

Someone shouted at Herbie, "Cut that out, numbskull!" So we carefully explained to Herbie that he could have killed some of us. After that event, we were often called out to unload ammunition from eighteen-wheelers. Quite a bit later, we were in another class when we were hauled out to unload the new 3.5 bazooka rockets. We decided to form a fire line and tossed the wooden boxes from one recruit to another, and the unloading went very quickly. All the rockets were stored very neatly, and very much later we were having a class on these new 3.5s. We learned that they must be handled with care, as they might explode if dropped about three feet onto the ground, whether the safety pin was in place or not.

One day we were taken to an old firing range, where we were allowed to fire one of the earlier bazooka rockets at some old Model T Ford-powered World War I tanks. The rockets didn't work like rifle bullets. The projectiles shot out of the launchers and rose in an erratic parabola arc, wandering off course, as they smoked toward the intended targets, dropping short of the tanks or shooting way beyond and exploding harm-lessly in the southern-pine forest. Our score for that day's trials must have been, "One tank destroyed, two knocked out of commission, and the rest escaped unharmed." We never got to fire the newer 3.5s. Eventually, we were taken out at night onto the firing range, and some practice 105 how-itzer rounds were fired over our positions, so that we would know what an artillery barrage was like if we were to ever come under enemy fire.

We were making roads in the swampy Alabama surroundings and needed to cross a small stream. I told Captain Young that we could build a Maine-type corduroy bridge using newly cut large trees. So Herbie Howe cut down four tall and straight trees with an axe. The captain was

LOUIS GUERTIN FROM RHODE ISLAND AND MCGUIRE, FORT BRAGG, NC.

impressed by Herbie's skill, "Every stroke cuts away; he doesn't waste energy!" We recruits, privates and one corporal, dragged the heavy logs into place, and we spiked smaller trees down onto the four timbers crosswise to make a rude culvert-type bridge. Blackie, the company six-by driver, was the first to try driving across the structure. It bent a little but sprang right back once the truck was across. I wrote about that adventure to my future bride, and she showed it to her father, who thought it was more of a feat than I did.

On our field marches, sometimes we came to really heavily wooded areas, where there were enormous black snakes.

HERBIE HOWE

AUTHOR WITH CAMERA AND THE CONSTRUCTION CREW
AT CAMP RUCKER, ALABAMA.

I had never been afraid of Maine's garter snakes, but these were almost six feet long and as big around as my wrist. I was not eager to walk into those woods! Also there were wild black pigs, whole litters of them. I imagine a wild boar could do some serious damage if he attacked one of us. However they seemed to be content to forage in the undergrowth.

There were wild grapes called scupper-

CAMP RUCKER, ALABAMA, 1951, MIKE DOW (LEFT),
AUTHOR (RIGHT).

nongs by the southern lads in our company. These grapes were large and quite sweet. They seemed to be cousins to Concord grapes, as we sucked the juices out and discarded the pulp and thick skins.

I was granted a leave at some point and went all the way to Bangor by train. The last three hundred miles were on the Flying Yankee. I managed to catch Barter's bus, which was a very stretched Chevrolet eight-door sedan powered with a six-cylinder engine and three-speed transmission. So it ground up the southeast hills in second then low gear, because the little six didn't have enough torque to wrestle the heavy vehicle up over those steep hills in high gear. Eventually, Norman Haskell dropped me off at our driveway. "My junky ol' '32 Plymouth sedan was outta commission, because Dick had taken the engine out and was rebuilding it to go into the *Scullpoogin*, Garland's lobstah boat." The only vehicle in use was Garland's '29 Ford Model A coach. "Not a spiffy gal-courtin' car at all at all!"

I made the mistake of wearing my uniform downtown and having a "cuppa coffee" at the local restaurant. Shall we say, I didn't get any congratulations from Punk Gray or the Dodges, who ran the little coffee shop at that time! From then on, I wore my beat-up levis and drove Garland's old '29 Ford Model A coach. Dick had sold his 1940 Nash long ago, as the '29 Chevy coach was good enough to drive on the Island. Well o' course, the Chevy's sheet-metal-covered wooden body had rotted away, and the only "wheels" available were Garland's Model A. I was almost glad to return to our military camp.

We were miserably cold in the Alabama winter weather, tramping around in our long military coats and woolen uniforms. We were carted to the railroad tracks in the olive-drab school buses and waited in the Alabama woods for a special train to come along. Eventually we saw it coming through the southern-pine forest, its searchlight swiveling around by some mechanical means, and it drew up hissing and wheezing, while we all climbed up into the passenger cars. I was sharing a sleeper with another recruit. I slept very well all the way to North Carolina, where we climbed onto the ubiquitous olive-drab school buses to ride to Ft. Bragg.

Spring in North Carolina was going to be much better! When we arrived, we had to occupy wooden barracks that had not been used since World War II. They were full of dust. So we fell to for a G. party, sweeping up the dust with stiff-bristled push-brooms; then we got our combat boots off and waded around in the lye- and soap-laced water, scrubbing the yellow-pine floors repeatedly until the sergeants were satisfied that they were clean enough. That was on a Friday night.

Saturday morning, we had to stand for inspection. For some reason, I was especially scrutinized by the commanding officer. He examined my shoes, which were not combat boots. "My feet are extra wide so that I can walk on top of the snow in Maine, sir!" He didn't laugh but must have been satisfied, as he hustled along from me.

The GI party had re-started my asthma, and I was laboring to breathe during the Saturday morning inspection. So on Sunday I went down to the company office and asked Sgt. Bulmer to put me on sick call. He erupted in anger, "You can't go on sick call on Sunday!"

I said, "I don't see why not, I'm sick!"

"Well," he said, "you'll have to go down to the hospital." So off I went, and the further I cuffed along the gravel-surfaced road the more I wheezed. So that by the time I got into the hospital, I was really in desperate shape. A young doctor examined me and asked me how I got into the army. "I was drafted!" I replied. Then he asked me if I would like to get out. Well o' course! I was tired of shoveling sand into empty ammo boxes and carting them from one ammo dump to another in simulated battleground deliveries. That was the time I needed a barracks lawyer to enlighten me about the GI Bill.

Nevertheless, some twenty days later, I was hitchhiking to Philadelphia to visit, however briefly, Pamela Haviland. With my discharge papers secured in my duffle bag, I stood by the road outside Ft. Bragg. In a mere minute or so, a Hillman Minx stopped, and I hopped in. Several stops and waits later, I was picked up by a family who were on their way to Upstate New York and were kind enough to detour through North Philadelphia to drop me off at a trolley stop. I climbed up into a trolley, and the conductor told me how to get to Germantown Avenue. He collected my fare and gave me a transfer slip, so I could get onto the 52 trolley line, that ran all the way to Chestnut Hill. The trolley ran up through Germantown and let me off at Johnson Street.

Near this northeast corner of Germantown Avenue and Johnson Street, the Battle of Germantown was fought on October 4, 1777. The Chew mansion at that corner has a cannonball embedded in the wall to this very day from that engagement!

I walked down to 130 West Johnson Street, to be warmly greeted by my future bride, Pamela Jean Haviland. Her parents were horrified that I had hitchhiked to Philadelphia from Ft. Bragg. A day or so later, they drove me down to 30th Street station and put me aboard a passenger train bound for Boston's South Station, where I had to take the infamous subway shuttle. It wheezed and whooshed, then ground noisily away to

Boston's North Station, where I boarded a late-running local to Bangor. It arrived well after Barter's bus had left for Stonington. So I asked a taxi driver how much he would drive me to Stonington for. Well o' course, he doubled the quote by the time we got to Sedgwick! I paid him off, but he didn't get a tip! He dropped me at the driveway, and I walked into the house: we didn't lock the doors in those days!

I called to my parents, who came sleepily downstairs, and we hugged and squeezed. I was mighty glad to be home. Marm warmed up some clam chowder on the old woodstove, and I was really, really home!

I went down to see the new superintendent at John L. Goss's main office, which overlooked the Eastern Steamship dock in those days, and asked to get my old job back, but John L's was in dire straits, and he said that he couldn't take me back on. So I went clamming all winter, in between cutting ten cords of firewood on shares at the old Stinson farm on Stinson's Point. Dick and I rowed around the Webb's Cove shore gathering wild apples and the apples from tired colonial apple trees on the old Seth Webb homestead and the three trees that were still producing at the old Stinson farmstead. Eventually we had three barrels full of rust-and-scale-covered apples. Deftly peeled and sliced, they made as nice an apple pie as store-bought apples. Oh sure, it took lots of labor and care, but we had lots of time! All winter, as it worked out.

I applied for unemployment benefits at the Stonington Town Hall, where the bureaucrats came down from Ellsworth to make me feel like a criminal. One little man always twitted me, "You haven't done a hand's turn all winter?" I replied, "Well, I cut ten cords of wood, split it in four-foot lengths; I go clamming for the larder three times a week right down through holes left by the saltwater ice cakes, but I don't get any money for that!" Then he signed my form, and eventually I received a check for $25 in the mail. Fortunately, I was never on unemployment again!

The snows stopped falling, and the early spring rains arrived in April, and by May Dick and I got the ancient 1932 Plymouth engine into Garland's *Scullpoogin*, lined it up with the propeller shaft using feeler gauges and shims under the engine mounts that Dick had made in his forge. He had overhauled the four-cylinder Plymouth engine, re-babbited the main bearings and scraped them in with a homemade scraper and Prussian bluing. It was a labor of love and skill. Eventually the bearings were true and tight enough, and Dad closed up the assembled lower end. He found some new valves somewhere and lapped them in by hand with a Montgomery Ward valve grinder, which I still have. We rigged up the ignition system and the Ford carburetor which Gumper Gray had fitted to the old Plymouth intake manifold; so we were about to try to start the old thing! I pulled the hand crank through two strokes at full choke, and then Dick turned on the ignition and tried the starter, while I pulled up on the hand crank. She fired right away. After two more tries she kept on running, and the cooling pump began pumping saltwater right through the engine. The oil pressure was thirty pounds per square inch, and she sounded great!

A few days later, we ran off to the Lowe Bottom, just a bit east of Great Spoon Island, and caught a load of cod and haddock. We sold most of the codfish at Colwell's in Stonington and kept some of the haddock for our freezer and gifts to our neighbors.

71. THE MODEL T TOURING CAR

I was twenty-two in 1950 until December; then I would be twenty-three for three whole days! We began the year with news that robbers had heisted a Brink's armored car and got away with almost three million dollars!

My huge Nash Advanced Six was needing a complete restoration, and I didn't earn enough money to finance the work. So I sold it for $50. I was riding around on the mainland with Duck Davis in his 1925 Model T Ford touring car, and we picked up a young man who was hitchhiking. He said, "I know where there is a car just like this, for sale." So away we went to Blue Hill, and the touring car turned out to be a 1927, the last year that Ford made the Model T. I bought it on the spot.

New adventures proceeded almost immediately. It seemed to take forever to find a used Model T Ford generator. The young lad who had the Ford had swapped an earlier rear axle onto the '27. Therefore, it had thirty-inch wooden wheels on back and twenty-one-inch wooden wheels on the front. The '26 and '27 Fords had a special intake manifold that had a very thin sheet-steel stamping "gas vaporizer" that enabled the Ford to start right up when the engine was hot by simply turning the switch to the "Battery" position and moving the spark control lever up or down on the steering column. The Ford vibrator coil system would fire any remaining gas vapors in the cylinder that had its piston in the proper top dead center firing position. This thin sheet-metal stamping had rusted away, and my Ford was very hard to start, until Alan Dunham or Alan Gott came up with a new one. (I forget which Alan had the nearly vital part.) But the generator was much harder to come by. Possibly, I got one in Brewer, Maine, where there was a locally famous source of antique car parts. It no longer exists, and the funny little proprietor with his equally funny little filthy beanie is also long gone.

72. ALL'S FAIR IN LOVE AND WAR

In 1950, the year of the great wife swap, Buster Sawyer, who lived on top of Thurlow's Hill next to the Square Deal Garage, got married. I think that his parents had just passed away, and he didn't like living alone, so he married a woman who had a young daughter. I asked the daughter for a date, and we went to the local movie show. That was on a Friday night. Saturday rolled around, and Norman "Nag" Robbins, Ken Robbins's son (to differentiate him from the Norman Robbins who lived on the Wheat Field Road, I suppose) came up to the house and asked me to look at his Pontiac straight-eight, two-door sedan. It didn't have any power, he thought. Well o' course, we opened the hood and discovered that the points were burned; the "sparkle plugs" had worn so badly that I was amazed that it even ran. So we hopped into my "wonderful" '32 Plymouth and drove down to Carlisle Webb's Garage and captured a set of points, an ignition-wire harness, distributor cap, ignition coil, and eight new Champion sparkplugs, and rattled back to our house. I replaced all the old ignition wiring and the coil, checked the gap on the new plugs and installed them, replaced the ignition points and set the gap, put on the new distributor cap, and replaced the really worn rotor button. After a while, I had the Pontiac running smoothly. I had set the timing with my new Sears timing light, and we took her for a little trial run. "Now she had some powah, deah!" The next thing I knew, there was Nag Robbins squiring the new gal around town in his 1939 Pontiac!

73. THE ANONYMOUS GIFT
AND THE ITINERARY

One Thursday evening, after working on the stone quarry, I had gone downtown and met Hutch, who was planning a prank on the Deer Isle Grange. Noona Bysher had been rummaging around in the family attic and had found a lady's rhinestone-and-pearl-decorated silk purse from the American flapper era, and after a giggly debate, we decided to fill it with fresh cow residue.

By the time we got Estelle's Buick Roadmaster straight-eight rolling, we had decided that Ralph Knowlton's pasture would be the most likely source of the desired still-steaming cow flaps. Hutch wheeled the big black sedan up the steep Tea Hill Road, down along the quiet houses, past my grandmother Knowlton's cemetery and over the small hummock by Zeke's little abode. Hutch backed and filled by Ralph's barn, and we were presently headed toward "Stonehaven." Another giggly debate ensued as to who should fill the bag with the odorous offal. I was annoyed at these pussycats, and exclaiming arrgghh! climbed out of the car and scooped up a generous morsel, while Arthur Snow held the gift open. Giggling all the while I filled the package. I washed my hands rudimentarily in a puddle that smelled as bad as the manure, wiped them off with a bunch of grass, and we resumed our travels.

Turning right at Tea Hill Corner, the Buick gathered speed, and we flashed past the Oceanville Corner intersection, lurched over the numerous thank-you-marms, slowed for the sharply radiused downhill turn onto Lover's Lane, and again for the equally-sharp left turn to cross the Holt Pond milldam bridge, which at that time may have still been wrought iron. We roared through the cluster of houses that constituted the southeast section of the island, and the big engine churned as we ascended the first rollercoaster hill.

The weight of the car overran the torque converter on the downhill slope, and the roar was subdued until Hutch accelerated for the uphill climb over the second southeast hill. We quickly passed the sharp right-hand turn at the bottom of the Long Cove Hill, where the high school principal had missed the turn and landed his Studebaker Land Cruiser in the mudflats on returning from a basketball game with a load of youngsters on board.

We churned past the old Settlers' Cemetery, where Cap'n Tristram Haskell lies to this day, up over the hilltop where the Deer Isle settlers went to Sunday services, and down past the remains of Cap'n Mark Haskell's house. (Legend implies six slaves brought up from Virginia built the foundation with handmade bricks, and the floor timbers and joists all hand-hewn. Once the house was completed, the slaves and their foreman returned to Virginia on one of the Haskell ships, possibly Cap'n Mark's own ship, the *Dolphin*.)

We swept around the curve at the intersection of Deer Isle village's only street and up the figure-S turn, past the war memorial, where its flowers had closed for the night, and Hutch really poured on the power as we fairly flew up the nearly straight North Deer Isle Road. By that time we had worked out a plan, and with Noona driving, she dropped us off at the Reach Road intersection. Arthur had been elected to deliver the odorous gift, and Hutch and I hid behind the roughly piled stones of the wall that ran along the north side of the Reach Road, while Noona and Charlene drove up to the Deer Isle-Sedgwick Bridge and waited a while before returning to pick us up.

Arthur gamely climbed the short flight of stairs to the entrance door of the Grange, put the bag on the floor, and knocked loudly, then ran down the steps and crouched, partly hidden. Dwayne Gray opened the door, looked up and down the road, and was about to close the door when he spied the prize. Hutch was whispering, "Pick it up!" as Dwayne picked up the silken object and disappeared inside.

Within a minute or so, the door flew open, and several men emerged, climbed into their cars and scooted up toward Little Deer Isle, while others roared off toward Stonington. Not one thought to drive down the Reach Road, not that it mattered. We were quite well hidden behind the jumbled stonework. Eventually, they all returned, and the Grange was as quiet as the rest of North Deer Isle.

74. Mike Dow and the Fall Snowshoe Rabbit Hunt

We became friends with Mike Dow, whose family ran a general store by the side of the Maine Route 15 road, just a few houses south of the old Settlers' Cemetery, and we used to go rabbit hunting with Mike, who used the family's fat old foxhound to scare them up. Mike would start the hound off from the old Morey farm, and we would stand in likely spots for the game to come hopping by. Every once in a while, I could hear Mike or Garland firing their shotguns; eventually, we had enough rabbits for a feast. Mike had an older sister, who married a local sea captain, who was overseas on a ship at that time; he also had a half-sister, Clara Howard, who would never speak to me. (I had a clam-digger's reputation to uphold!) Eventually, she married Frankie Pickering, a distant cousin, I suspect, on my mother's side. He didn't want to talk to me either. However, his father Lawrence Pickering was the local Chevrolet dealer, and he was very friendly!

Mike caught his older sister with a young dude on a very back road somewhere, and he backed out quite a distance, climbed out of his ancient '35 Ford pickup truck, hauled out his two-man crosscut logging saw, and felled a large spruce tree right across the roadway. He told me all about it with great glee! There was no escape route.

On one of our frisky hunting trips, Hutch was with us; Garland was in the front, and Hutch and I were sitting in the truck's bed, and as we roared along the road, having just negotiated the sharp curve at the bottom of Long Cove's hill, Hutch signaled me to fire off the old Meridian double-barreled shotgun. Kerblam! Mike jumped on the brakes, and the Ford almost spun out of control, as mechanical brakes were seldom perfectly evenly applied, by their brake rods not being exactly evenly tight. Hutch and I had a wicked wild ride there for a moment! When Mike figured out that he didn't have a tire blowout, he laughed as much as we did.

Mike must have had nearly perfect eyesight. We were driving down to Stonington, and he saw a rabbit sitting in the woods, so he turned around and went back and got his shotgun; when we returned, the rabbit was still there. So we added it to our game bag for the day.

The day I walked over to Mike's barracks at Camp Rucker in Alabama, he was so homesick that he wasn't any fun at all at all. Eventually, Mike got married and had some children, one of each, I think, a daughter and a son. As we grew older, we kind of drifted apart. The last time I saw Mike, he was on a yacht with Cap'n Alton Torrey; they had come into Morehead City, North Carolina, and were taking on stores, fuel and water. Mike told me about rescuing a downed fighter pilot, whose jet had splashed down offshore. Mike and Alton hauled him aboard the sailboat and got him out of his parachute. The pilot thought that he had a broken back. About then, a helicopter came along, and the crewmen hoisted the pilot up, stowed him away inside and flew off like a dragonfly. I was on the *Antonia*, and we were also getting stores and diesel fuel for the last leg of the trip to the North Palm Beach Marina.

75. LOBSTERING FROM MONTAUK

William Torrey emigrated from Combe, Somerset County, England, to Massachusetts in 1644. He was my mother's ancestor. One nice sunny afternoon, when my brother Wink and I were walking along Main Street in Stonington, Captain George Torrey, most likely related to us, came driving along and stopped to ask if we would like to go down to Montauk and work for the summer, so we accepted the offer.

We arrived at the *Perry B.*, a converted 110-foot wooden sub chaser, built in Canada and berthed at Billings Marine on Moose Island, which is connected to West Stonington by a narrow causeway. We had brought along an assortment of clothes and bedding. Collis Holland, the engineer, arrived and proceeded to start the two Caterpillar diesels with the little two-cylinder pony engines, and after these had churned away for awhile, the big six-cylinder Caterpillars began to rumble and chatter.

Captain George swung her out away from the dock on a spring line, and after Collis and Lynn Eaton, the cook, had pulled the lines on board, we were running out to sea past Desert Rock Light, and then sometime early in the morning, past Cape Sable. Wink was seasick all the way to Arichat, Nova Scotia.

We loaded lobsters all day, although I was mostly a spectator to the operation. The *Perry B.*'s engine-driven pumps fed cold seawater into large wooden tanks, and other pumps scavenged the overflow, so the lobsters were constantly receiving fresh seawater. After we completed loading, we set out for Montauk, just a few miles from the very east end of Long Island, New York. With the diesels churning away, we averaged ten miles per hour and ran along about a mile and a half offshore, where we could see that Nova Scotia was not mountainous and not very different from Deer Isle. Eventually, we arrived at the Cape Cod Canal, motored through it and into Buzzard's Bay, crossed Long Island Sound, and arrived at Duryea's dock after dark. The staff had turned on the dock lights, and we proceeded to unload the lobsters right away.

The *Perry B.*'s derrick hoisted the wooden tanks out of the smack onto flatbed trolleys. The crew then rolled them into the tank room, where there were even larger tanks. The experienced staff unloaded the tanks, sorting the lobsters according to weight, rapidly emptying tank after tank. Eventually, they were all emptied and returned to the hold of the *Perry B.*

The crew turned in for the night, and Wink and I moved into the barracks, converted from a henhouse at some point in time. The doors didn't have locks, and there were two bunks, one above the other. So we settled in and began work in the morning. Perry B. Duryea, Jr. began cooking lobsters that had died on the trip, and we learned how to pick out lobster meat, New York fashion. The lobster meat was sold to restaurants along the Long Island shore, and sometimes I drove one of the delivery trucks.

During the winter, I had borrowed $100 to buy a 1936 Ford five-window coupe that had been bought brand-new for the local postmaster's wife. It had never had an oil change, and the motor sounded rough. She had driven it in low gear, I think, and never let the clutch fully engage! Being complete amateurs, my friend Digger and I removed the engine to replace the clutch. The flywheel looked like a blued gun barrel and was all heat checked. We removed the flywheel and then decided to replace the motor with one from a junked 1935 Ford that I had bought before I went into service. We bolted on a new pressure plate, a throwout bearing and clutch disc, and reassembled the coupe.

I wanted to take the Ford to Montauk, so I went home on the *Lynn*, one of Duryea's two lobster smacks. I had to rush a brake job onto the car. It had never had the brakes replaced! I worked all day and riveted the new linings onto the brake shoes myself. Then I adjusted the mechanical linkages, preloading the clevises by an eighth of an inch. This procedure eliminated any slop in the mechanical brake system but still allowed one-half of an inch "free pedal" from the driver's seat. I went down to Carlisle Webb's in Stonington and bought four new tires from stock on hand. He gave me a good price, but the tires had been in for stock a long time. I changed the oil in the engine, filled up with gas, and started for Montauk the next morning, right after breakfast. I enjoyed pulling into a gas station and telling the attendant to, "Fill her with oil and check the gas!"

Being an amateur, I had done a valve job on the V8 engine but hadn't enough experience to know it was a waste of time and money. I should have put in a new short block. So I trundled along at forty miles per hour, leaving a thin blue smokescreen behind me all the way to Bridgeport, Connecticut, where I took the ferry to Port Jefferson, on Long Island.

I enjoyed watching the three-cylinder compound steam engine rocking away on its mounts as we steamed along, crossing Long Island Sound. We were soon at the dock, and as the Ford and I climbed the exit ramp from the ferry, the engine began to skip and finally died. I had expected trouble from the fuel pump, and I managed to coast to the side of the road and out of the way of traffic. I had rigged up a Stewart-Warner vacuum tank while I was home, to see if it would work. So I pulled it out of the trunk and assembled the Rube-Goldberg apparatus, using the copper tubing that I had made for it while I was at Tea Hill Corner. I removed the fuel pump pushrod and put the pump back on to retain the check valves. I blew air into the gas tank with my mouth, which filled the vacuum tank. After a few anxious moments' grinding the starter, it started again, and I resumed my adventure. I made a mistake at Riverhead and took the road to Greenport, not knowing that I could keep on going and take the ferry to Shelter Island, then to Sag Harbor, and from there continue to Montauk.

At Cutchogue I had a flat tire on the right rear. So I jacked the old girl up and put on the spare, which hung off the back on a bracket and had a metal weather cover. (This feature was reintroduced on the Lincoln continental coupes in 1940-48.) After that exercise, I returned to Riverhead and took the road to Southampton and then the Montauk highway, which at that time ran along a barren, narrow, sand-dune area close to the Atlantic Ocean. (The last time I drove out there, all but Hither Hills State Park had been transformed into miles of beachfront homes.) I arrived at Duryea's late in the afternoon and returned to work in the morning.

There were a lot of unattached girls vacationing in Montauk from all over the country. I met one, and being young and foolish, asked her to marry me. Lady Luck had other events in store for me. I took my friend to Maine twice, once to meet my parents. Once there, she wanted to get married while we were in Maine, but returned to sanity once she saw the spires of New York again, and later she dumped me.

I had planned to replace the tired Ford V8 engine with a 1948 short block and set the coupe up with new cylinder heads and all the goodies to make it meet 1948 specifications. I was going to drive to Florida and find a job down there for the winter! Things didn't work out that way, and I foolishly traded the Ford for a 1940 Buick Special straight-eight convertible coupe. It was even more of an oil-burner than the Ford. The water pump had a steel plate on the back with a pinhole-sized rust-out, and it overheated on the way back to Montauk. I removed the water-pump and engineered a temporary repair to the steel plate. I spent the winter in Yonkers working in a cable plant that made telephone cables and other things of that nature. About then my love of the moment gave me my walking papers, and I started for home, back to the clam-flats and woodpile.

In 1953 I started going as cook on the *Lynn*, with Captain Maurice "Squire" Eaton and George "Buck" Pickering as engineer. I remember that on our first trip we ran over to Gus Heanssler's in Sunshine (connected to Deer Isle by a causeway) and loaded there. The voyage was like crossing a millpond all the way to Montauk and back. On the second trip, we left Billings Marine and ran out past Isle au Haut, churning along at six knots. We raised Mt. Desert Rock light and set a new course for Seal Island off the Nova Scotia coast, where we arrived with the

ALVIN "DIGGER" JONES ON AUTHOR'S INDIAN VERTICAL TWIN MOTORCYCLE, DIGGER'S STUDEBAKER PICKUP AND AUTHOR'S 1940 BUICK CONVERTIBLE, A CLAM HOE, AND MARM'S IRIS PATCH, 1953.

approaching dawn the next morning. Squire eased the *Lynn* into Clark's Harbour, and sometime between seven and eight o'clock, the Canadian workmen arrived, and we began to load 26,000 lbs of live lobsters.

We left for Montauk almost immediately after closing the hatch covers and began crossing the Gulf of Maine during the remainder of the day, running on through the night, making landfall at the Race Point sea buoy off Cape Cod. The smack was very lively, and I was seasick, but eventually I got used to the pitching and rolling of the not-so-good-ship *Lynn*. I took advantage of the calm waters of Cape Cod Bay as we ran toward the canal to cook up a dinner for the three of us. Two ate while the third steered.

We traversed the Cape Cod Canal and emerged into Buzzards Bay, which has very strong currents, and Squire manned the wheel. After a while, we picked up the Point Judith light and changed course to pass the lightship and continue past Block Island and on toward the Montauk Point light. Once we saw that, we changed course to run into Fort Point Bay and tied up at Duryea's dock to commence unloading immediately! My brother Wink was there to help, and we had a mini-visit. We loaded groceries for the return trip and left in the morning, having had a good quiet rest at the dock.

On one of our trips, we docked in Lake Montauk, which was actually a saltwater inlet. We were there quite a while because the big Caterpillar diesel was being rebuilt. I was still on good terms with my ex-girlfriend's Yonkers family, and they gave me a used Model A Ford truck motor. Squire said that he would go to Yonkers if I would go to a baseball game. So we borrowed Perry Duryea's Chevy station wagon, and the Cap'n got a speeding ticket somewhere on the Sunrise highway. We went to the ball game in the old Dodgers Stadium. Then we drove over to Yonkers, where my old flame's father, Otto, put on a beer party. After a while, we loaded the Ford motor into the Chevy, and when we returned to Montauk, we wrapped the engine in an old tarp, because Squire didn't want any grease stains on his "beautiful" dull-gray, anti-skid painted deck. We lashed the engine to the mast to make sure it didn't roll over and damage the deck!

When we got back to Moose Island and the shipyard, we tied up to await the next trip. Buck and Squire bailed the lobster well and got nearly a bushel of lobsters, but I single-mindedly didn't want any, not thinking of Dad, who would've liked to have some for a "Pinkham" stew (Mel Stinson's name for a stew made with short, illegal-sized lobsters), but on subsequent trips I took some home for Dad!

The summer slipped past, and with fall weather we made one trip that was so rough I couldn't keep anything on the little shipmate stove. I went forward to check things out, closed the forecastle's sliding hatch, and when I opened the oven door on the stove, seawater ran out! About then a huge sea hit a quartering blow, smashed the smokestack and carried it away, guy wires and all. Squire hauled the *Lynn* up into the wind and held her steady. We rushed out of the pilothouse and re-secured the dory, which was to be used as a lifeboat, as it was threatening to go adrift. The *Lynn* had a steadying sail that rattled and slatted all the while we were hove to. I dove down into the galley and quickly assembled some canned corned-beef sandwiches and carried them back to the pilothouse, made a trip for mugs, and then went aft to the icebox and brought back some milk. We ate standing up while holding onto something for support, because the old boat was thrashing around so much that without supports we would be thrown to the deck. Buck and I spent many hours lying beside the six-cylinder Cat, he on the starboard decking and me on the port side, hardly sleeping with that diesel chattering away. It wasn't quite as loud as a jackhammer but still too loud to manage any sleep!

Every four hours one of us would have to climb up and take the wheel. Eventually, we saw the Race Point sea buoy, and after we had gotten into the lee of Cape Cod the sea was almost flat calm in comparison. I went down and made breakfast after mopping out the shipmate stove. We were ready to eat almost anything.

Once in a while, Perry would have something in the lobster tanks like fresh oysters, and I wasn't ashamed to ask him for some. Once he gave us half a bushel, and I opened them as best I could, with a hammer and a big screwdriver. I had to pick pieces of shell out, but once I was into the inner sanctum, I scooped the oysters out with one of Dad's homemade clam knives. I crushed some Ritz crackers on a breadboard with a rolling pin, dipped the oysters into an egg batter and then rolled them into the cracker crumbs and slowly sautéed them in a cast-iron spider in a liberal amount of butter over the coal fire. There weren't any leftovers that time!

I wasn't afraid to try anything in the cookbook, but cornbread and the coal fire did me in. Possibly it would have worked if I had left the batter in a lot longer, but eventually I heaved it over the side, and Squire shouted as he opened the pilothouse door, "Hold on, Cab, we'll eat it!" Too late, of course.

Along about November, I asked Squire if Perry would keep me on half-pay for the winter. The answer was, "No soap," so I washed my hands of the whole operation and went deer hunting with Alan Gott. I didn't have any luck at that, either. Maurice was a little perturbed, because it would be hard to get another hand for just a few more trips.

I was told years later that the *Lynn* was sold, converted to a dragger, and that she went down with all hands in a storm. Captain George Torrey of the *Perry B.* and many other ships passed away in 2001 in Deer isle, and Captain Maurice Eaton passed away in 2002 in Texas. George "Buck" Pickering had passed away years before. Perry B. Duryea, Jr. became a senator in New York State, and his son now runs the business in Montauk.

Garland married Catherine Benton and lived in Miami, where he worked on aircraft hydraulic systems until he moved to Ogden, Utah, then to Allen, Texas, where he rebuilt aircraft jet engines until the company was sold. He retired and continues to live in Allen with his second wife, Betty. Kathy died as a young woman. They had one son, Leroy "Dickie" who lives in Colorado.

My youngest brother, Leon "Wink," worked at Duryea's until he was drafted for the Korean "police action." During the Truman administration he crossed the Pacific four times on the same troop ship and toured the American Southwest by bus on his way back to Maine, after serving his second session on the "exact same Korean mountaintop" during the Cuban Missile Crisis. He is unmarried and continues to work on heavy equipment in the "boonies" of Pennsylvania.

76. Rifles and Pistols

During the Great Depression, many of the island's menfolk used to poach a deer now and then. There were almost no jobs, and one scratched out an existence anyhow one could manage without coming afoul of the State of Maine game wardens! My father Dick kept a loaded .32 special lever-action Winchester in the corner by his platform rocker. One Saturday morning in the fall of 1953, he was sitting in his chair when a big doe ran through the dooryard. Dick grabbed up the Winchester and levered a cartridge into the firing chamber, but that deer was running from feral dogs or something; she was at full speed and disappeared into the alders and birch saplings before he could get the front door open!

Bob McGuffie, our uncle by marriage to Dick's half-sister Florence (Knowlton), had a High Standard .22 caliber long-barreled pistol that he kept in his boot as he stalked through the woods. One day he came over to the house and wanted Dick to help him bring out a buck deer that he had shot with the pistol. So Dick went off with Uncle Bob in his 1937 Dodge coupe that Bob used for ordinary island transportation. For real serious trips to Bangor or Ellsworth, they used his brother's 1939 Oldsmobile six-cylinder sedan, although Uncle Bob took me to Ellsworth when I reported for the draft in 1950 in his Dodge coupe.

Albert Nevells had a Civil War vintage Springfield .45-70 single-shot rifle with the flying breech, an advanced type that appeared on the front lines in 1864, I believe. Al would sell me the rifle for $2 and two eider ducks—imagine that! Garland and I went over to a ledge just west of Sheep Island, and put out some decoys. Eider ducks flew past that ledge all day long in the fall duck-hunting season and would swing in closer to look at our decoys, but they did not land, so every duck that was bagged had to be shot while flying by. Garland was better at leading his shot, but I did knock down three that morning; we picked up the game, we had a total of eight ducks, then loaded the decoys on board the ancient peapod and rowed back to Webb's Cove, tied the peapod onto the outhaul, and hiked up through Ralph Knowlton's abandoned colonial settlers' apple orchard. I climbed the only russet apple tree and captured several russets, which were excellent to gnaw on! We loaded the ducks and shotguns into the ancient six-cylinder Chevrolet coach and drove home. I took my three ducks down to Albert's and came back with the .45-70.

Dick made a real effort to sight in the rifle, and we annoyed "Aunt"

Ruth Carter Williams no end! She even walked over to the house to complain about our "shooting the rifle in back of her house" which was brand-new at that time (1948, I think, but surely before 1950, when I went into the army), although we were on our own little piece of land. After her father died, she inherited the remainder of the forty acres that her dad, Arthur Carter, had bought for a pittance in 1936 or '37. We did discover that the rifle would shoot clear through an eight-inch diameter red-spruce tree, but not through a ten-inch tree!

In the fall of 1948, my distant cousin Alan Gott came over and wanted to go deer hunting on the Mines Road in Blue Hill. We hunted for several days and never saw a deer. One Saturday we took Ethelbert Morey along, and he had a twelve-gauge shotgun loaded with double-aught buckshot. Well o' course! the only deer that came anywhere near our stands came right past Thalbert, and he let go with a blast from his shotgun; a mini-second later he fired again. Uh-oh! I thought, that deer has gotten away! It ran into the oak trees west of the Mines Road, and we tracked it for about a hundred yards, but it wasn't wounded enough to fall and escaped. There had been too much traffic through the fallen leaves to track any further, and it had stopped bleeding. If it had been hit anywhere with the .45-70, it would have dropped in its tracks!

What happened to the valuable Civil War rifle, you may ask? When our second daughter was born, she was a blue baby, because Pam has O-negative-type blood, and I am O-positive. Jennifer was put under the McBurnie lights, and I traded the Springfield with one of the Bell switchmen for a donation of rare O-type blood for our baby. Fortunately it wasn't used, as the donor, later in time, was diagnosed with a rare blood disease! Jen turned out fine and has two children in Upper Moreland schools, near Willow Grove in Pennsylvania, in 2009.

I had a 1947 Ford which had very good stump clearance, and we drove her right into the woods on a soggy logging road. Somewhere along this rough cart-way, we found a nearly flat granite ledge and parked the car on that, so it wouldn't sink.

After a quick discussion, we decided that the Jones boys would stand spaced quite a distance apart along the woods road, and the Haskell lads would make a drive from the river's west bank up through the swampy woods, in hopes of flushing a white-tailed deer. As we walked along the riverbank past a summer cottage, Garland said, "I think I'll walk up by that pump house," a small wooden building painted red and standing on a granite foundation up the slope to our right.

Within seconds we heard his .32 Winchester lever-action fire one shot.

FROM LEFT: FUDD, AUTHOR, AND DIGGER, 1954, WITH
ALAN GOTT's PIPER CUB.

"I got him, I got him!" he shouted, and we walked up to see an eight-
point buck lying on the slope behind the building. Within minutes, Bill,
Collis, and Alvin arrived, and Bill began to clean the deer. Meanwhile,
I walked up and brought the Ford right down to the pump house. We
loaded the game onto the right front fender and lashed it on with some
pot-warp (it never hurts to have a length of salvaged line in the car). We
all climbed into the sedan, and I drove her out of the woods in low gear.
After we had gained the asphalt surface, we moved right along to the
tagging station, where the registration formalities were performed. Then
we set out for Stonington.

A dog decided to chase the car, and Digger opened the right rear
door and gave the dog a kick, forgetting that the force of the blow would
be multiplied by the speed of the car, and he nearly broke his leg as it was
kicked back against the door. Bill was highly amused as Digger yelped
in pain. Bill began to tell about a well-known local poacher who finally
shot a deer legally and was so proud of the feat that he carried the deer
around on the right front fender of his ancient vehicle so long that it

must have been maggoty. Of course, we had all seen the car and knew full well that there must have been at least one illegal deer hanging in his woodshed. We crossed the bridge to Little Deer Isle and trundled down to Stonington at a pretty good clip. I backed the flathead six up beside Dad's shop, and we strung the game up to hang from an overhead beam. Later we divided it into shares.

Except for the deer hunting experience with the Jones boys, I haven't been deer hunting, legally or otherwise, except for a trip from Yonkers, New York, in 1954 with two New Yorkers. We stopped in L. L. Bean's in Freeport to procure out-of-state hunting licenses, and we three traipsed through the woods on Deer Isle and even went on the mainland one day, without any success. After my dad passed away, I sold all my guns. I didn't want any accidents due to children playing with my firearms!

Virgil Gross had a Zenith windmill generator that kept his batteries charged in Head Harbor on Isle au Haut. They were housed in a separate building and provided the electricity for all the lights in the one-story summer home. When Fudd's mother turned on a water faucet, a Briggs & Stratton-powered water pump started right up and ran until the faucet was turned off. I imagine the house in Head Harbor was sold after Virgil passed away. Fudd went to Embry Riddle School of Aviation in Miami, Florida, with my brother Garland in 1953 and 1954. I was on the *Antonia* serving as waiter and rented a Ford to drive up to the aviation school to see Fudd and Garland sometime during that winter.

77. Marm's Flower Garden

My mother had flowers growing in every conceivable little spot that wasn't a solid granite ledge. There is a small sheltered triangular plot beside the road where she grew annuals that anyone driving towards Deer Isle could see in bloom as they passed by. There is a Japanese barberry growing in a shallow loamy spot directly in front of the east windows, but at the edge of the road it is accompanied by a cluster of red-maple saplings that are showy red and yellow in the fall. There are less than six inches of topsoil on the ledge that runs east from the house and slopes down to lie under the main road at that point.

Mother had tuberous begonias all along the north side of Dick's shop, where he sharpened saws for the fishermen and local carpenters. She also planted iris along the front of the henhouse. Up against the house our mother had planted beautiful dahlias and iris here and there on the west side of the front doorstep and mini-deck. On the east side, there are yellow lilies that still bloom in June and seem to thrive in the poor granite-dust and leaf-mulch soil. There are several quite large red maples growing in a cluster behind the old shop. Several hackmatack trees have grown along the south property line. These American larch are susceptible to wooly adelgid, which kills the trees eventually.

In 1950 I had "captured" in the woods of Little Deer Isle an evenly cone-shaped cedar sapling about six feet tall and planted it close to the house on the east side; one nice Fourth of July, a local lad returned "from away" and celebrated with just a few too many. He came down from the direction of Deer Isle, but some little distance south of Tea Hill Corner, he strayed off the road, bounced off a few granite boulders and then crashed through our neighbor's fence, barely missing a large apple tree, their yard, and several children who were playing outside in the sunny weather. He continued through the wire fence that ran along our property line, taking two metal posts along as decorations. He just missed crashing into our little house, flattened my little cedar tree right to the ground, swerved off toward the ice house, which was still in evidence at the time, tearing Mother's rugosa roses out by the roots as he continued to drive off the top of the granite ledge, crashing down three or four feet onto the asphalt; then the Chevy lurched across Route 15 to knock down Dad's mailbox, post and all. One would think that the Chevy would remain stuck in the ditch, but after a few wheel spins, some banging and crashing noises, the driver managed to get the sedan moving towards Stonington again, with Marm's prize rugosas sticking out of the radiator grille. As he weaved down Thurlow's Hill, Officer Ralph Pinkham, our Maine State Fish and Game Warden, saw the bright red blossoms adorning the battered car and managed to corral the wild beast and bring the danger and mass destruction to an end. The fireworks over Stonington Harbor that evening were merely anticlimactic.

78. There's Gotta Be Somethin' Better 'n This

Gumper Gray and I both agreed that "there's gotta be somethin' better 'n this," when we were pounding away with the Ingersoll-Rand plug drills, making holes in the sheets of granite on hot windless days, the stone dust hanging around in the quarry hole like fog on a July morning. I had gotten engaged to a girl from Yonkers, New York, while working in Montauk, way out on the tip of Long Island. As fall approached, I had planned to drive my 1936 Ford coupe to Florida and find some menial job to get me through the winter. But romance intervened, and I spent the winter in Yonkers working in the cable plant, making telephone cables, and my intended kept trying to get me a job with the New York Telephone Company, a division of AT&T at that time.

By then the Florida dream had dissipated, and I was living on the fourth floor, high up on the ridge-top of Yonkers, and I had to drive down to the Phelps-Dodge plant, just a few feet above the Hudson. Some cable reels were shipped out by barge from the dock that was an essential part of the operations. My girlfriend dumped me unceremoniously, and sometime late in the winter I chucked the whole works and drove home; back to clamming and daydreaming of better things to come.

I had worked as cook on the lobster smack *Lynn*, and after a season of walloping around back and forth between Billings Marine's dock in Stonington, the run to Clark's Harbour, Nova Scotia, and the long crossing of the Gulf of Maine, sometimes lying beside the noisy Cat diesel all the way across to the Race Point sea buoy, I decided that there's gotta be somethin' better than this!

I quit the job and went deer hunting with my cousin, Alan Gott. Sometime just before Christmas, I started working on Deer Isle Granite, and Fuller Eaton, also a distant cousin on the Haskell side, asked me if I would like to work on a yacht going to Florida for the winter. And after two days of an Ingersoll Rand's plug drill pounding away on my chest, I decided it would be first-rate. After the third day, I drove up to Fuller's house in North Deer Isle, and he called Captain Hollett. After the captain had questioned me about my summer's job and about Captain Maurice "Squire" Eaton, whom he knew, he said, "You've got the job!"

I borrowed some money from Dad and some from Garland, who drove me to the Bangor airport in my old Ford. Northeast Airlines was a pioneer serving New England, including "outback Maine." The ticket office and flight center was a low, wooden building, almost like a roadside vegetable stand, which gave the impression that the airline was rustic, rough-and-ready. In the flight office, there was one baggage handler and one attendant, who was as down-homey as an old friend.

I boarded the Convair, and we took off and flew to Boston. There were views out of the left-hand windows of the mainland towns, beaches, and some islands lying offshore all along the coast of Maine.

We landed uneventfully in Boston and were supposed to stay on the plane for the flight to Washington, DC, but when the pilot tried to restart the starboard engine, it caught fire. The ground crew put it out with a carbon dioxide fire extinguisher, which promptly fouled the complex carburetor, and we had to climb down and file inside to await another plane, which happened to be a DC-3 that started right up and flapped, wobbled, vibrated, and shook all the way to the capital airport. I suspect it might still be flying passengers somewhere today. I waited for my luggage, which consisted of my old army duffle bag and one Sears suitcase. As it turned out, I didn't use most of the contents.

I captured a taxi that took me to the Capital Yacht Club, which was at that time on the north side of the Potomac, along Maine Avenue, lined with crumbling stone houses along the riverbanks.

79. THE *ANTONIA*

I found the yacht *Antonia* tied up to a narrow wooden dock and met Captain Hollett, who seemed to have a southern accent. However, I later learned that he was from Newfoundland, a small outport destroyed by a tsunami in the early 1900's.

The *Antonia* was an eighty-two-foot houseboat, built at New York Ship and Light on the east side of the Hudson, and in 1956 the buildings were still in existence. The yacht had a dining room forward of the pilothouse, and the galley was below that, "up by the eyes of the boat." The four crew bunks were below and aft of the galley. And there was a tiny washbasin and crew's toilet in a space no larger than a closet. There were no facilities for taking a bath or shower. The skipper's (captain's) bunk was out on the starboard side of the pilothouse, aft of the door to the main deck. There was a ladder on the port side that gave access to the boat deck and flying bridge, where the owner had auxiliary controls installed, so he could operate the yacht from up there like a sport fisherman. Aft of the pilothouse, there were also wicker chairs and a table. The boat deck ran all the way aft, providing shade or shelter in sudden rain squalls for the occupants of the wicker deckchairs. Below the main deck, aft of the engine room, there were two tiny staterooms, one to port and one to starboard. The master stateroom was all the way aft, under the quarterdeck. Each stateroom had its own tiny bathroom. We had city water under pressure while tied up to a marina's dock or at the better yacht clubs, with an ordinary garden hose attached to a spigot on the dock and to special fittings on the *Antonia*'s hull, port and starboard: either side could be used.

A day or so after I arrived, Al Jorgenson came aboard as chef. And after we had loaded food and supplies for the trip and topped off with No. 2 diesel, Captain Benny Johnson came aboard as supercargo. We promptly got underway. Cap'n Hollett backed the *Antonia* out into the channel, and as she slowly turned to the right, we started southward for the long journey to the West Palm Beach Marina in Florida.

There were no bands, no one to wave goodbye, just a cold, dismal overcast December day, as we churned down the Potomac at ten miles per hour. There were lots of things to see along the banks of the river as we whined along, the Rootes blowers on the diesels always making their presence known. George Washington's Mt. Vernon peeked out above the trees, and a little further south an old iron steamship lay in the mud, leaning toward the west riverbank.

There was an early Herreshoff racing sloop hauled out, also on the west side of the river, somewhere near Quantico, Virginia, and at a future date it was patched up and with a Chrysler marine engine appeared at

THE *ANTONIA* MAKING TEN KNOTS IN FLORIDA'S INLAND WATERWAY; THE BOSS IS AT THE WHEEL UP ON THE FLYING BRIDGE.

the Hunting Park Marina, owned by Julian, a "bird colonel" in the Air Force. He was a handsome duck and went through wives like most of us go through ice-cream cones. One day he set out for a sail carrying a load of "straphangers," and as the big sloop came back into the marina, the colonel at the helm attempted to put the engine in reverse; the shift lever fell into the bilges, and the clumsy old wreck "sailed" right into Mr. Fallowfield's little sloop, carrying away the bowsprit and its standing rigging. The owner issued a distressed, "Oh my!" (He was a gentleman and not a hardened sailor.) Cap'n Hollett and I rushed over to the other T dock to throw some lines to the gaggle of hopeless deckhand guests and eventually warped the ancient Herreshoff into her berth.

The colonel had re-decked the old boat with common planks in a rough pattern which left wide gaps down to the bilges below. Sometime after that adventure, Julian took the big old leaky craft down the Chesapeake and ran aground on the remains of Billy Mitchell's attempt to prove that the old battleships could be sunk with aerial bombs. They lay there on the bottom, a hazard to navigation, and Billy's lesson was forgotten until the Japanese sank two capital ships off Singapore with dive bombers in minutes, during the opening salvos of the Japanese attempt to colonize all the Pacific Islands. Julian promptly sued the Government for the loss of his sloop. The next time we heard about Colonel Julian was in *Newsweek*, when he was indicted for murdering most of a family on a chartered sailboat trip in the Caribbean; a teenage daughter escaped in a rubber dinghy and was rescued in a badly sunburned and dehydrated condition to survive to testify in the trial that followed. But like all sensational news stories, there was never any follow-up, and his fate is unknown to me.

One day, the skipper hired two Scandinavian sailors; Hans was from Sweden, and Arne was a Norwegian. Mr. Bryant decided to run down the Potomac and have a weekend anchored off of Virginia Beach. Arne was to be the waiter, and he and I worked like fiends to deliver a satisfying dinner onboard. One of the female guests was alcoholic, as we were to discover, in a loud screaming manner. She asked Arne to put a little whisky in her coffee. He asked me if we should do that, and unsuspecting what could ensue, I told him to "lace it with the scotch from the aft deck salon's liquor cabinet." He smuggled a bottle up to the galley, and we doctored up her coffee. Everything was going quite smoothly, for amateurs, and when the dinner was over, we were still cleaning up the dining-room dishes when the lush came staggering down into the crew's quarters, demanding more whiskey. We were quite alarmed and did not know what to do, when providentially her husband and Mr. Bryant came to our rescue. They escorted her aft, she protesting loudly, and we were greatly relieved to be rid of her.

The *Antonia* wallowed all night on oily swells, and I'm sure that we were all happy to haul up the anchor and waddle back up the Potomac at ten miles an hour the following morning. This adventure must have left a bad taste in Mr. Bryant's memory, and the *Antonia* didn't venture forth again until the return trip to Florida.

We ran down Chesapeake Bay and just at dusk entered the Dismal Swamp locks, which raised us to the water level of the Swamp. I seem to remember that we tied up to a fuel dock and topped off the tanks. The owner didn't charge us dockage because we bought a lot of fuel. Early the next morning, we started running in the Intracoastal Waterway Canal. We had breakfast in shifts, as someone had to steer as we navigated the narrow channel, guided by numbered signs on channel markers that consisted of stout posts driven into the bottom.

We entered Albemarle Sound in a thick fog, and since I had the youngest eyes, I was instructed to look for the channel markers. Sometime during the morning, the fog burned off, and we could see the beaches east of us and low-lying saltwater grassland running along the sides of the sound. I had an eight-millimeter Kodak Brownie movie camera and took panoramic views of this monotonous marshland and the beach areas. My future father-in-law always teased me that it was a waste of film. There were a few houses and small buildings on the outer island at Nags Head.

We entered Pamlico Sound and saw Cape Hatteras Lighthouse tower coming into view, and I took some picture frames of that. I began to see a few black skimmers. They were comical to see, flying with their elongated lower bill sticking into the water, scooping up any food item close to the surface. There were also many laughing gulls and some oyster catchers, all new to me.

Eventually, we reached Morehead City, where Al bought some fresh groceries, and the skipper and I topped off the fuel tanks, and after a while we turned in for the night. Early next morning we ran out through the inlet, staying just inside the Gulf Stream, which swirled along, a beautiful emerald blue-green. Captain Hollett said there was a counter-current running south at about a mile and a half an hour, close to the shore, and we took advantage of that little boost.

Captain Benny could steer for hours and hours with nothing to sustain him but cigarettes and coffee. He loved to tease me by talking to me in Norwegian and laughing because I didn't know what he was saying. He had a wife in Philadelphia, but they "fought like cats and dogs," and he hadn't seen her in years. He was a well-known yacht finisher and earned a respectable living working on the brightwork of private yachts in the marinas in the Washington, DC area and in marinas in Florida. He kept himself looking clean, neat, and well-dressed after finishing for the day. He told me about trips to Russia during World War II and the dreaded Focke-Wulf Condors shadowing the convoys and radioing information to the German submarines and shore bases in Norway. He was first mate under Captain Hollett.

We cruised southward all day and all night, taking turns at the helm. Sometime late on the following afternoon we were approaching San Fernandina Inlet in Florida. Captain Hollett took the wheel, and we roller-coastered into the inlet. The *Antonia* labored up the huge smooth seas, and the engines raced as she surfed down the landward face, the beach looming closer and closer until, like a huge surfboard, we slid down the last mighty sea, the 671s racing, and abruptly we were inside, into the quiet waters of the St. Mary's River mouth and slowly reentering the Inland Waterway, to continue cruising southward. We tied up at a fuel dock earlier than usual and topped off with diesel and water. Al and Captain Benny dared me to drink the water out of a faucet sticking up out of the ground. Ugh! Sulphur water! They both thought it was the funniest sight since Laurel and Hardy. I didn't swallow and spat it out.

There were numerous eastern American birds, including anhingas and double-crested cormorants, fishing in the canals and inlets as we ran south "in the ditch" for several more days. Eventually, we came to areas where construction crews were cutting down mangroves and erecting interlocking steel bulkhead plates. Where the bulkheads had been completed, huge dredges were pumping sand out of the canal bottom into the voids where the mangroves had been, to make new land. Elsewhere along the canal banks, houses were already under construction. I suspect by now there are very few mangroves left in the inland waters on the east coast of Florida. We arrived at the West Palm Beach marina, where many yachts were tied up, the crews waiting for their owners to come south or east for their winter vacations.

One day, as we were lying in the marina, a man on the particularly ugly yacht docked next to us heard me talking and asked, "What part of Maine are you from?" I told him I was from Stonington on Deer Isle, as I expected he would know about Deer Isle but not necessarily about the south end of the island. Then he proceeded to tell me about one of his experiences in Wiscasset, Maine. It seems an old-timer was down beside the dock digging clams. So he had kindly asked the old salt, "How do you tell the clams from the lumps of mud?" The crotchety old Downeaster didn't even look up or slack off his pace, but he replied, "Clams are edible." and kept right on digging. The stranger was highly amused. The yacht belonged to a famous Chicago newspaper publisher.

Captain Benny had to find a new berth, as the boss was expected very soon, and we had a particularly fine supper for him on his last night with us at West Palm Beach. On March 15th, Mr. Herbert Bryant arrived with his wife, Margo, and as she approached, I could see she had the most intensely blue eyes I had ever seen. She exclaimed, "Oh, she just sparkles!" It was her impression of all our work, sanding, varnishing, and scrubbing the teak decks using citric acid and a floor-scrubbing machine that bleached the wood to a golden color.

After I had carried the luggage down below, Captain Hollett started the twin diesels, and we maneuvered out into the Inland Waterway to start our run down to the Flamingo Club in Miami Beach. Mr. Bryant was changing into his yachting attire and soon came up and climbed up onto the flying bridge, where he took the controls for a while.

Al began preparing lunch, and I set the dining room table. Al came up to supervise, as he wanted everything to be perfect. We fussed with the tablecloth and the silver napkin holders. I was sent to find Mr. Bryant to announce that lunch was ready. The consommé was sent up in a tureen, and I ladled it out very carefully as lunch commenced. I wore a white jacket and black trousers, a white shirt and a clip-on black bow tie while serving lunch. I stood silently while they ate, and cleared away the dishes as they were ready. Al and I worked silently with hand signals, and it went very well.

That evening, after we had tied up at the Flamingo Club, Mr. Bryant and Margo went ashore to eat at the club, and I went to take a shower, so I wouldn't smell sour when serving meals. One had to ask Rex, the dock master, for permission to use the shower, which he always granted, but I had the impression he didn't like the idea. He was not a friendly guy!

We soon had our first guests, Mr. and Mrs. Bowersocks, and began the runs to the Key Largo Yacht Club, that became something like a shuttle. The guests would stay a week, and new guests would come aboard for the run down Biscayne Bay to Key Largo. Mr. Bryant jogged around the club grounds every morning, took a shower at the club, and after breakfast all of them went golfing, returning for lunch and dinner.

I was on the *Antonia* from 1953 till she was sold. When we returned to Washington, DC and the Capital Yacht Club, Al's wife drove down from New York in the family Buick. He was sorry to leave us, but his wife had cashed the "half pay" checks from the other "Luft boat job in Annapolis." So he was morally obliged to return. They left promptly, and Mrs. Hollett came to pick up her hubby. I cooked dinner that evening. Captain Benny and I ate quietly. He talked about looking for work. The very next morning the skipper came aboard and told me that I could go home for a week with pay. He cleverly told me that he was reducing my pay for the summer, as there was little activity during that time. Since my possessions were still on the boat, I meekly accepted this news. Ah! but today I would have had all my gear packed up and been taking it with me. "Too lade schmardt we get," an old Pennsylvania Dutch proverb, but how true! If I hadn't left so many of my belongings on board, I would have just gone home to stay; it seemed to me to be underhanded and an insult.

80. A Trip Home Between Cruises

We flew to Boston and landed but did not get off the plane, and the Convair took off again for Bangor. It was an overcast day, the New England towns along the flight path were white with snow, and as we approached the airport I could see that there was plenty of snow on the ground on April first 1954. When I climbed down the loading ladder, I realized it was below freezing. Wink had driven up to pick me up in his '36 Ford five-window coupe. The car didn't have a heater, so we wrapped ourselves in an army-surplus blanket, and we scooted through downtown Bangor, an ugly collection of old brick buildings arranged helter-skelter on the west side of the Penobscot River.

We crossed the river on the old wrought-iron bridge and straggled down through Brewer, south on Route 15 to Bucksport, then Blue Hill, left onto Route 172 through the beautiful white-pine forest, past the Punchbowl farm and across the suspension bridge to Little Deer Isle. I noticed that the neatly-piled home-heating woodpiles were pretty well depleted this late in the winter. There were a few oldsquaw ducks rafted in Bow Cat Cove, and a solitary merganser.

We rumbled across the little Deer Isle bar, climbed Hardy's Hill and churned down the island, past the old Settlers' Cemetery, where my ancestor Captain Tristram Haskell is interred, down and up and down again on the rollercoaster southeast hills, across the bridge over the site of the colonial Holt Mill Pond dam. The colonial grindstones were still lying on Joe Judkins's embankment at that time. The old coupe climbed the crooked "lovers lane," and a few minutes later Wink pulled into the driveway after about an hour and three quarters' drive from the airport. It was two below zero, Fahrenheit. My '47 Ford six was just barely sticking out of a snow bank beside the house. Dad didn't bother using it, as it wouldn't start unless it was towed about twenty feet. Wink preferred his V8, which would start at twenty below. Dad had just been clamming, and Marm had made a clam chowder and biscuits for supper. Quite a treat for me, after all the rich food on the *Antonia*.

I dug the Ford out of the snow, determined to drive it back to Washington, DC. But after we towed it and got it running, it had a clanging noise in the torque-tube driveshaft assembly. The local mechanics weren't too interested in repairing it, so I drove over to Ellsworth and found an English 1952 Sunbeam Talbot 90, and I bought it on time payments. It was a joy to drive, and after my week was nearly up, I set out for the Capital Yacht Club at ten at night.

There were only two turnpikes in 1954. The Maine Turnpike was forty-six miles long, and one entered it at Portland after a drive out into the boonies. And there was the New Jersey Turnpike. I zoomed down that to pick up the two-lane roads to Washington, arriving at the Yacht Club in fourteen hours flat. As the trip to Florida neared, I asked Bob Dobbins if he knew where I could store the Sunbeam Talbot until spring. He knew of a row of single rental garages, and I backed her in there, disconnected the battery, and Bob drove me back to the marina.

Sometimes they had dinner ashore, and Al and I had a break. I used the time to vacuum, dust and clean the windows, guest rooms and bathrooms, trying to keep up with wear and tear. The skipper was always checking to see that things were "up to snuff."

Al was watery-blue-eyed, about five foot ten, gray-headed and just a tiny bit paunchy, a little round-shouldered, and he liked a "li'l snifter" when he was working hard, cooking for the boss and the usual four guests. He usually asked me to sneak aft and bring up a glass of scotch from the liquor cabinet, which I accomplished with the ruse of bringing the dirty glasses from the salon and quarterdeck forward to be washed. Only once did he get sloshed and sent up the soup in the cook pot, signaling me to serve it! I knew that there would be repercussions from that episode, and the skipper had a few words with Al out of my hearing. Dinner that evening was especially well done.

We became used to seeing manta rays leap out of the water, and once, I saw a huge sunfish as we were running along in Biscayne Bay. I looked again and saw the huge silvery fish, which seemed to swim slowly along with its mouth open all the while. Sometimes, dolphins leaped and cavorted near the bow. Schools of mullet swam close to the surface, and stone crabs climbed on the sides of the concrete dock, all very interesting sights for me.

We had a midwinter break, when the Bryants went home. There was a single woman staying on board for a few days, a cousin to Mr. B., I was told. She left, and we went to the dog track several evenings with Captain Benny Johnson, who found us after the skipper had made a phone call. They thought it would be wonderful if I bought a used car, so that "we" wouldn't have to take a taxi. But I silently resisted.

Eventually, it was time to take the *Antonia* north again, and as we approached San Fernandina the skipper checked the marine weather reports and decided to try running outside in the Gulf Stream, and we were doing famously until I noticed a change in the engines' sound, which awoke me early for my turn at the wheel. One diesel was just running at an idle and loping (it would speed up a little then slow right down to idle speed). I got dressed and went up to the pilothouse. Captain Benny was at the helm, Al was standing by, and the skipper was pondering what to do. We had changed course and were very slowly running into Charleston, South Carolina, where we dropped the starboard anchor well out of the shipping channels.

In the morning, everyone slept late, but I was up prowling around looking at Fort Sumter through binoculars. Soon, Captain Hollett went down into the engine room; then he came up and started the 671s, and they seemed to be perfectly fine to me. We winched the anchor up, and I went over the side to stand on the anchor, hanging onto the rail with my left hand while cleaning all the mud off of the flukes with a long-handled brush, which I dipped into the water every so often. The skipper, satisfied with that, went back inside, and I went down to clean up while the engines were run up to cruising speed. Later, I learned that he had removed the fuel-filter elements, and the diesels were running on unfiltered fuel. When we entered Morehead City's harbor, we tied up, and Captain Hollett found a diesel mechanic, who came and installed new filter elements and checked out the diesels. We were soon churning up the ditch, and the rest of the return trip was uneventful.

Cecil Bannon was dock master and had waited up for us. Bob Dobbins (Capital Airlines) came down, and we drove off to retrieve my Sunbeam Talbot. The garage roof had been shingled during the winter, and the garage was full of shingle nails. I found a stub of a corn broom and swept it all up both sides and forward. Of course, the battery was flat, but I cranked the big four-cylinder engine, and she jumped into life on the third pull-up!

As it turned out, Al Jorgensen was gone for less than a week, and Captain Hollett hired a new chef, who arrived on a Friday. He had been working on yachts in his youth, but after he got married, he went ashore and found work on land in Maryland. He was a mild-mannered man, and he arrived after I had washed up the supper dishes and cooking equipment. He settled in, but after an hour or so, he began to fidget and lament about being away from his wife and children. Then he bundled all his clothes back into his bags and was about to take a trolley to the bus station. So I offered to drive him there. In a few minutes, we had traversed the worst of downtown traffic, and I dropped him off at the bus station. I became the cook, reinstated to my former pay, but not a chef's remuneration by any means. Mr. Bryant seemed to be satisfied with my attempts to cook for parties of six.

Shortly after that, we moved the *Antonia* down to the new Hunting Park Marina at Hunting Towers, Alexandria, Virginia; not a great distance, but closer to Mr. B.'s estate. I liked the new place. There was a swimming pool, nice landscaped grounds, red-winged blackbirds nesting in the rushes along Hunting Creek, and mockingbirds singing in the black locust trees along the parking lot driveway.

81. THE *TONGA*

To liven up the summer's events, Mr. B. found a sixty-foot sail yacht that was reported to have belonged to Errol Flynn. Like Mr. Toad in *The Wind in the Willows*, Mr. B. just had to have that new toy! The *Tonga* looked impressive, with baggywrinkle on all the standing rigging. She was a gaff-rigged ketch with a square sail on the foremast, and the hull was shaped like a watermelon sliced lengthwise when seen on a marine railway. She had a huge centerboard and a small Chrysler six-cylinder marine gasoline engine for auxiliary power. The batteries were out under the stern's overhang, and I had to keep them topped off with water using an extension device with a trigger-operated filling valve. (Stay tuned for further adventures with this apparatus!)

Captain Hollett and Captain Benny Johnson flew down to Miami and

CAPTAIN LLEWELLIN HOLLETT ON THE *TONGA*, 1954.

brought her up partly in the inland waterway. Somewhere along the way, the skipper picked up some friends and family for the short trip up the Chesapeake and the Potomac. I was alone on the *Antonia* when I head the *Tonga* coming in under power in a pouring rain. I slipped on my oilskins and went up onto the dock to help moor the sailboat. About then, an ambulance arrived in the parking area, and I was surprised to see one lady with a splint on her leg. A squall had suddenly arrived, tossing the *Tonga* about, and the heavy lady had slipped on the varnished white-pine deck

THE *TONGA* AT HUNTING TOWERS MARINA, 1954.

and bounced off a bitt-head, sustaining a painful fracture. Everyone was soaked to the skin and apparently very anxious to get ashore. I carried baggage and helped stow it away in the various cars that kept arriving. Eventually, they had all gone away, and I was left to clean up and make things tidy again.

After a while, the *Antonia* was sold, and I moved my duffle into the *Tonga*'s narrow crew's quarters, which were forward of the galley on the port side of the centerboard trunk. The master stateroom was up in the bow of the *Tonga*. There were two huge bunks, one to port and the other to starboard in the main cabin aft of the centerboard trunk. There was a shower and bathroom on the starboard side in the narrow passageway that ran forward past the centerboard housing; there were linen closets along this passageway against the hull and under the fantail; there was a Onan generator driven by a small gasoline four-cylinder engine which had a magneto, which was very handy when the starting battery was flat. The yacht's batteries were also stuffed in under the deck, and it was difficult to fill them with distilled water. There was a "magic wand" that allowed me to reach out over the first two banks to reach the filler ports in the other two banks. But it wasn't perfect, and once I managed to short out some cells with this gadget, and battery acid flew into my eyes and face. I rammed out through the access hatch into the main cabin, scraping my ear painfully, and raced to the galley sink, which had a faucet that had a tall, hospital-type loop. So I opened the cold-water valve and let the water run into my eyes for quite a while. It was déjà vu, as Raymond Poitras had slapped me in the face with that burlap swab soaked with sulphuric acid, when we were washing off stone slabs that had just come out of the gang saws, back in 1949. Raymond thought it was as funny as a Three Stooges act, and it nearly was; he didn't take any care and just let go of the long handle, and the swab bounced off of something and hit me in the face.

Even so, I had to start the Onan generator once in a while, or the separate starting battery would go flat. However, it had a magneto, and during Hurricane Carol I crawled in there when the dock's power went off and cranked the Onan to get it started. Thus, we had lights all through the worst of the storm.

We went outside at Fernandina outlet and ran up to Morehead City, where we topped off the tanks (water and fuel oil) and proceeded in the ditch. I seem to remember that we tied up in the Pamlico River, where the shad fishermen were generous and didn't charge us a dockage fee. We had breakfast together below deck and started for Norfolk before daylight. We emerged from the hidden swamp to skim ice in the Chesapeake and churned up the Potomac to tie up at Hunting Park Marina way after dark.

Bob Dobbins had decided to go along as an extra helmsman, and we set out on a nice day on the same routines as before. When we arrived at Morehead City, we tied up next to a modern sailboat. I was surprised to see Elmer "Mike" Dow as deckhand and Captain Alton Torrey, both from Deer Isle, Maine (Alton was a distant relative on my mother's side).

After we topped off the fuel and water tanks, I walked up the dock, found a store, and brought back some fresh milk and groceries, and we poked the *Tonga* out through the inlet, south past Cape Lookout, to run down to the Ft. George Inlet at Jacksonville. This time there were no huge seas, and we entered the inlet at low tide, and promptly ran aground on shifting sand at the sea buoy. A small tug ran by and tooted a salute. After a while the tide came up a little, and we backed to where the tug had been running. The little Chrysler burbled along, and at the first dock that we saw, Dobbins wanted to get off. The skipper sidled the *Tonga* up beside a wooden ladder, which was fastened to the concrete surface, and Bob climbed up; I heaved up his bag, and he walked away to find a cab to the airport where he could "deadhead" to DC on a Capital turboprop Viscount. He didn't like the *Tonga;* she was difficult to keep on course under power.

For days, Hurricane Carol was in the news, and we put out all the hawsers and fenders that we could find, beg, borrow or steal. It came right up the river and heaved us about somethin' wicked. Eventually, the eye of the storm arrived, and everything was very very quiet. The lights were still working in the marina, and Bob Dobbins, a Capital Airlines pilot, came rowing out to the *Tonga* right over the planking on the docks, as the river was backed up quite a bit. Robert had no more than made himself comfortable than the backside of the storm arrived, and the marina lights went out. I climbed into the battery room cubby hole and started the generator on the magneto. Then I made coffee, and we hung on to anything solid until the hurricane blew out to the northwest.

The next morning, there were small boats all through the marsh north of the Hunting Park Marina, and I unwittingly waded out into what turned out to be raw sewage to retrieve about ten of them. We had gathered a small flotilla of boats and tied them up inside the marina. Lieutenant Brown from the Alexandria Police Department was out there wading around with me, retrieving these small boats. I punctured my foot on a seed pod and got some kind of horrible infection that put me down for two or three days. Possibly the raw-sewage problem has been cleared up by now, but I was a very sick pup for awhile. Modern antibiotics saved the day, and I was soon climbing the rigging again.

I rescued a nice hydroplane, powered with a big four-cylinder Mercury outboard. One of the Chris-Craft cruisers had sunk at the dock, so the skipper called someone for a gasoline-powered pump. It was located on a dredge in the river, and I ran over there in the hydroplane to arrange for the gasoline-powered pump to be brought to the Hunting Park Marina. Shortly after that, two men in a flatbed truck arrived with a pump, hoses and know-how. Two mechanics managed to lift it out of the truck and set it on the walkway, where they rigged up the hoses and pumped the sunken cruiser "up offa the bottom." It took a while, and they fussed with the boat's engine even longer, but eventually, even that ran again.

We tied up at the West Palm Beach Marina again, and we washed every line on the *Tonga* in soap and water. We pulled the lines through the blocks by sewing another line onto the tail end of each halyard and washed them, one at a time.

When the B.'s came aboard, we ran down to Miami, and shortly after that the skipper and I sailed to Havana. Captain Hollett fastened a fishing reel to the rail, and just before noon he shouted, "Carroll, we caught a fish!" So I ran up onto the deck and reeled it in, a small tuna. Since it was lunchtime, I filleted the yellowfin and fried him up in lotsa butter! We didn't leave anything for the nonexistent cat. After dark, I was busy throwing flying fish back into the Gulf Stream. In the morning there were many dead ones, as they were trapped inside the rails. Perhaps a few managed to slither through the scupper holes. Sometime near midnight, we caught a larger tuna, and I slid it right into the huge chest-type freezer. But we never ate that one.

We moored the *Tonga* by dropping two bow anchors and backing in to secure the yacht with two stern lines, and then rigged a gangplank onto the aft rail. Then the skipper ran a safety line. Sometime after lunch the next day, we saw El Morro, the Spanish fortress that guarded the harbor of ancient Havana. The English captured El Morro by climbing over the low rear walls and defeating the garrison quite easily. (However, the Brits forgot all that when they designed the fortifications at Singapore. Not one naval gun could be brought to bear on the road into the city, and the Japanese came rattling down the road on bicycles to take the defenders from the rear.)

We explored Havana, and I took a guided tour of El Morro from a huge black man who spoke English well enough for me to understand. I paid him in U.S. dollars, and he beamed; then I bought him a drink at the bar in El Morro and a cigar; he was pleased. I had a Coke! I took the next little ferry back to the central park and explored some more. Once in a while, someone would try to talk to me in broken English. I was amused by one black man who boasted, "Me no negro, me Cubano!" At that time Americans weren't giving hi-fives, but I smiled and shook hands to let him know that I understood what he had said.

82. THE *MARGO* AND THE *ADDONAWAY*

After we had sailed the *Tonga* back to Miami, everything was sort of anticlimactic, and Mr. B. bought a newer yacht, a sixty-foot Trumpy houseboat. The *Tonga* was sold in Miami, if my memory does not fail me. I remember that I captured the radio direction finder to use on the Trumpy. At any rate, we went north in the new yacht, renamed *Margo*. We stopped in Fort Pierce, where the skipper had an old friend, and they got totally smashed. In the morning, Captain Hollett got the *Margo* under way and left me to steer the Intracoastal Waterway by myself. Sometime after noontime he came up, took the helm, and I went back to the galley to make lunch. The galley was above deck, aft of the pilothouse, and ran crosswise to the hull with a companionway on the starboard side to the crew's quarters below. There was a Perkins diesel generator set that started automatically, and it ran all the while we were underway. It shut down automatically when we plugged into shore current.

Once we were back in Alexandria, we tied up in our old *Antonia*'s berth. I found Bob Dobbins, and he drove me up to retrieve the Sunbeam. The boss came down to the *Margo* one day, complaining about the price of food (for the crew—me!). I decided that I needed a change of scenery and drove up to City Island, New York, and got a waiter's job immediately on the *Addonaway*, another eighty-two-foot New York Ship and

Addonaway, Boston "habbah," 1955.

Light day-cruiser-cum-houseboat. I climbed up a wooden ladder to talk to Captain William Hinch on the *Addonaway*. She was hauled out for work on the hull. She was almost a twin to the *Antonia*, another eighty-two-footer, built in the same yard on the Hudson, and was owned by Donnelly Outdoor Advertising. We spent the summer cruising up and down Long Island Sound, trips to Hyannis Port, Nantucket, and Block Island, Rhode Island. The company yacht crew was not the least like the *Antonia's*. It was not a happy crew. We had beer-company representatives on board, but they only drank scotch! Once, Howard Johnson came on board, and I was quite sure that he was used to having his own way on anything! He was just average in height, losing some of his red hair, and when we returned to the dock, he was almost running in his haste to leave! An-

CAPTAIN WILLIAM HINCH (LEFT), ENGINEER AND DECKHAND, 1955.

other time, there was a very beautiful young lady that came aboard with a large group for a day's cruise, and she told me that she was afraid that she would get seasick, so I slipped down into Benny Zera's galley and sliced off a wedge of lemon. I presented it to her and told her to suck on it, so that she wouldn't get nauseous—all blarney, but it worked!

Once, we went into Lake Montauk, and Captain Hinch asked me if I could get some lobsters. I went ashore in the yacht club launch, called my brother Wink, who still worked at Duryea's, and he brought over the order of lobsters for the owners, who were trying to host a party onboard. I was surprised to see Rex as dock master again. Wink loaned us his '49 Ford, which was in need of major engine repairs. Captain Hinch and I went somewhere in the poorly-running thing, but I don't remember where. The party was a flop; no guests arrived, and in the morning the owners slept to way past noon. The chef, Benny Zera, was a ten-percenter; he asked me to hit up the laundry operators for a ten percent commission on everything that they did for us. I told him flat out, "If you wanna do anything like that, I don't wanna know anything about it!" I was already itching to leave.

In September, after the summer cruises were over, I quit the job and drove to Boston to see if I could board with my mother's sister. Aunt Franscene had become a widow, and I thought that we could both benefit by that kind of arrangement. I got a job in an automatic screw machine shop in Cambridge, and at first I liked operating the machines. It is a mind-numbing job, though. The machines shape little pins from solid brass rod material, and the pins were used in the manufacture of circuit boards for television sets and other electric gadgets at that time.

83. THE *ELECTRON*

But late in 1955, Captain Hollett wrote to me via Stonington to come to work on the *Electron*, a new yacht under construction in Nevins's yard on City Island. It was being built for RCA (the Radio Corporation of America). Captain Hollett managed to secure the captain's berth. He wrote to me via "Stonehaven," asking me to come aboard as sailor on deck!

I flew down to New York's La Guardia Airport, a terrible place to land. The Convair came in like a load of bricks and landed nearly as hard. I made my way through the city and took the elevated to the end of its run, where I caught a bus to City Island. (The El has been torn down since then.) I walked into Nevins's and went aboard the *Electron*. We soon went out on sea trials to correct the magnetic compass and test other things. Captain Walter "Dan" Billings from Little Deer Isle was in the temporary crew.

The chef was to be James Horba from Wilmington, Delaware. Cousin Captain Walter Dan Billings was in the trials crew. Cap'n Hollett hired a lad, Roger, and an even younger lad from Oceanville, Maine, who lasted about a week. He went back to the island and became a lobster fisherman. I wish him well! He was replaced by Walter Robson, "Porky," from City Island. We had a professional waiter from Scotland. He didn't like certain ethnic groups. Angus couldn't disguise his dislikes, and David Sarnoff (Chairman of the Board of Directors at RCA) soon dismissed Angus. Captain Hollett discussed promoting me to waiter with General Sarnoff, and I was soon attending a school of sorts at the RCA building in New York. I rode down there every day on the old elevated line, where a real English butler, Marsland, proceeded to teach me how to mix drinks for the legal cadre at RCA's company dining room. I was taught how to serve these exalted persons by Marsland, and eventually I was accepted for the waiter's job on the *Electron*.

The *Electron* had the best of RCA equipment, a huge radar set, a deluxe ship-to-shore radio telephone, and in the aft salon, a large and ornate stereo console, upon which David liked to play records of *Aïda* and other operas at a very loud volume, to entertain the curious on the Nantucket dock. However, a New York tourist loudly insulted the General by referring to his religion, and Sarnoff angrily exclaimed, "Take up the lines! We're leaving!" The crowd ooh'd and ah'd, while we rushed to get underway. Very late that evening, we tied up at our berth in City Island, and the Filipino chauffeur was waiting patiently at the dock with the huge black Cadillac limousine, while we carried the Sarnoffs' luggage up the ramp and helped load it into the trunk.

Mrs. Sarnoff was a character; she insisted on having me serve her morning coffee with all the attendant containers jammed onto a tiny silver serving tray hardly wide enough for the coffee urn. I managed, clumsily, to succeed for many mornings, but one morning the *Electron* gave a lurch or something, and the urn tumbled right into her lap! "Oh," she said, and she dashed down the companionway to the master stateroom, but promptly returned while I was busy mopping up the mini-disaster. She didn't scold me or say anything other than, "I'm blue!" She had put on another beautiful blue dressing gown. Jim Horba, the chef, had soon equipped me with another silver tray, large enough to hold all the items securely, and she never requested the tiny one again!

She wasn't a good sailor and got seasick in the slightest of seas. We were crossing the often-choppy stretch between Martha's Vineyard and Nantucket when she rang the bell, and I dashed aft to see what she wanted. She pointed to the starboard outside deck forward and said plaintively, "I got a little sick!" In minutes I had that cleaned up, and she seemed to feel better lying down.

Sometimes we had RCA's president, Mr. Folsom, on board with Cardinal Spellman and other church personages. We always picked him up in Hyannis Port and dropped him off there. The clergy were very appreciative of any favors. I was amused that they used the bar on the quarter deck as a place to conduct the mass. Jim and Sinbad went aft to join in the celebration. We sinners stayed for'ard and were very quiet. After mass, the business of running the yacht commenced in earnest.

We cruised up and down Long Island Sound, taking General David Sarnoff to Nantucket, where we were tied up to a dock when the *Andrea Doria* and the *Stockholm* collided in a dense fog, and the General wanted to go out to help in the rescue. Cap'n Hollett didn't want any part of rescue work, so we stayed at the dock while Sarnoff listened to the news reports on his brand-new toy, a solar-powered radio, especially made for him by Radio Corporation of America research engineers.

Another time, we were tied up at Nantucket, and a young girl came to the dock and asked to come aboard, explaining that she was Mrs. Sarnoff's maid. She was quite pretty, "Irish as Paddy's pig," and wanted to talk to me while she waited for Mrs. Sarnoff's return. Soon, the General and his bride came aboard, and the minute he saw me talking to the young beauty, his face screwed up into a storm cloud, but Mrs. Sarnoff saved the day by embracing the girl, and I escaped forward while the going was good!

I survived as waiter, serving meals, making beds, and cleaning bathrooms all summer, and was cook for the crew, as we churned down the inland waterway, while Jim had some time off.

Once, in Havana, the Boss had arrived by plane from Miami, and late in the evening they came aboard. They had been at a casino, and Mrs. S. was well into her cups. I was asleep in the crew's quarters, and all of a sudden I heard the skipper shouting for me to get up. I hauled on a pair of pants and ran up on deck in time to see Mrs. S. dripping water onto the deck. She had fallen into the incredibly dirty harbor and lost her mink stole! There was quite a bit of excitement, and after awhile everyone retired for the night.

The next day, divers came to look for the lost garment, but I suspect that it had washed up into the filthy harbor with the incoming tide, which was moving along at a good clip at the time she fell in. All good things must end, and we prepared to return to Miami. Sometime during the night, I found Mr. S. standing in the main cabin as we surged along under sail with a free boost from the Gulf Stream. He wanted to return to Havana and fly back to Miami. Captain Hollett assured him that we would be in Miami sooner than Havana, as we had to buck the strong current. But he prevailed, and we turned around and ran back under power, as the wind was against us. They all went ashore to catch a flight to Miami.

One day, while we were tied up at the Flamingo Club, without the Sarnoffs, I walked up to mail a letter to Marm, and I espied a huge empty Beefeater gin bottle on top of the trash cans in the back alley of the club building. I promptly gaffed it and scampered back to the yacht, washed it out very carefully and later poured the Gilbey's gin into the bottle, so that I could display it prominently for General Sarnoff's imperious and disagreeable lawyer. He beamed with pleasure as I mixed his martini, never the wiser. The rascal strikes again!

Later, we were tied up at the King Cole Club in Miami, and the manager came out to tell us that we could use the huge swimming pool after dark if we didn't make any disturbing noises. So we did! We younger crew members liked the King Cole much better than the Flamingo Club, where we could not ever use the pool.

Christmas came around, and the General came to wish us a merry Christmas and gave each one of us a cold, limp handshake, then promptly disappeared into another huge black Cadillac limousine. Captain Hollett just as promptly packed an overnight bag and had a cab take him to the airport, leaving us to fend for ourselves. "When the cat's away, the mice will play!" Pamela Haviland had flown down from Philadelphia, and she stayed with my brother Garland and his bride, Kathy (Benton) Haskell, in North Miami. Jim decided that we should have a Christmas dinner aboard the *Electron*. So his bride, Hope Horba, came aboard, and Garland and Kathy, with Pamela in tow. With the two sailors we may have also had Cap'n Benny Johnson; at any rate, the dining room was full, and I wore my waiter's uniform as I served the guests! Jim put on an enormous turkey dinner. Pamela and I were engaged in October of that same year, 1956.

The next day, Garland, Kathy, Pam and I drove to Key West on the Overseas Highway. Garland had a brand-new six-cylinder Chevrolet coupe, and we had a picnic cooler full of New York cut steaks, which we grilled on the Key West public picnic grills, fired with convenience-store charcoal briquettes. There were hopeful fishermen and ladies with expensive rods trying to catch sports fish in the very fast-running tides from the bridges that connected the Keys together, all parts of the Overseas Highway. Way off to the west, Fort Jefferson lay almost out of sight below the horizon, where the good Dr. Mudd was incarcerated for setting the broken leg of President Lincoln's assassin, John Wilkes Booth.

Later that winter, the RCA manager Mr. Lynch organized a charter party for the *Electron*, and the skipper didn't think I was capable of serving the Canadians who came aboard, "all pomp and circumstance." He decided that I, the "Downeaster," wasn't polished enough to be waiter for the Canadians, so I was demoted to sailor on deck. That was the ultimate insult. The new waiter was a troublemaker and riled up the entire crew, including Jim, who could get along with almost anyone. He soon had Captain Hollett gnashing his teeth, and I said to myself, "Good enough for ya!"

Captain Hollett proposed to run all night to enter the Bahama Island waters at Bimini. We promptly set out for Nassau, crossing the Florida Straits at night. When we entered the first small outpost, I was sent up on the bow to watch for coral formations and conned the *Electron* through the gaps by hand signals. The Canadians all went ashore, and the skipper had a nap. There were sharks swimming in the crystal-clear waters inside the coral reefs.

Lord Bader was on board with a beautiful Hollywood star, and we holed up in Frazier's Hog Cay, while a hurricane passed through. Porky and I explored the island, which seemed to have only cacti, sea grape plants, and small grasses; there were some small birds that were new to me, and the ubiquitous brown pelicans, some tropical terns, egrets, and local natives fishing with a small purse seine. We watched as they caught some fish, which they transferred to the wet well of their homemade sloop. They talked in Bajan, a dialect using English words but with native meanings. They had caught an armored tile fish, which they reverently released into the ocean, while chanting a prayer: "Another Mary go with God." They walked barefooted on the razor-sharp coral rocks! Porky and I were amazed to find the soles of our topsiders cut to ribbons when we got back onboard ship!

Lord Bader had a Grumman twin-engine flying boat come out and pick him up, as he had a hot date with Florence Henderson, the Hollywood beauty in the limelight at that time (1956). The Grumman bounced along atop the waves until it lifted off and was soon out of sight, headed for New Providence Island.

Once underway again and before dawn, the skipper rammed the sea buoy in the channel, as we approached Nassau in the dark. Porky told me about it with a delighted grin. We tied up at the Royal Yacht Club, and the following morning I happened to be up topside swabbing the dew off the teak decks and cleaning windows when I spied Clayton Robbins on a sailboat just ahead of us by a boat length, so I hailed him: "Well, old son, this beats haulin' traps offa Brimstone in January, deah!"

Clayton looked at me for a second or two and finally figured out who I was, and he replied, "Can yew get a li'l time off?" So I found Cap'n Hollett and arranged to go ashore with Clayton for an hour or so. We met outside the club's entrance, which was wreathed in beautiful pink blossoms on vines that I had never seen before, breadfruit trees growing beside the dock; I later read that the slaves wouldn't eat the fruit after Captain Bligh, famous for the mutiny on the *Bounty*, had successfully made a second voyage, west to east, around the horn to transplant breadfruit trees to the Caribbean. How ironic! There must have been a flaw in his makeup, as he also failed as governor of New South Wales when the Rum Corps mutinied!

Very soon a 1950 DeSoto Club coupe pulled up, and we climbed in. The Bajan driver seemed to know exactly where Clayton wanted to go.

The big six-cylinder DeSoto surged up the hills and deposited us at King Dick's establishment. We entered, and Clayton made a bee-line for a corner table, and King Dick himself came over to take Clayton's order. He was a huge, very, very black man with a prominently noticeable long scar running from above his right eye to below his chin. I can only surmise where and how he had acquired that! Very quickly, an elderly, small black man brought over two long-necked bottles of beer, and Clayton tipped back his wooden chair to lean on the wall and said, "This is the only place in th' world where I can sit back and feel just one step above everybody else!"

I was amused but didn't laugh or let on that I was surprised. Just about then, an ancient and wizened tiny black female danced over into our corner, clicking her tongue and snapping her fingers, and spoke to me in the Bajan dialect. I didn't understand a word, but I divined her intent, so I shook my head; then she went into a little dance. She was lithe and sinuous, but I wasn't buying any, whatever it was, so she glided away, snapping her fingers and clicking her tongue, trying to entice someone else, I hoped! About an hour later, the big DeSoto returned, and we left for the Royal Yacht Club.

Clayton and I shook hands, and I never saw him again. He lived in a small two-story house nearly on top of Russ's Hill, where Church Street meets the hillside street in Stonington. It has been over fifty years since I was supposed to go as stern man with him in 1947 during the winter months. Every time I drove over to see if he was going out to haul, he would come outside and sniff at the weather like my father did; then Clayton would announce, "It's gonna blow somethin' wicked, deah. We won't be going out today, ol' son!" So I drove down to Clayton's house the very next Monday morning. It was about eighteen below zero, and the sea smoke was a-flyin'. We couldn't even see Two Bush Island. Clayton came out on the sundeck and said, "I guess we'll stay ashore today, ol' son!" So I returned in my ancient 1929 Nash Advanced Six on Tuesday. After three frosty morning trips to Clayton's house in a row, I figured that he didn't need me! So I went clamming instead.

I never saw Clayton again, but I did see Cap'n Dan Robbins, who bought a very nice house on Moose Island in Stonington for his retirement years. Clayton's house has been acquired by people from away, and it has had three huge windows installed on the second floor, providing an excellent view out over the Stonington Harbor and the islands between Stonington and Isle au Haut.

Cap'n Dan and Cap'n Hollett both passed away quite some time ago.

84. FAREWELL *ELECTRON,* STARTING A NEW LIFE

The Canadians wanted to go to a small island nearby and have a picnic. Jim Horba and the new waiter arranged all the foodstuffs, and Walter Robeson and I lowered the starboard launch. It had a tiny four-cylinder Universal marine engine with a marine transmission. I was to be the coxswain, and we ferried the Canadians ashore onto a beautiful broken-seashell beach. The broken shells were pink, and the tiny little pieces stuck to our skin. Walter and I held the tiny launch off the beach by jumping in barefooted and leaning up against the hull to keep her from grounding out. There was a palm-frond ramada up on top of the little island, and the Canadians sat on benches in the palm-frond roof's shade and enjoyed themselves. Eventually, we ran them back to the port-side boarding ladder, and Walter and I hoisted the starboard launch up into her davits. Meanwhile, the new waiter and chef Jim Horba had raised the boarding ladder, and the next chore was to bring up the anchor. I went over the side and cleaned off the anchor with a long-handled scrub brush, using seawater to aid the process

Eventually, the Canadians went back to ice and snow, and we returned to the Flamingo Club. Dock master Rex was almost glad to see us. I sent my paycheck up to Miami Groceries, and they cashed it for me. I was going to need all the cash I could get my hands on for my planned escape. My brother Garland came over to pick me up. I had packed all my treasures into an old U.S. Army duffle bag, and Garland and I went aft to get what cash I had coming to me from Cap'n Hollett. In parting I only said, "You don't need me anymore, and I won't see you again!"

With some more money onboard, Garland and I drove off to West Miami in his new Chevy six-cylinder coupe. The next day, I started calling around for a delivery job to Philly or close by. Most of the deliveries were going to New York; one to Atlantic City, but my last phone call netted a Mr. Lyon, who had a 1955 DeSoto coupe going to West Philly. The owner of the delivery agency said that Mr. Lyon definitely wanted to meet the driver of his pride and joy! So he drove me over to meet Mr. Lyon. The DeSoto had a hemi V8 and would cruise at 80 knots. Mr. Lyon asked me how I planned to go. He had a set of AAA road maps, and I pointed out my route. "No, no! Go up 301, but be careful at Ludowici, Georgia: the township cop sits on the sidewalk with a traffic light control button to trap out-of-state drivers!"

He turned me loose with the big DeSoto and the road maps, and I got back to Garland's house in the outback of Miami. I set out for Philly about 7 p.m. Kathy had made me two sandwiches and put two nice oranges in the paper bag. I kept below the speed limit to the Georgia state line; then I hookered her up to seventy knots. The DeSoto was thirsty at thirteen miles to the gallon, but it ran on junk gas, zip at thirteen cents a gallon and zap at fourteen. I had to put in a quart of oil somewhere in Georgia and a quart of transmission fluid. Eventually, I came to Ludowici and the speed-trap cop! I noticed a 1938 Chevy coupe bouncing past the intersection on a red dirt road, so I followed the Chevy and came out on 301 north of Ludowici. "Good on em!" But when I got to South Carolina, every curve in the road had two rubber hoses crossing the highway. Tires passing over the hoses broke a pressure flow and registered as speed. So I was careful to be well below the fifty-five-mile-per-hour speed limit until I got to Virginia; then I pushed her up to seventy again.

I picked up a hitchhiking sailor near Norfolk, and he was a greenhorn driver. He could handle forty, so I relaxed for several hours, while he puttered along. We came to Baltimore, and navigating through Baltimore is bad news unless one lives there, but I asked a cabbie how to get onto Route 40 north, and he must have been feelin' good, as he hollered, "Follow me!" My sailor boy could barely keep the cabbie in sight, but we were waved right, and there was the Route 40 sign. A left turn, and we were toddling along at forty knots forever. The sailor lad wanted to get out in some little gunk-hole town, and he shouldered his canvas bag and was off. I kept along, very tired by that time, and finally found my way to West Johnson Street. The Havilands were glad to see me, and Pam and I were married in the First Church at 22nd and Chestnut Streets on May 11th, 1957. We were about to set sail on all-new adventures!

85. ADVENTURES IN THE NINETEEN-FIFTIES

Pam had a new '55 VW Beetle; I had an older '52 Sunbeam Talbot 90 series sedan. I had just started as a splicer's helper in the construction department of the Bell Telephone Company of Pennsylvania. I was the oldest helper in the North City Division. We moved into Rosemary Lane Garden, in a first-floor, one-bedroom apartment, just off Lincoln Drive, on March 28th, in a very large snowstorm.

Some time later, we drove to Deer Isle for a three-day weekend. My old buddy Alvin "Digger" Jones had just finished building a little carvel-planked skiff. He was in the air force and stationed in Bangor at the time and built a sixteen-and-a-half-foot, outboard-powered skiff in an old cow barn in Orrington, near where he and his bride Barbara (Bartlett) Jones lived. It was delivered for Thanksgiving the following year.

It had native red-oak ribs, stem and transom, and he had clamped a big 25-horse Evinrude onto the transom. After a very fast and wild ride in it, we decided to have Alvin build one for us. My memory fails, but I think that it was more than a year later that it was ready to launch at Thanksgiving. I had found a used 30-horse Evinrude at Borghesi's in North Philly, and I loaded it into the "Roachwagen" by taking the passenger seat out and then lowering the Evinrude into the Bug, with the lower unit tucked up under the dash on the passenger side and the power head rammed up against the rear seat. The front passenger seat was put in upside-down on top of the outboard motor, and Pam's brother's cat went inside the seat frames in her carrier.

In those days, before the Interstate system, we used to cross the Delaware via the Burlington-Bristol or Tacony-Palmyra bridge and eventually got onto the New Jersey Turnpike. Those VW Beetles were so noisy, with the squirrel-cage cooling fan screaming away amidst the noise of the engine, that we really needed an intercom system with headphones just to make conversation. We averaged a door-to-door trip, just over 612 miles, in twelve hours, twenty minutes, with one stop for gasoline in Kittery, Maine. Pam sat behind me, until it was time for her to drive awhile.

After Marm had put on a huge Maine breakfast, we drove down to Stonington to see Digger and the new skiff. It was sixteen feet long and painted Pettit's Seamist Green. Three of us lowered the Evinrude down over the edge of Mickey Webber's dock onto the transom and clamped it on tightly; I borrowed one of Alvin's two-hose fuel tanks and skimmed up to Webb's Cove. With the help of Guy Eaton, Alvin, my dad and myself, we carried the skiff up to my grandmother's house, where we stored it inside, upside-down on sawhorses in Dad's homemade Model T Ford garage, for the winter. The skiff is forty-eight years old now; it has taken us on many marine picnic adventures.

We towed home enough driftwood timbers to build the first fog deck on our log cabin. The second deck was supported on hatmatack timbers, harvested from Bill Schoettle's driveway project. The huge tree was right in the path of the proposed driveway. So I climbed up and tied a three-quarter-inch manila line onto the tree, so that we could get a nice strain on it while Pam's brother sawed away with his chainsaw. I towed the tamarack right down into the proposed roadway with our family Ford Fairlane station wagon. Bill whacked the tree into twelve-foot lengths, and it yielded four deck-support timbers, twelve feet by five inches by three inches. It is very rot-resistant wood, and the cross-members are Canadian white spruce from Barter's lumber, right on Deer Isle. The deck planking is partly driftwood and partly red oak from a huge tree that stood close to the northeast corner of the log cabin (see Chapter 94).

Budget Eaton and his son were building a new driveway for us, as Mrs. Minerva Young demanded that we stop using the Haviland driveway, which belonged to her at the time, and part of Grover Small's old woods road which ran along what became her stone wall, when she bought the old "Poofie" Hardy homestead.*

So we asked Budget to come down, and he loaded the logs onto his

---

*Built about 1779 by Peter Hardy, who married Elizabeth Wheeler Haskell and came to Deer Isle in 1700 with Elizabeth's father, Deacon Francis Haskell, first-born child of Captain Mark Haskell, who came to Deer Isle in 1765. —Win A. Haskell, *The Haskell Family Anthology*, Volume 1.

dump-truck with his front loader and hauled them down to Joe Judkins's sawmill. Joe sawed them into the oak planks that we are still using for the fog decking. Bill Haviland and I helped Joe saw these planks, and we carted them to North Deer Isle on a homemade boat trailer towed by the Ford Fairlane wagon. It took several trips to carry all the wood back to North Deer Isle.

Ironically, I received a letter from a local realtor asking if I would be interested in buying Minerva Young's shore properties. I called him and said, "No I couldn't buy it, but I knew someone who might be able to!" Dr. William Haviland, Pam's brother, bought the entire package. Minerva balked at selling the right-of-way, but Bill said, "All or nothing!" and she folded. Now we all use either driveway, whichever is convenient. Minerva retained a small separate house lot on the old steamboat landing road, and her son-in-law has built a summer home on it, which is well away from our properties. Amen!

86. WHEN ONE MUST HAVE A BOAT

Somehow Pam and I both managed to get the Friday after Thanksgiving off, and we drove her little "Roachwagen" beetle to Maine with the used 30-horse Evinrude outboard motor loaded on the passenger side of the VW, with the power head resting on the floor, jammed up against the back seat.

Wednesday after dinner (in Pennsylvania, dinner is the evening meal; on the island dinner is at noontime, and supper is the evening meal), we set out for the island and battled up the East Coast on whatever seemed to be the fastest route. We used to drive right through New York City on the so-called Pelham Parkway and pick up the Hutchinson River Parkway, which became the Merritt Parkway in Connecticut. Eventually we picked up Route 20 and then Route 9, ending on Route 128 around Boston. From there we followed Route 1. We stopped in Portsmouth, New Hampshire, just across the Kittery bridge, where we almost always stopped for gas. The attendant looked in and saw the Evinrude and exclaimed. "You've got more power in there than under the hood!" We used to bypass Rockland on Route 90 and eventually arrive on Deer Isle on Route 15 in anywhere from twelve and a half hours to fourteen hours, depending on traffic and weather.

We tried out the Evinrude on the new boat. It was a dark, overcast day, so we didn't play with the boat at all. I ran it up to Webb's Cove, and with a lot of help from the neighbors we carried the skiff up the slope and stored it in Dick's old garage.

We used that Evinrude for many summers, and we went out as far as the Big Cod Shoal south of Great Spoon Island, Dick and I, with our great friend Dr. William Krogman, fishing for haddock or cod or whatever bit our bait; eventually the Evinrude corroded and gave all sorts of trouble. The final adventure with it was that it would start, but I couldn't shift it into gear. Upon examination we found that the shift rod inside the housing had rusted away and could not be repaired from the outside. Attempts to remove the bolts resulted in a collection of bolt heads, as they sheared right off. The steel bolts seize right to the alloy castings.

I never intended writing about my thirty-four years with the Bell Telephone Company of Pennsylvania, but this little adventure involves my short friendship with Jack Sablich, of the East Oak Lane Section of Philadelphia. It was a very short friendship, because Jack passed away several years before I retired. He was very smart, very Polish, and very Roman Catholic, and I was not. However, we worked very closely together all the while I was in "buildings," as we named our titles, "Futility Foremen."

Unlike cable-splicer Bob Lewis and his bride Jean, Jack Sablich never got to visit Deer Isle. But he enjoyed my stories of life on the Island, like when our slightly used 40-horse Evinrude broke its crankshaft, right off Calvin "Kelp" Dunham's little cove on the west side of Moose Island. Tony Broncatto, who was on the Bell Telephone Credit Union board of directors had the big 40-horse Evinrude, and I had bought it and carted it to Deer Isle in our 1966 Ford Fairlane wagon. We didn't have any trouble fitting the motor into the back with all the rest of the cargo. However, that motor had a very short life with us, as the crankshaft sheared right off. Luckily, we were abreast of Kelp Dunham's at the time, and I got out the oars and rowed in there. Bessie Dunham let me call Dick, and he came over with his Plymouth sedan towing the boat trailer; with a lot of help from James "Casey" Robbins and another man, we managed to get the skiff onto the trailer, and Dick hauled us all over to the old homestead. The local Evinrude dealer's advice was to buy another used motor, as the repairs on the broken one would be more than it was worth. Next, we tried to transplant a used power head onto the late-model Evinrude that had broken its crankshaft. That worked, but not perfectly.

Pam's brother Bill and his bride Anita went with Pam and me on a trip to Marshall's Island, which lies east of Webb's Cove about seven miles. So I carried two six-gallon Evinrude tanks full of gas-and-oil mix down through an abandoned farmstead and through the alder patch, to straggle out Cyrus's Point, where we kept the sixteen-and-a-half-foot skiff on a homemade outhaul. We pulled her in, and I bailed her out; then we loaded up with picnic gear and the two tanks of fuel. The junky Evinrude fired up reluctantly, and we started out for Marshall's; as we passed Shingle Island, I noticed that the motor was running very smoothly. But just as we were getting close to Marshall's, a connecting rod snapped off inside the crankcase, and some pieces flew right out through the crankcase casting with a tremendous bang, then rattled around inside the plastic engine cover. Anita shouted, "Turn the boat around!" But the old motor simply died just as I twisted the steering handle. We went ashore and had our picnic. While we were discussing how to conduct the return trip with only two oars, a young mink ran right through our picnic spot!

After we had eaten and rested a bit, we looked around to see if we could make a sail of any kind. We only found a few tattered pieces of plastic and erected a mast with this fragile rig, and we loaded everything aboard the skiff. It was flat calm, which was a help. We began to row toward Webb's Cove. We labored away hour after hour, and when we passed Millet Island a breeze sprang up, and we actually sailed as far as the Shivers, a tiny granite isle with a few straggly spruce trees on top. Of course, the breeze fell off to nothing, and we continued to row up through the gap between Bold Island and Devil's Half Acre, exactly where we had run out of luck years ago when Kelp and Eugene Dunham had towed Garland, Mike Dow, and me up to Clam City's shore and cast us off, safely "outta th' wind." This time it was flat calm, and we were tiring. However, we labored along and reached the outhaul just as the sun settled down behind Tea Hill. We left everything in the boat and straggled up the hill to fall into the Ford with a great sigh of relief. When we pulled into Dick's yard and Bill went into the house, Dick asked Bill, "How far did ya row, Bill?" and he replied, "All the way!" And Dick clapped his hands and laughed. But I know that he was worried when we didn't return by four or five o'clock.

Of course, that was the end of boating that summer. But at work in the fall, Bob Angelow gave me a used 40-horse Mercury outboard. Several of us Bell employees built a sixteen-foot plywood skiff in our tiny Model T Ford garage, and we used Bob's little Scott outboard motor for many fishing trips in Barnegat Bay in New Jersey, where we caught mostly blowfish and sometimes kingfish and winter flounders.

I used the big Mercury on the wooden skiff for several years, until the lower unit began to leak oil into the water. I took it to the Mercury repair shop in Ellsworth and left it over the winter. In the following year's vacation trip, I drove over to Ellsworth, and young John Haskell said that they couldn't get the lower unit apart. Then, he wanted storage money, to add insult to injury, so I said, "keep it, John."

Nathan was working by then, and he bought a used 1974 Evinrude from Gene Eaton, who was selling Evinrudes at that time, and we used that little 15-horse on the old wooden skiff until the old eighteen-foot *Nessie* sank on its mooring. When gasoline got to $4.249 a gallon, we thought that the little Evinrude would be just right. But it had been neglected, and the power head had seized up, as well as the lower unit. So that ended up in Dean Eaton's used-parts department.

Bob Angelow came to the rescue again, when the 40-horse Evinrude died, and he gave us his old tri-hulled eighteen-footer fiberglass boat and trailer. I drove over to Angelow's house in Berlin, New Jersey, and cleaned the trailer's wheel bearings in gasoline, dried everything out well, and repacked the bearings with Castrol wheel bearing grease, obtained at Pep Boys in Philadelphia. (Yes! I took the used gasoline back and gave the mess, five-gallon can and all, to the hazardous-waste collection folks later in the year!) Eventually, Bill Schoettle and I hooked onto the trailer and started off. We stopped for ice for our picnic cooler and again for air to bring the tiny trailer tires up to fifty pounds per square inch. Stay tuned: that was too much pressure for the very old tires. Bill towed for hours and hours with his little red Jeep. We poked along and eventually stopped at the last rest area on 1-84 before the Massachusetts Turnpike entrance. Fortunately, I had bought two used wheels with used tires before we left New Jersey. Bill and I inspected the rig and found that one tire was about ready to burst. The sidewalls were all agap! I had thrown into the boat with the spares and tools a scissors jack from a Renault Ten that I had bought, well used and abused, for our kids to learn to drive, as it seemed an excellent little "bombe." The car lasted long enough to serve Jennifer as a set of wheels to drive to State College to visit her sister, Melinda. Shortly after that, it began to have brake problems. So Nathan and I towed it to a boneyard and waved goodbye.

With the little jack and its very long operating handle, I jacked the rig up and put on one of the wheels that Angelow had found for me. I let some air out of the other tire to register forty pounds, checked and rechecked, and once we were on the Massachusetts Turnpike (I-90), Bill decided that we should speed up, so that we could get to the Island before dark! Traffic was light, and in about five more hours we drove down through the oak forest that girds our long driveway. Bill backed the boat into a parking spot by the Cabbage Patch log cabin, and we unloaded the *Nessie* and trailer. I found that she was a monster trying to get into the dock. It took me many tries to get the hang of it. Bob had given me his old three-cylinder, 60-horse Evinrude, which worked very well until the electric shift began to act up. The shift is accomplished underwater in the lower unit, which eventually leaks saltwater into the workings and finally fails to shift. Dean Eaton told me to junk it.

Eventually we had Kevin Grindle at the Dry Marina on Little Deer Isle put a brand-new Tohatsu three-cylinder on the *Nessie*. That worked even better, as it had power tilt! Well o' course, Kevin gave up the Marine sales and repair business, and we tried someone else. Somehow the old fiberglass hull got a hole in it, and the *Nessie* sank on the mooring. That didn't do the Tohatsu any good. Walter Gottschalk was the first one to volunteer to help raise the *Nessie*. The whole operation was straight out of the Three Stooges, but with a couple boat-trailer winches and lots of muscle provided by two of Walter's cousins, who we haven't seen since that event, we raised her and moved her to Carney's Island's sand bar. "We left 'er there, because with a nine-foot rise and fall of th' tide, the boat would be high and somewhat dryer at low wattah, deah!" Paul Sewall had come in from hauling his traps, and he joined us. We bailed her out with two five-gallon plastic buckets and floated her off. Paul was towing, rowing Dick's old peapod, and Bill Haviland was a-bailing, trying to keep ahead of the incoming leakage! Paul managed to get the *Nessie* onto her trailer, but my little Lone Ranger couldn't muckle her. About then a complete stranger came along with his high-rise Chevrolet homemade flatbed four-wheel-drive truck and backed right down into that soft sticky muck, hooked onto the trailer, and hauled it up onto the hard-packed beach. He hopped out and shook hands all around and left! Only in Maine would that kind of thing happen! He wouldn't take a penny. He was just glad to help, simply amazing! The Lone Ranger could tow the *Nessie*, now that we were on solid ground.

Eventually, Bill Schoettle gave us his old Aquasport, which had been stored in our blueberry field for three or four winters. I sandpapered the bottom and sloshed on two coats of antifouling paint; then we launched her. The old Johnson lasted two or three summers, but after our Babbidge's Island adventure (Chapter 98), the ignition and/or the shifting mechanism failed in 2007. I was just about ready to give up on powerboats. But Pam bought a used Ebbtide fiberglass boat, complete with a big 140-horse Johnson, oil-injected, and it has power tilt, for my eightieth-birthday present, which was right after Christmas. We were at our house celebrating with ice cream and cake when Nathan handed me the envelope; I opened it up, and there were several pictures of a fiberglass boat on a new-looking trailer. I was completely mystified! "This ain't my boat !" I said, and they all shouted, "It is now!"

87. CARS AND HOMES IN THE 1960S

I was still a splicer's helper in 1960, as there had been a minor depression in the American economy in 1958. Pam was still working as a librarian, and I was earning just enough to pay the rent at Rosemary Gardens, a nice little collection of rental units just a few feet off Lincoln Drive in the West Mt. Airy section of Philly. Cars were showing bumper stickers that read, "This car climbed Mt. Airy," which was all of 440 feet above sea level, *más o menos*. If one is going to live in Philadelphia, one might as well learn some Spanish! It comes in handy in some areas of the city. Especially if one is going to be standing over a manhole all day and someone comes up asking questions in Spanish! *"No hablo español"* is good, because they walk away! *"De nada"* is also handy, as it means "It's nothing" or "you're welcome," depending on the situation.

I began to see the new Chevrolet Corvair sedans running around and wanted one to replace the tiny VW beetle that Pam had bought before we got married. Her brother Bill bought my treasured Sunbeam Talbot 90 that I had bought from Harold De Lait in Ellsworth. It would cruise all day at seventy miles per hour. Not very fast by today's standards, when Lexus and Mercedes sedans whiz past on the Interstates at close to a hundred and five and are "hull down" on the horizon in a matter of a minute or two!

Late in 1960, we bought our first General Motors product, a Chevrolet Corvair 500 (the plain-Jane series). The seats were so poor that I transplanted the cotton padding from a 1950 Plymouth into the front bench-type seat. The GM turn-signal flasher was so cheap that if I put the brakes on while the turn signal was flashing, the flasher quit! I looked around and found a Sylvania flasher, which I put into the Corvair, and that worked. The brakes were so poor that I took the car to a mechanic who did some Bell Telephone Company automotive work, and he put metallic linings into the drums. Next he put in special shock absorbers to tame the front-end shimmy. At 20,000 miles the valves were leaking, and my brother Wink brought down a salvaged Corvair engine from Montauk, N.Y., where he had a service station. So I took the cylinder heads to a machine shop that specialized in engine work, and they ground in a new set of valves, and I tore the engine in our car down and transferred the refurbished cylinder heads onto it. However, when I reassembled the engine, one of the hydraulic valve lifters collapsed, and the engine knocked all winter! By then, we were about fed up with Chevrolet. I took the original cylinder heads to the same machine shop, and they put in twelve sodium-cooled valves. I installed Thompson Roto-Caps and special hydraulic lifters. When I put her back together, she ran very nicely and got one more mile per gallon than she did new! The ignition switch caught fire while Pam was driving, and she managed to dump the Corvair into a parking spot in East Oak Lane, and someone disconnected the battery for her. By then, I had been promoted to the line gang and was working out of Washington Lane in the Germantown section of Philly. Somehow we got the Corvair home, and I replaced the ignition switch by making a special tool to accomplish the job. By the time the Corvair had 66,000 miles on it, the engine was burning oil.

We bought a used Plymouth Valiant station wagon, which was also a bummer. One day Pam came into the garage, which was built under the kitchen in that block of row houses. There was a raised water-stop strip of concrete, and when Pam drove into the garage the brakes made the font end dip, and it banged onto the concrete strip and tore a sheet-metal brace right off the lower front end sheet-metal assembly. She came into the house very angry and said, "I hate that car." So right then and there we drove over to the Ford dealership on Chelten Ave. in Germantown and bought a leftover 1966 Ford Fairlane 500 station wagon. It had Ford's miserable slave-cylinder power steering, and one sawed away every inch of the way to anywhere, trying to keep the thing on track. However, the Fairlane never failed us all the while we had it. It had the little 289 V8, and it was good for seventy all day long for 77,000 miles. Around that time, I took it out of the Ford and had it re-bored and rebuilt at an engine shop on Fairmount Ave. in Philly. The shop manager advised me to take the pieces home and reassemble it myself. It lasted until we bought a 1974 Dodge Coronet Wagon.

Sometime in the 1960s Pam's parents bought Cap'n Montaford Haskell's house, and we were to share it with Pam's brother, Bill, and his bride, Anita. Also, sometime after Pam's father, Thomas Philip Haviland, passed away, we started thinking about building a Ward's log cabin down on the shore of Bow Cat Cove. Pam's mother gave us a piece of land, and Bill advised us to buy a Ward's cabin. George Fifield dug the foundation hole for us in 1969, and a contractor in Bucksport set up plywood forms and poured a concrete foundation. Herb Carter built a rough floor platform that the cabin was to be erected upon. We drove to the island for Christmas that year and walked down through the woods on top of the party-line stone wall to take pictures of the building site with about three feet of snow covering the foundation.

88. FROM DICK'S 1963 JOURNAL

Got my withholding tax return this Friday, Jan. 11, 1963; made $3,885.47
    FICA Tax, $121.41
    Federal Income Tax, $459.90

Monday, Jan. 14, 1963: Mild, nice for this time of the year. Some snow.

Ethel Knowlton died this day @ 4:15 pm., Feb. 4th, 1963 [Dick paid his half-sister's funeral bill, $455.00. No help from Elroy or half-brothers. Dick retrieved $245.61 from Ethel's savings bank in Cambridge, Mass. —CMH]

Friday, March 1, 1963: Worked this day, D.I.G. payday $51.33.

Saturday, March 2, 1963: The snow is piled up 12 feet high on each side of the road up to Bangor.

Tuesday, May 14th, 1963: Eddie Villecca turned the Stone Truck upside down with a roof stone aboard. [Mack truck, I remember. —CMH]

Found a record of the times on page for Sunday, June 30, 1963, of Ethel and Raymond's death [Due to trying to survive in the old Knowlton-Haskell homestead. *Not* a pretty story. —CMH]

Special entry: Carroll, Pam and Melinda came from Phila for two weeks vacation. [In the 1960 Corvair, Melinda slept behind the back seat in the little cubby hole over the transmission. —CMH] Melinda beginning to talk a bit.

Lobsters 65 cents per pound, 4 cents for hake in Vinalhaven. [June 1963]

89. CAMPING TRIP TO KATAHDIN

Dr. Thomas Philip Haviland talked about a trip to climb Mt. Katahdin in Baxter State Park in 1956. He yarned about rattling his cast-iron frying pans to scare off any moose that might be nearby. He actually did meet a cow moose and her calf on the trail down.

In 1962, Pamela and I drove the little Roachwagen to Deer Isle, and I seem to remember that Bill had a new Rambler American. When George Willauer arrived for his vacation, we three decided to go up to Baxter State Park to climb the Mountain.

We assembled an assortment of camping gear and planned to camp in one of the shelters that had been built for the purpose at the edge of a tarn, Chimney Pond, a three-mile climb from the road's end, up on the side of the mountain. I don't remember much about the drive up there. But we must have been laughing about some of our other adventures, as we were in a jolly mood all the way up there and back.

We signed in at the Ranger Station and left the American in the parking lot. Then we straggled up the trail, pausing to check out Basin Pond, a large lake part of the way up, that lies close to the trail. We skinny-dipped in the lake, as we had worked up a sweat climbing up the trail. The water was refreshingly cold, and we were very shortly dressed again to continue climbing. Eventually, we arrived at the campsite and found an empty shelter, where we unloaded our equipment. We had read enough about black bears to know that they would raid our food supplies if they happened to wander into the campsite. However, our food was canned, so we merely stowed it in the shelter. We cooked our first night's supper of hamburgers and washed up the dishes, and were tired enough to drop off to sleep very quickly.

Sometime in the night George got up to use the privy that was a short hike away, and when he returned I was awakened by his disheveled form and very dark hair, thinking in my half-awake state that he was a bear. Then I was alarmed enough to shout, "Here comes a bear!"

That set George off laughing, and I was annoyed that the joke was on me! However we were all very quickly asleep again. We didn't have air mattresses, and I was young enough that I could sleep on a rock. (But quite some time later we acquired air mattresses, and I did not sleep well when the air leaked out ever so slowly during the night.) Bill and I awoke very early, and George didn't like being awakened at half-past daylight at all, at all!

Bill and I decided to climb up to the top in the fog, and we climbed up the Cathedral Trail, direct but quite a climb, where we were surprised to meet some others from downeast (Machias, I think), who had carried a partly-filled, smoked-herring box all the way to the top. They offered us some, and since we had not had breakfast, we ate a few.

There was nothing to see except a wooden signpost, and Bill and I were soon scrambling carefully down the Saddle Trail. About halfway down, the herrings were desperate for some drinking water (I remember a Coors TV ad that had two Western men refusing water from a prospector's canteen as they stomped off through the desert to find some Coors, and the two prospectors exclaiming, "They must have a powerful thirst!") We found a brook tumbling noisily down over the rocks, and we drank and drank, using our hands as drinking vessels. By the time we reentered the campsite, George was almost ready to get up. I mixed up some pancake batter, and George cooked them in our cast-iron frying pan. I seem to remember that we had difficulties finding enough dry brush and firewood to build a fire. All the dead wood within the campsite had been harvested, and we foraged wide and far to gather up enough fallen twigs and conifer boughs to make a satisfactory fire. We did succeed, and George was now ready to climb to the top. I think that the fog had cleared off by then, and we started out again, Bill and I, accompanied by George.

Of course, we could now see out over the trees, and the forest seemed endless. It was becoming a very nice day. We were becoming very warm and would have welcomed another dip in a lake. But now we were meeting other climbers, and it would not be acceptable to swim in the buff with complete strangers wandering around hither and yon. We encountered a lady who was trying to watch birds. She was not happy with our chatter! So we kept on climbing. There were several climbers at the peak, happily inquiring, "Where are you from?" One asked me, "Where is Stonington?" So I regaled her with stories about living on an island off the coast of Maine. I wondered at the time if she would ever get to see our island.

We went up to Pamola Peak and across the 1.1-mile Knife Edge to

Baxter Peak. On the way up we met "Dr. Caribou," whose companions were turning back, and he asked if he could join us. On the Knife Edge, he fell further and further behind (he was not in good shape, rather pudgy). We got to Baxter Peak and met some other people, and told them we were waiting for Dr. Caribou. He could be seen lumbering along in the distance. The reply was, "What's the doctor's specialty? My knee has been giving me trouble." The guy evidently wanted a free consult. We had to explain that "the doctor" was in fact an usher in a movie house!

90. ISLE AU HAUT CAMPING TRIP

I have been requested to relate our adventures on Isle au Haut, which lies approximately seven nautical miles south of "Stonehaven," a name I use freely for what used to be Green's Landing and is now called Stonington. Once upon a time, it was a mere granite rock projecting from the sea, where a little coastal steamer could unload some passengers who had come aboard in Rockland, which was long ago the center of commerce for almost all of downeast. There were a few houses perched upon the granite of Green's Landing monolith, and a rudimentary tote road wound around the shore, dodging between the granite erratics.

Fred Eaton's store, as told in Chapters 2 and 8, was the first in Stonehaven and sold all kinds of general merchandise: dry goods, flour, sugar and salt, coarsely ground rye and cornmeal; products of the tide mills at the Holt Pond, Torrey's Mill on the Reach, and the tide mill at the Falls at the mouth of Crockett's Cove, near the present Stonington-Deer Isle town line. Fred was the shrewd operator who bought clams from the diggers, paying them with goods "out of the store," which resulted in the story of the clam digger who called Fred "outta th'stoah" to get paid in cash. Roy Jones, who told me this story, said his great-grandfather was digging clams for bait used by the fishermen, who fished offshore for cod, haddock, and the occasional halibut.

Now that I have established the rock-solid base for "Stonehaven," I'll proceed to relate our camping-trip story at Deep Cove on Isle au Haut. We had a used Evinrude 30-horse outboard mounted on the sixteen-foot carvel-planked skiff that Alvin "Digger" Jones had built for Pam and me. We moored it on an outhaul at the tip of Cyrus's Point in Webb's Cove. We four adventurers: my bride, Pamela; George Willauer;

William Haviland (Pam's brother); and myself, loaded the boat to the gunwales with crude camping gear, two six-gallon Evinrude fuel tanks, mosquito spray, and food enough for a Boy Scout troop paddling down the Bagaduce River on an overnight trip, with George Willauer as scout troop leader. Fortunately, we were able to moor the skiff between two ledges not far from the "popplestone" (pebble-stone) beach at Deep Cove by running pot-warp lines between two trees and a third line to "Morris's Mistake." (During the Revolutionary War, Captain Morris was cruising the coast of Maine in a dense fog and found Deep Cove just a tiny bit too late! The frigate crashed onto the rocks and was destroyed. The Isle au Haut natives rescued the crew and salvaged some of the cannon and stores, but the frigate was lost.)

For all of two days, the sea was quiet enough to keep our little boat moored there while we camped in under some spruce trees. We slung a driftwood sapling nearly level between two red spruce trees and draped a tarpaulin over the ridgepole to make a small squad-type tent. The triangular ends overlapped nicely, and we laced them together on the west end with ravelings of a hunk of pot-warp. Bug spray quelled the ever-present mosquitoes, and we slept quite well all night.

The next morning, we made breakfast, discovering that we had enough "fog" (store-bought bread) for an entire Boy Scout troop! I don't remember what exactly we cooked over the beach-stone fireplace, but we were filled, as it were. After washing up, we started to hike along the rudimentary trail to Western Head. We even managed to cross to Western Ear, a tiny island that marks the southwestern limits of Acadia National Park. At that time, there were the remains of a fisherman's shack, a very small abode or bait shed. It would be a lonely outpost in any event, a difficult place to land supplies on most days, as there are no islands to break the surge of seas coming all the way from the Antarctic. (Look it up in your atlas, and convince yourselves that this is a true statement!)

Sated with the landscape, we re-crossed the narrow rocky neck and straggled along the shore to our campsite. Tourists were very thin on the ground on Isle au Haut before the Aldrich brothers started ferrying folks to Duck Harbor, where there was at one time a colonial farm. (You might want to read *The World of Carrick's Cove* by Gerald Warner Brace, who taught creative writing at Boston University. It's excellent reading.)

On the way back, we disturbed a hornets' nest, and as George was the tail end of our hikers, he got stung several times! Pam, Bill and I ran like thieves and escaped. We hiked to Long Pond and swam in the glacial tarn. The pond water was quite warm, and of course, by the time we had returned to Deep Cove, we needed another swim. However, the ocean water at that spot is very cool. The pebble-stone beach is difficult to walk on, and we didn't dive in. We made an evening meal. I seem to remember that it was not high cuisine, but we would have eaten a dogfish, we were so hungry! Again we slept like rocks on the beach.

In the morning, we made pancakes of sorts and reloaded all our camping gear for the run up to Webb's Cove. We ran east to pass between Eastern Ear and Eastern Head, where there were great cormorants; one American kestrel flew up into a pine tree that was growing close to the shore. There were many dovekies, murres and guillemots all along the shore as we threaded up through York Island Harbor, where my father spent part of his summers with his father, Freeman Charles Haskell, from 1906 to 1912, while he was growing up. Just north of York Island, we saw a solitary gannet dive like an arrow into the sea to catch a fish. As we passed Burnt Island, we saw a willet calling as it flew into the tall grasses on the eastern tip of the island. We passed west of Fog Island and up past McGlathery Island, where there is a huge glacial erratic boulder resting on the flat ledges of the tiny islet east of McGlathery; we scooted up past the west end of Devil's Island and just west of Humpkins Ledge as we zipped along, arriving in Webb's Cove, and made for the old Haskell homestead's shore at nearly high tide, where we unloaded all our camping gear and spare gas tanks; and then alone, I ran over to tie up to the outhaul again. I carried the remaining gas tank back along the shore, hopping and skipping from stone to stone. I couldn't do it now, at eighty-one years of age. I would fall onto these rocks and most likely lie there waiting to be rescued!

We carried some of the camping gear up to the Roachwagen, Dad's name for Pam's little VW beetle. But the bulky tarp and gas tanks were stored in Dick's old shop-cum-forge.

I seem to remember that we had a delicious supper with Marm and Dick, and then we scooted up the Island to the Havilands' cottage in North Deer Isle. Some time later, we had the use of Captain Montaford Haskell's house, close by the Havilands' cottage, which was down overlooking the Cat Cove shore, in North Deer Isle.

91. You Ain't a Native No More!

Captain Arthur Cabot Haskell lives in his father's old homestead on the North Deer Isle Road, very close to the Deer Isle Memorial Monument that stands in the intersection of the Quacko Road and the North Deer Isle Road. He went to sea, as many Deer Isle men did, throughout our history. He married Mabel Dow. Like most seagoing captains, he wasn't home very often, and I guess that you can figure out what that all led to. He lives alone, but when he has the cow-barn door open, he is holding court, as it were. He has many visitors, and I only visit when the doors are open and there are no cars or trucks in his driveway.

My bride's parents, Dr. Thomas P. Haviland and Annie Theodosia (Cushing) Haviland, bought Captain Montaford Haskell's house after Monty passed away, so that Bill and Anita could share it with us for vacations on the Island. We had been keeping the sixteen-foot wooden skiff at my father's house, located below Tea Hill Corner on Route 15 in Stonington. I had made a boat trailer by bolting a Model A Ford front-axle assembly to two long two-by-fours, which I forced together to form a V-shaped front end. My dad devised a trailer-hitch metal plate assembly in his forge that joined the two timbers securely and also fastened the trailer hitch to the steel plate. A driftwood timber bolted to the spruce side rails with galvanized angle irons closed the rear. The skiff nestled in-between the side rails, and I used it for years.

My cousin Melvin borrowed the trailer one day, and like all things, the right-hand tie rod end fell off and triggered the trailer, when the right wheel twisted up against the spruce side-rails. Melvin was about halfway from the boat-launching site at the head of Webb's Cove to Oceanville Corner, where the Oceanville Road meets Route 15. I don't know how Melvin got his boat back to Tea Hill, but that event was the end for that trailer.

I had junked a VW front-wheel-drive sedan in Philadelphia, and I brought the rear suspension cross-member and rear-axle assembly up to Deer Isle in the 1966 Ford Fairlane wagon. I made a new boat trailer using that rear suspension and some oak boards that Joe Judkins had sawn out for me with his sawing machine. It is an ugly trailer, but it worked well enough, and I have used it for many things.

The Galley used to be a grocery store in Deer Isle village, and there used to be a cast-iron-framed wooden bench out in front, where Captain Arthur Haskell and others would gather to pass the time of day, gossiping and telling stories. I drove into the village to mail some letters, and Captain Arthur, known as "Dud," hollered at me, "Hey, Cabbage! You ain't a native no more!"

I asked, "Why's that, Arthur?"

"Well you've been away; ya hafta be back here fifty years to be a native agin!" ignoring that he had been away at sea almost all his adult years.

Several days later, I hauled a load of brush down to the Deer Isle recycling center (read "dump"), and Dud was down there fibbing with Frankie Davis, the attendant at that time. Arthur saw me, and as I was getting ready to leave, he shouted, "Cabbage, did ya make that thing?" (indicating my crude-but-it-works trailer.)

"Why yes, Arthur, I did."

"Well, then! You're a native!" he replied, with emphasis on the last three words. Undeterred, I went back for another load.

Captain Dud is eighty-eight years old, and his health and stamina have deteriorated. But he doesn't give up. He still opens the cow-barn door to hold court, but not every nice day!

92. Christmas at the Haskell Homestead, When I Was Grown

After Pamela and I were married, we drove all the way to Deer Isle in an all-night marathon drive. It took between 12 and 14 hours, depending on how many drunken-driver crashes we encountered on the highways near and around New York City on Christmas Eve.

There was only the New Jersey Turnpike and a partial Maine Turnpike in 1957. Dwight Eisenhower's Interstate system was barely started at that time. Pam's little VW beetle got thirty-three miles to the gallon. So if we started with a full tank, we topped off on Route 1 in Kittery, Maine, and topped off again in Bucksport, so that we would have gas enough for Christmas Day and the weekend, if Christmas fell on a Saturday.

Sometimes we arrived before Christmas, if I had vacation days coming. Then the two of us went out into our own backwoods, and Pam was never happy with the local balsam firs because they were not clipped to make them grow fuller. One time we were out behind the vacant henhouse, and not one tree satisfied her. I looked up at a very tall fir and asked her, "How do ya like the top o' that one?" So I cut it down with a Swedish-type bow saw, cut the top off to a 6-foot length,

LEON'S 1949 FORD, GARLAND'S 1929 FORD; HOME FOR CHRISTMAS
C. 1954 (LEFT TO RIGHT): GARLAND, LEROY, LEON, CHARLOTTE
MILDRED (TORREY) HASKELL, AUTHOR.

and we dragged it down to the house through the deep snow. Set it up after shaking the snow out of it, and Pam declared it, "almost perfect!" We soon had lights, tinsel and grandfather's ornaments plus new ones on the tree.

Our all-time great Christmas trip to the old homestead was when we drove up in our newer 1966 Ford Fairlane station wagon. When we crested Caterpillar Hill, the road was all black ice with a thin coating of fresh powdery snow. Near the end of Route 15 there is an intersection with Route 172. It is a dead-end intersection, and there was a granite pillar right in the middle of Route 15. As I crested the little hill south of Caterpillar Hill, the Ford was barely creeping along. When we got onto the south side of the hill the thin powder on the black ice sent the Ford sliding downhill, picking up speed as she slid along. I kept tapping the brakes, trying to slow the car and maintain the middle of the crowned road. As we approached the granite pillar, I had to move off the crown to avoid a crash. The Ford slid right across Route 172 into a deep snow pile pushed up by the snowplow. The wagon stopped quite abruptly! My brother Wink hollered, "You better hop out to see if the radiator hoses didn't pop off. I ripped the hood open, and with a flashlight I could see that all was intact. I had to get out of there quite quickly because the local snowplow was coming along. I put the shift lever into reverse and the Ford backed right out without spinning the rear wheels! I swung 'er around to the right as I backed, and the snowplow swept past with a toot toot de toot! on the horn.

The grand finale was when we captured six balsam firs from Aunt Ruth's swamp. She was always trying to put something over on us, and it gave us great pleasure to put one over on her. We lashed the trees onto the roof-rack rails of the Ford and had no trouble until we crossed the George Washington Bridge, with its crosswinds baffling about, and the trees threatened to fly off, tethers and all. I grabbed one tree with my hand out the driver's window, and Wink captured the other. By holding onto the outside tree on my side with my arm out the driver's door window, and Wink did the same on his side, we managed to get them all back to Philly intact.

After our parents passed away, Marm in April, 1986, and Dad in November, 1990, there was no reason to drive to Deer Isle for Christmas anymore, and we celebrate here with our three children and seven grandchildren. Merry Christmas to you all.

93. CAMPING ADVENTURES

When we were married, in Philadelphia's First Unitarian Church on Chestnut Street in 1957, Pam had the Volkswagen Beetle, and I still had the Sunbeam Talbot 90 sedan. I was just beginning a lifetime job with the Bell Telephone Company of Pennsylvania as a splicer's helper. There were several of us helpers sprinkled around the North Philadelphia garages. There was a small Bell garage on Clearfield Street in Kensington. I rode the trolleys down Germantown Avenue to Allegheny Avenue and rode that line to Clearfield Street; then I walked down to the garage.

One week we decided to go camping on Long Island. Pam's brother Bill and his friend John Watt went along. There were four of us and a Dalmatian dog jammed into the little bug. Somehow, we navigated to the Staten Island ferry, which set us ashore on Long Island. The ferry trip is a great weekend trip anytime, as the large ferries churn along at a good clip, and one can see the marine traffic in New York's harbor. There is marine traffic through Hell's Gate Narrows to Long Island Sound, and there is marine traffic up and down the Hudson. We debarked up the ferry ramp and headed out to Montauk.

Just about then the "damnation" dog got sick and messed up the back seat with dog dew. What a mess! Then Pam spied a public drinking fountain, and I quickly pulled the Roachwagen off the parkway, and we removed the front passenger seat and the rear seat cushion. With some rags from the front luggage compartment, we washed down the rear seat cushion, which was upholstered with a durable plastic fabric in the early VWs. The dog dew had run down into our L.L.Bean stainless-steel pots-and-pans camping gear. We just had to wash them out right then and there. Fortunately the foul liquid had not run onto the battery, which resides under the rear seat in the early VW Beetles. We had to load the rear seat in through the starboard door opening and reinstall the front passenger seat in that order, but we quickly resumed our trip eastward, with both vent windows wide open, and the larger door windows all the way down, and eventually arrived at Hither Hills State Park, which consisted of a forest of low scrub pines, acres and acres of sand, and a magnificent, miles-long sand beach.

At that time there were no houses or buildings the entire length of the beach from East Hampton to the Montauk Hills (which were scrub pine and poison-ivy-clad sand dunes). My brother Wink had a service station in Montauk Village, and he found some heavy-duty canvas that we used as a tent. Montauk Point has mosquitoes, and the "damnation" wandered in and out of the makeshift tent all night long, taking the mosquito netting along with him. It rained in the night, and the camping was deteriorating to a soggy horror story.

In the morning, we tried to get some scrub pine deadwood to burn, with no success. However, desperation was the mother of invention. The early VW Beetles had huge gas-tank filler caps, and I stuffed a rag down into the gasoline, pulled it out all dripping, and shoved the rag in under the wet pine branches. We flicked lighted wooden matches into the makeshift fireplace until the gasoline-soaked rag caught on fire with a whoosh! Aha! Instant heat! Once lit, the scrub pine burned rapidly, and we soon had some hot coals ready to cook our breakfast.

John dropped the butter into the sand, and he became instantly known as "John-whatnot." I don't remember that we went in swimming, but we surely must have waded in the Atlantic. We returned to the Germantown section of Philly, and John went on to become a psychiatrist and is newly retired. We never went camping with a dog again, but we did have camping adventures with our three children, and it almost always rained.

The next most memorable camping adventure was sometime after we had bought a brand-new 1966 Ford Fairlane station wagon. We drove down the Delmarva Peninsula, crossed the Chesapeake on the brand-new bridge-tunnel complex, and eventually camped on the beach camping grounds near Nags Head. By then we had a large tent and sleeping bags, but not air mattresses. As nighttime approached, flash lightning was fluttering all around, mostly out over the Atlantic, but the wind increased as the rain arrived. Our unlit gas lantern was dancing on its cotton support line, and as the wind increased the tent threatened to fly off into the ocean. We decided to try to get into the Ford, and just as I tried to open the tailgate I was struck by lightning, which knocked me down. Pam was horrified, as she was standing in the tent opening, thinking that I had been electrocuted! Fortunately, most of the electrical charge followed the water on my skin down into the ground, and I arose like Lazarus and managed to get everyone inside the Ford. We left the tent and its contents to its fate. At that terrifying moment I didn't care a whit if it crossed the Atlantic, airborne.

Sometime later, the moon came out and shined in my face over the edge of the wagon's steel roof. So I got everyone awake, and we folded the soaking-wet tent and stuffed it all higgledy-piggledy into the canvas-covered roof rack, poles and all, quickly checked the campsite for valuables, and set out at once for Philly. Somewhere along our northward route in eastern Virginia, we spied a restaurant that was just opening up for the day. We all piled in there looking something like drowned rats and ordered a very satisfying breakfast. The sausage patties and eggs were just coming onto our table, when the also wet and disheveled campsite crowd arrived en masse. A Cadillac load of New Yorkers came in and were complaining about the sausage patties when we were leaving. "Oh! Good on 'em," as the Aussies say (this time with sarcasm). That little trip pretty well satisfied any yearning for the wide-open spaces and camping for quite some time.

But there's always one more camping story. Barbara (Brace) Gottschalk Seeley and her second husband, Ralph Seely, decided to invite us along on a camping trip to the Ripogenus Dam site in the Maine woods. Ralph drove up I-95, and somewhere along the superhighway I saw a black bear come running out of the woods; its fur was very shiny in the sunlight. The bear seemed to be young and very sleek. I shouted, "Look! There's a bear!" The creature bolted into the woods as soon as it heard or saw the car.

After we signed into the paper company's log book at the entrance gate, we soon encountered huge truckloads of limbed-up trees coming down the wood roads at great speed. I suppose they were loaded onto rail cars, but we never saw what exactly happened to the tree-length logs.

At the campsite overlooking the West Branch of the Penobscot River, we spent some time watching outdoors folks rafting down the rapids. There seemed to be little control of the huge rubber rafts; they spun around and went down over the falls every which way, the crews laughing and shouting heartily. It was a nice, warm, sunny day. We sat on the smooth, black rocks amongst the huckleberry and serviceberry bushes overlooking the river and enjoyed the show. At the base of the rapids falls, there is a sheer-walled black stone passage, where the river becomes very quiet, with little currents boiling up from the activity of the water rushing down through the falls. At that point, the waters look deep and dark.

I was camp cook! I made a stir-fry for our evening meal. I had chopped all the ingredients beforehand. And I had made, in our early camping days, a nice little wanigan, which held our portable kitchen, plastic dishes, and stainless-steel tableware; the safety-latched lid dropped down to become the kitchen countertop. Our L.L.Bean portable stainless pots and pans worked well over the campground's cast-iron fire grate, which spanned the stonework fireplace. The steak stir-fry was excellent, but I think we were so hungry that we would have even enjoyed very bitter dandelion greens.

Pam and I set up our little tent, and Ralph and Barbara were off a ways. But Ralph snored so loudly that I couldn't sleep a wink. All the way back down I-95, I kept falling asleep in the midsized Chevy wagon. I was never before so glad to return to my bed.

94. ITEMS FROM THE NINETEEN-SEVENTIES

I was working in Bell of Pennsylvania's engineering department in Center City, Philadelphia, and would remain in engineering until I retired on December 15th, 1991. Vince O'Hearn, an Irish Catholic, took me under his wing and taught me some things about getting telephone service to the floors of downtown's high-rise buildings. The installation and repair foremen always wanted new house cable and terminals wherever a new business and/or department set up housekeeping. Sometimes I was able to shift some wires around in the huge house cable terminals and get service where it was needed, without placing new facilities, thanks to Vince. Unfortunately, he had a heart attack and died while working in his vegetable garden in New Jersey, and from that time on, I was on my own.

He took great pleasure in calling me "the farmer." I guess that he had no idea of what life was like on an island off the coast of Maine. At that time, Northern Ireland was in a vicious religious war, and Vince made no bones about where his sentiments were.

About 1976, I was transferred to the Oxford Avenue engineering office and rode SEPTA transportation trolleys down Wayne Avenue to Chelten Avenue, where I caught the H bus to Overington Avenue, which dropped me off a mere block from the office. The engineers had to share company cars, which were at that time 1969 Plymouth Valiants and one Chevy Nova V8, a gas-guzzling beast. It used a quarter of a tank of gas driving to the farthest central office and returning. There was one six-cylinder Ford Maverick, which was used by the rights-of-way agent, Gino Weber. These cars were all housed in a row of wooden garages a short walk from the Bell Telephone business center on Oxford Avenue.

Once in a while, the SEPTA buses could not operate in deep snow, and we had to hoof it from wherever the bus got stuck and could not move. Several of us plowed along in company, laughing at our problems and/or grousing about someone who was an obstructionist in the office. Therefore, I met A. Eugene "Gino" Weber, and we have been friends ever since.

Eventually, there was an opening in Rights-of-Way in Germantown, and my boss at that time wanted me to put my name in for it. After talking it over with Pam, I put my name in the hat; several others really wanted that position, but I was leery of working with the public. I was really surprised to walk in one morning, quite soon after that, to be told to report to Domino Lane in the Roxboro section of Philadelphia. I was to replace Robert Motson, who was retiring. Bob taught me some of the methods of securing rights-of–way. One of my engineering bosses had always maintained that I would be "handicapped working with the public because of my heavy downeast accent!" However, in Chestnut Hill, it was an asset. I was frequently asked, "What part of Maine do you come from?" And sometimes I would be asked if I knew so and so, "who lived in Southwest Habbah?" (twenty-five miles east of Stonington by water, further by the mainland routes). Once I was invited to visit a family who had a summer home on Vinalhaven, about seventeen miles west of Stonington by water. (It was an eighty-mile drive just to get to the ferry that served Vinalhaven, starting from Stonington.)

We still had the 1966 Ford Fairlane 500 station wagon, and it had almost a hundred thousand miles on the odometer. We were driving all night—very close to six hundred miles—from West Mt. Airy to North

Deer Isle in ten to twelve hours. We planned to build the Ward's log cabin kit on the aforementioned concrete foundation down on the high banking of Bow Cat Cove, overlooking Carney's Island. The Ward's Cabin Kit was delivered in a large trailer by a driver who simply sat and ate his lunch while Almond "Zeke" Eaton, Herb Carter and his son helped my dad and me unload the contents directly onto the ground on July 4th, 1969. Dick started building the cabin right away, with Pam locating the code-numbered logs and her brother Bill and Dick doing the heavy lifting. I had to fly back to Philadelphia to help other management personnel on strike duty. The day that the strike was over, I caught an airport limousine in front of the Franklin Hotel, and I was in Bangor being picked up by Pam accompanied by our three children. My brother had flown up from Allen, Texas (just twenty-eight miles north of Dallas). He had brought his adopted son Carl along, so that he would have an idea of what Maine was like, compared to the flatness of Texas in the Dallas area.

We sheathed the log-cabin roof with plywood panels, and I caulked the seams, so that we could work inside on rainy days. Garland, Betty, and Carl flew back to Texas, and Dick and I shingled the roof. We finished the roof's edge-trim boards and started working on the inside partitions and had to quit when my vacation time ran out.

95. EVENTS OF THE NINETEEN-EIGHTIES

We continued to vacation on Deer Isle at the Cabbage Patch. The Ward's log-cabin basement still had a sand floor. Sometime in the '70s we had Budget Eaton's son dig a trench to bury the electric service wires and telephone wires from Charlie Bartlett's driveway and electric pole to our basement. He and his wife, Anita (Torrey) Bartlett, granted me the rights-of-way for a bottle of gin for Anita and a large live lobster for Charlie.

It was sometime in the 1980s that Minerva Young decided that we could not use Grover Small's short tote road from the Haviland's right-of-way driveway through Grover's stone wall and short driveway to our log cabin. So Budget and his son built us a new driveway that exactly paralleled the Haviland right-of-way driveway that was grandfathered. Pam's brother Bill and I massacred all the small trees along that route! Budget and his son tore most of the stumps out of the ground to put in a coarse gravel roadbed, which has held up very nicely. Eddy Nevells, who worked on John L. Goss with me, needled me, "She got ya real good,

Cabbage!" He was pleased with himself at my discomfort! However, Eddie and I were good friends all his life, from our first meeting in the stone quarry days.

Eventually, we had a concrete floor poured into the log cabin's basement by the Reverend Cormier and his stalwart church-member crew. One was Nilo, an older man who was born in Finland. He was a character, and his precise English led us to believe that he had more than a high-school education. But he would never tell us anything about his past. He lived in a house that sat in some woods off the road to Ellsworth. He had several cats. The peak of the roof was just visible from the highway as we passed by from time to time.

Pam and I drove the Ford to Deer Isle on all-night marathon drives, and I stayed a week, then flew back to Philly on Northeast Airlines, which was always an adventure while they had radial piston engines. The airfare was $49, and we landed in Boston but did not get off the plane if we were continuing to Philly. I lived all by myself for the summer and flew back to Bangor when it was time to come back and get the children into school. The trip back to Philly was always in the daytime, as I had to shut down the cabin's plumbing. I engineered it so that all the drains were in the basement, making it easy to shut the cabin down in an hour! We began to stop overnight in Southington, Connecticut, as traffic built up over the daytime trip, and we always hit I-84 during the early rush hours. We got back on the road early in the following morning and were back in West Mt. Airy by noontime. With one day to rest up before returning to work.

My brother Garland flew up from Texas with his new bride, Betty, and they stayed in the Bridge End Motel every year until Betty's health went into decline.

In 1989, Melinda and Edward Adams were married on July 8th on the lawn at the Cabbage Patch cabin. Brian Kopke flew down from Canada to perform the ceremony. Ed's sister and her husband flew in from Phoenix, Arizona. Ed's brother Frank drove up from Pennsylvania with his bride and Katelyn and their daughter. Ed's other brother flew in from California.

On the 17th of September Jennifer married Daniel Perry at a Synagogue in the 600 block of Broad Street, Philadelphia, and later we bought a leftover Ford Taurus station wagon. Actually, it turned out to be a rental car, and it had been abused. It used oil from the get-go. Parts failed all the while we had it. We traded it on a 1995 leftover Taurus sedan, which was even worse! We traded that bomb on a used '95 Audi V6 wagon, which has been a very nice car!

96. JOE JUDKINS:
A LOCAL MECHANICAL GENIUS

I don't know when Joe was born, but he bought a World War I surplus Curtis Jenny and established a record number of forced landings bringing the Flying Jenny home from Bangor to Stonington after the Great War. Joe equipped the Curtis JN4 with wooden floats, and he flew it out of Holt Pond, a tidal estuary at the Stonington-Deer Isle town line.

Of course, by the time I was driving around the island in my 1929 Nash Ambassador Advanced Six long-wheel-based sedan, the ancient airplane had fallen apart, and local children living in the southeast section of the island were using the old laminated wooden floats as a diving platform as they swam in Holt Pond.

There were many stories about Joe Judkins that I will not repeat, but my personal experiences with Joe begin with the sad discovery that our huge red-oak tree, that had been growing just south of our Ward's Log Cabin, was dying due to so many roots being cut off by the bulldozer's scoop. Dick came up and engineered the felling of the old monster. I climbed up and sawed a huge branch off with the large Lombard chainsaw that my brother Wink had sent up from Montauk, New York, where he still worked for Duryea. After the branch came crashing down, I tied a heavy-duty manila line to the red oak with a clove hitch and a half hitch on top of that; then we put the line through a snatch block that we rigged with a manila sling to a large white-ash tree down toward the beach. We then fastened the line to our '66 Ford Fairlane station wagon with an anchor hitch, so that we could untie it again after taking a strain on the line. Dick cut a kerf in the big oak and then proceeded to make the felling cut from the backside, away from the kerf. I kept a strain on the line. The left rear wheel turned a bit but grabbed on again, and after a while the big tree began to topple, as I goosed the throttle to hasten the fall. Down it went, within inches of the snatch block.

Budget came down and loaded the three sections of the red oak onto his dump truck and carted them off to Joe Judkins's sawmill in "Southeast." Dick and I drove down to see Joe Judkins, as Joe owed Dick a few favors. Dick had helped Joe set up his mill quite some time before. Joe had trouble getting the big Buda diesel marine engine to start. Dick worked on the fuel injection system and retimed the injection pump to the best operating setting. Joe had utilized an old steam boiler to act as a coolant radiator. He finally buried the boiler in his sawdust pile. This kept the coolant warm overnight. Joe simply warmed up the Buda's water jackets by turning on an auxiliary electric water pump, and the Buda fired right up on frosty mornings.

However, at the time I wanted to have the old tree sawed into two-inch planks to make a fog deck for the Ward's cabin. He had found a used four-cylinder Hill diesel, which didn't have enough torque to wag the large circular saw blade through the red oak rapidly. Pam's brother Bill and I took my homemade boat trailer down to Joe's peckerwood sawmill. Bill helped Joe set up the logs on the saw frame, and I took the sawn planks off the out-feed end and loaded them onto the boat trailer. Of course, we had too many planks for the little homemade trailer and had to stack the planks and three-quarter-inch boards for a second and third load. Dick wanted the slabs for firewood, so I made another trip to accomplish that little errand.

The fog deck was erected using salvaged timbers found on George's Head Island off of Stonington. We were towing three logs to Webb's Cove when we were overhauled by the local game warden, Ralph Pinkham, and another younger warden, who checked our papers and saw that we had not been hauling someone's lobster traps. Hey! I have enough troubles without looking for whatever that offense would entail. Just about then we drifted into a pot-warp and head buoy of a local fisherman's trap. Even Ralph helped us unsnarl that mess. Once free of that entanglement, we towed to the head of Webb's Cove and snaked the three slender logs onto the trailer. I worked the wooden skiff down the creek with the stout ash oars to deeper water and ran back to Cyrus's Point with the Evinrude 30-horse outboard, where we kept the skiff on Dick's homemade outhaul.

I climbed up through the woods on Ralph Knowlton's tote road, and Bill picked me up. We reloaded the boat trailer onto the '66 Fairlane wagon and proceeded to North Deer Isle and the Cabbage Patch cabin, where we sawed the logs to suitable lengths with a handsaw. Dad kept my saws in good shape, working in his little saw-sharpening shop that stands unused today, August 2009.

But we were not through with Joe Judkins's help yet! Bill had a project that required some sawing by Joe and his peckerwood mill. I don't remember how we got the logs to Joe's loading frame, but I remember the actual sawing operation very well. Somehow the fuel injectors had leaked back to the fuel tank, and we had to prime the system. This took a bit of time, as we had to open the bleeder valves for each injector and activate the hand pump until the lines and injectors had fuel weeping out. Once the fuel system was primed, the Hill diesel started right up using two batteries to wag the engine over fast enough to get compression heat in the cylinders. It started up with a belch of blue-black diesel smoke, and the exhaust pipe promptly fell off. Bill held the pieces together while Joe set up the logs, and Bill had to keep changing leather gloved hands because the exhaust began to get very warm!

We completed the sawing operation, and Bill wanted the boards planed. This is where Joe's ingenuity showed up very well. His salvaged industrial planer had been belt-driven in the shop where Joe had found and bought it. However, Joe didn't have the means to re-create the original setup. He backed a beat-up 1949 vintage Chevrolet sedan up into his mill, fastened it in place, and welded an extension onto the Chevy's driveshaft to power the industrial planer. As our son Nathan would say, "It's crude, but it works!" Joe showed Bill how to get the Chevy started, and by using the hand throttle knob, he kept the Chevy running at a steady indicated thirty miles per hour on the speedometer in high gear, which kept the planer blades whirling at the best cutting speed. Joe fed the boards through the planer, and I took them off and stacked them onto the old boat trailer. The rest was easy; we hooked the trailer to the Fairlane wagon and lashed everything down securely with salvaged pot-warp. "It's always handy to have a length of pot-warp in the car! You never know when ya might have to tow someone outta th' ditch in a snowstorm, for instance!" The trip up the island was uneventful, almost serene. But every once in a while we still love to laugh and retell the Joe Judkins sawmill story, especially Bill doing the hand-dancing act holding the exhaust system together.

97. EXPIRATION DATES, AND REV. FRANCIS CORMIER'S WORK CREW

I used to keep rough notes in my daily journals, but I have no expiration date on my neck—not like plastic milk bottles. Therefore, I do not know when I must cross the Styx. I'm sure that the crossing will be close enough to Hell for me to feel the heat! But on the other hand, would any of you want to be in heaven with Richard Nixon flashing his sickly "V for victory" hand signs? And "Spiral" Agnew with his alliterations?

Give me the brimstone; at least it's honest heat! So my memory of the exact date of the following story is sometime after erecting the Ward's log cabin, that began in 1968.

These projects, built on time payments and short summer vacations, run on and on until our personal expiration dates! I had discovered that Maine contractors and builders can work on indefinite schedules that are determined by the phases of the moon, weather cycles, and immediate needs for income. None of these things are acceptable to "people from away." They expect to see their project completed and in move-in condition on the very first day that they arrive from the Hades of Philadelphia's first summer heat wave, for instance.

I discovered that the Reverend Francis Cormier would complete a task, chore, or project on a given date, for a price! Something that had not occurred to the native contractors yet. So I'm not sure of the exact date when Pam and I decided to have a well dug up in Grover Small's previous shallow hand-dug well site. Which was uphill from the Ward's log cabin erected in 1970, on a concrete foundation that was poured by a Bucksport contractor in 1969. However, we decided to have Reverend Francis Cormier dig the well hole there and install, or erect, if you will, three sections of precast concrete rings to make a useful well. That project was successful, and I engineered a siphon that provided water under atmospheric pressure to the cabin. Further experimentation revealed that the water heater could be moved to the basement, and there would be plenty of water pressure from the faucets and water closet. Some fifteen years after we had a roof and plumbing at the cabin, we decided to try to get the Reverend to pour a concrete floor in the cabin's basement.

With his collection of laborers, skilled and unskilled, we contacted the Reverend to have him and his crew construct, make or pour a concrete floor in our cabin's basement, as mentioned above. There were problems! The floor finishing machine would not slide down into the basement through the hatch that had been planned to be the foundation for a fireplace chimney, which was changed when we liked the view through what was supposed to be a temporary window. That's when my father's skill with granite workings came to the rescue, and I drilled a series of plug drill holes by hand with plug drills sharpened by my father in his Tea Hill forge. With a set of half-rounds and wedges (quoins), we broke the concrete foundation into two roughly parallel sloping sides to make a hatch opening wide enough to slip the polishing machine down onto the proposed floor. One of Reginal Greenlaw's sons brought a load or two of rough crushed stone, and we made a driftwood ramp, as he was afraid that his dump truck would sink, really sink, into the lawn. Eventually, the Reverend's crew had smoothed out the stones, and a concrete delivery truck arrived and backed laboriously down to the building site, and the laborers proceeded to arrange chutes. Then the concrete began to flow down into the basement.

One of the laborers was the Finnish man who answered to the name of Nilo. We could not entice him to talk about his past. But we determined that he lived almost directly opposite Wendall Davis' cousin's faded, red-painted house. This same cousin owning the extensive sand and gravel pit that lies just south of the recycle center on Route 172, northeast of Blue Hill village. Nilo was an interesting character, who drove an ancient Chevrolet pickup truck, which was so reliable that Nilo carried a lifeboat of sorts, a girl's bicycle equipped with balloon tires, in case he had to abandon ship and ride off for help. He carried a cargo of salvaged items that might be useful in case one or even two of his salvaged junkyard tires failed. They also had no expiration date imprinted in the sidewalls.

98. COLONIAL STONEWORKS WERE CALLED "PAVING MOTIONS"

When I was a lad, there were very few automobiles driving about on our remote gravel-surfaced roads. Our house sat upon a granite ledge with a view out over the Deer Isle Thoroughfare to the islands beyond, and behind the house to the north there stood the landlord's house sitting higher upon its granite outcrop, and higher still there was an extensive forest of mixed softwood trees: balsam fir, red spruce, white spruce, and white and gray birches were sort of sprinkled in. There was and still is an old cart-way which ran up past Cap'n Al Shepard's house through the spruce forest to two small stone quarries that had been abandoned years and years ago. These were called "paving motions" in the colonial period. An entire family might have been engaged in quarrying the granite and breaking it into paving blocks.

Holes were drilled in straight lines, which were "traced" with a sharp chisel and a heavy hammer, to help the stone break along these chiseled lines. I have been told by old-timers that oak wedges were inserted into the holes, and before there were inexpensive steel quoins, water was poured into the holes around the wooden wedges, which expanded enough to split the stones. When the winter temperatures were in the low ten- and twenty-degree range, the water froze hard enough to split the stones. It must have taken a very long time to quarry and work out enough paving blocks to make up a cargo.

Then all the good blocks were carted to a loading area, which could be as crude as a granite ledge at the edge of a quiet cove, where the shallow-draft stone sloops and pinkies could ground out without damaging their hulls. Once the stone was loaded, and supplies for a trip to Boston or New York were laid aboard, several of the family's menfolk would cast off on the rising tide and work their way slowly out into the channels, possibly being towed by two of the family's sons or relatives rowing a smaller boat, to a passage between the islands. The sails would be hoisted and the tow line cast off or taken aboard; then the little ship would tack back and forth, if the wind was out of the southwest, as it usually was; the laden ship would be making its way slowly toward Boston or New York. If they were lucky and caught a southeaster, its winds would push the heavily-loaded craft along quite nicely. If the wind stayed southeast or even better, northeast, and there wasn't a storm accompanying it, the crew might sail all night, as winds out of the east were unusual along the Maine coast.

It's about three hundred miles from Deer Isle to Boston, so it would take at least three days of sailing round the clock to reach Boston's harbor, but a southeaster would most likely blow out in two days, and then the wind should come around from the southwest, and the sloop would have to tack in order to make any headway toward port. Once the little ship had cleared the offshore islands, it might work offshore to a point where it could run into Boston on a long reach. But if they were lucky, there would be a strong northeaster, and they would then have a fair wind into Boston's docks.

Usually, the cargo was sold for a letter of credit or bartered for items that were hard to come by on the coastal islands. Currency of gold and silver coins was very scarce in the Colonies. The return trip would be started directly after a storm had blown itself out. I can imagine starting in a fresh northwester and the lightly-loaded sloop surging along under reefed sails and possibly one jib, heeling over with the rails just clear of the water. The winds were most predictably reliable from the southwest day after day when sailing downeast.

Imagine the trading that went on when the little sloop or pinky reentered Deer Isle's Northwest Harbor or Green's Landing or Webb's

Cove: both the latter were on the south end of Deer Isle. There is a well-defined paving motion quarry's remains visible to this day in Webb's Cove. The little ship might be loaded with animals, sheep, a cow or two, textiles from England, iron and steel tools, cast-iron pots and cauldrons, copper kettles, furniture made in Boston, and other items that could not be grown or manufactured on the island.

On one of our marine picnics, sometime after 1989, we went to Brimstone Island, and while exploring the ledges that comprise Little Brimstone Island, we found some paving blocks that were obviously very old, so we salvaged all that could be found lying about hither and yon on the wave-polished "popplestone" beach. At a much later date, we were outlining Pam's flower garden with these paving stones and wished that we had more, so we thought that possibly there might still be some on Little Brimstone Island. Pam's brother, Bill, volunteered to make a day-trip to Brimstone, and we towed Bill's new aluminum skiff behind to use as a tender and to ferry any stones that might be found, out to Bill's lobster yacht, the *Cormorant*.

Our son-in-law Edward Adams, Theodore Haviland, Bill and I made up the work party. Upon beaching the skiff, we searched the beach and found one or two stones; it happened to be the low-water slack period, and deep in the water we found many more paving blocks, and we waded in and lifted them up, piled them on the beach at a place that was accessible for loading into the skiff. Ted was the skiff pilot, and we loaded eight stones for each trip out to the *Cormorant*, that was anchored in safer and deeper water. Sometimes the sea would surge into the area and carry the skiff way up the beach, stones and all. We were forced to hold the boat as steady as possible while standing hip-deep in the very cold water; eventually we had loaded most of the paving blocks and promptly set out for North Deer Isle, towing the skiff, which was loaded with eight more pavers, for a total of thirty-two. It was such a beautiful day that Bill ran over to Saddleback Light before making his course slowly through the gap at Dunham's point and on to Bowcat Cove.

I suppose that one of the small homemade paving-motion sloops had run aground or had hit the Little Brimstone ledges in a storm, possibly in foggy conditions, losing the ship and cargo and possibly their lives, as Brimstone Island is not a hospitable place, even if they were fortunate enough to reach its steep southeast beach. There may have been a driftwood shack erected there for castaways, but with only a driftwood fire, if they could make one with a flint and steel striker, it would have been extremely uncomfortable, especially in the winter. In any event, we were happy to salvage as much of the long-lost cargo as we could safely carry. Upon reaching Bill's homemade dock, we decided to drop me off, so that I could take the Rustoleum Roachwagen (a Rabbit diesel) up to the Little Deer Isle bar, and we could transfer the blocks directly to my little sedan and carry them back to the garden area, ten or twelve blocks at a time. Ed climbed overboard, and he and I waded thigh-deep, carrying two stones at a time to load the car, while Bill kept the lobster yacht from grounding out. Eventually, we had all the booty unloaded at the garden area. Ed rode up the hill, wringing wet, perched on top of the last load consisting of ten blocks. Bill returned the *Cormorant* to the mooring, and once the tin skiff was pulled out on the outhaul, we called it a day!

99. CRUISES AND TREKS IN 2006

We had Promised Walter Gottschalk a trip to Babbidge's Island. We had a weather report that September 2nd, 2006, was to be a very nice day for a boat trip. I filled up three Evinrude six-gallon tanks with gasoline and a pint of Evinrude outboard oil in each tank. We rowed over and got the Aquasport off her mooring and tied her up to our makeshift dock, leaving Dick's ancient peapod on the mooring in the lee of Carney's island. We proceeded to load Pam's tiny 2.5-horse Yamaha outboard (just in case the big Johnson failed; we could at least get home with that). We loaded the three tanks of gas and safety equipment and were shortly under way running down past Heart Island and through the gap between the ledge off Dunham's Point and the point itself. We pounded across the rips north of the next island south and shaped a course for the east end of Babbidge's Island.

The beach that we wanted to land on was occupied by tourists, so we ran east a bit and landed on a cup-shaped beach and had trouble getting the Aquasport nineteen-and-a-half-footer to push off, as the wind immediately spun her around. Finally we thought that she was far enough off, and I tripped the killick stone to anchor her. Thinking we had time to cross to the south beach, Walter and I hacked a path through the fallen dead spruce trees, and after a while got onto a beach much further east than ever before; there were hundreds of nickels lying around as refunds on returnable bottles and cans.

Eventually we had to return, but the path that we had used for years was blocked by recent blow-downs. We crawled under and climbed over them to reach the old menhaden factory dock and walked as fast as we could to get back to the boat. Much too late! The Aquasport was high and dry. Pam couldn't push it off alone, and we had to wait till way after sunset for the tide to return. Eventually, Walter and I together moved her an inch, then another inch. We kept pushing on each surge of the sea. At last, we got her to swivel off, and we reloaded the gas tanks. I poled her off as Walter clambered onboard over the bow, and the big Johnson fired right up. I put her in reverse too early, and she stalled. I lifted off the engine cover and Walter cranked while I fiddled with the choke. Eventually, it fired up again, and we let it rumble, cough and sneeze a bit, pushed her into forward, and she gargled and spit but held onto the revs.

Walter steered, and we ran up "Lake Penobscot" in as dark a time as I want ever to do by myself. Walter is out there in all kinds of weather, alone in his fiberglass Pixel, so he was more familiar with the western Bay than I will ever be; besides, he could see! After a while, we banged over a pot buoy, kerthump, and continued at 5,000 rpms. Of all the hundreds of pot buoys in Eastern Penobscot Bay we found only that one in our run up past Eagle Island Light—which was a most welcome and comforting sight about five hundred yards off our port side! Somewhere about abreast of Dunham's Point, the throttle or ignition began to produce a wobble in the revolutions, as it did when Nathan was running the boat. Walter kept the speed as even as he could, but it would race up to maximum, then he would ease it off a bit but couldn't find the 5000 rpm setting. We got north of Dunham's Point, and Walter kept her far enough west to be clear of the ledges, then joggled east to clear the half-tide ledge north of Heart Island.

Bill Haviland had left their outside porch light on, and we ran up past the *Cormorant* (his lobster yacht) till we could see right into the porch. Then we ran down the reflection in the water till we could make out the white peapod (Bill's). Then I could see the dock in the light from the porch, and Walter put her in there as nice as can be. I secured a bowline and swung her around with an oar, so that she was facing out again. The Aquasport was then secured with a stem line and spring line, and we got Pam ashore onto the squared-log parts of our homemade dock.

I set out immediately to get some flashlights, and after I had climbed up the steep staircase from the beach, I stumbled over through the woods in the darkness and nearly poked myself in the eye on a dead skunk-spruce limb; I was way off the path.

Eventually, I found and climbed the fog deck stairs to open the cabin's porch door by feel. I fumbled around in the dark and found the lighted ceiling-fan switch, and with the unlighted switch I turned on the lights! I grabbed up all three flashlights, and with these we got Pam safely over to the stairs, and equipped with one flashlight she climbed up and straggled over to the cabin. Walter hauled in Bill's peapod, and I bent a bowline on the bight after taking a loop of line through the mooring eye. I turned the bight end loop back through the eye and wormed it over the horns of the bow fitting. Walter and I pulled the boats out as far as they would go and then backed the pod off about a yard, secured the outhaul lines, and we climbed up the stairs. We left all the clobber on board, including the baby Yamaha, locked into the cuddy. I would deal with that later in the morning. And, just maybe, I could get the Aquasport hauled out the very next day by Travis Eaton.

In 2007, we never got a boat trip in the Aquasport. Our boating adventures were limited to the ancient (over one hundred years old) peapod, powered with Pam's tiny Yamaha 2.5-horse outboard. We ran over to nearby Pickering Island and sailed back. The wind always picks up in the afternoons, and Pam wasn't comfortable with the rail just clearing the water, as the little boat heeled over. It took just thirty minutes to run out to the Island and thirty-eight to return. Landing on the lee shore is always adventuresome. The wind pushed the peapod against us, and we both ended up in the water. However, we weren't hurt or in danger, and after we had unloaded the Yamaha and all the picnic items, Pam climbed the staircase from the beach, while I attended to mooring the peapod and carrying stuff up the steep stairway. There is a rest area at the top of the first flight of steps, where I was glad to rest for a while. Then I loaded all the stuff into our tin wheelbarrow and pushed it over to the boat shed.

Pam was unhappy with expensive attempts to restore the big Johnson to service, and for my birthday in 2007 she bought a used Ebbtide eighteen-and-a-half-foot fiberglass boat with a 140-horse Johnson V4 with power tilt and oil injection. The boat was in Ambler, Pennsylvania. The original plan was to have a Deer Isle lobster fisherman's family tow the boat to Deer Isle with their big SUV. They had planned to drive down to visit our daughter's family near Christmastime. However, the SUV was out of commission due to a crash. Bill Schoettle, one of my fellow Bell retirees, volunteered to tow the boat to the island if we could do it on the Presidents Day holiday weekend. We made the trip in fourteen hours door-to-door. When we drove down to Pam's brother's new house, Anita and Bill Haviland had supper all ready for us! The weather had been beautifully clear, and the price of gasoline had kept weekend traffic very light.

We awoke in the morning, and it was still beautiful weather, so we went sightseeing, took some photos of Bill and his little Nissan pickup truck and the frozen surface of Northwest Harbor of Deer Isle village. I could see storm clouds coming up from the southwest, and by nightfall it was very overcast and threatening. We four discussed departure plans, and Anita suggested that we wait until daylight to see if we would have rain, freezing rain, sleet and hail, or just snow.

After breakfast, we loaded up, said our thank-yous for the hospitality, and trundled out their very long, ice-coated driveway through the Reach woods to the Reach Road and made our way north to Interstate 95 southbound in a steady rain. It rained all day, and we returned in thirteen hours door-to-door.

100. Adventures With the Gnu Nessie

We flew up to Bangor late in May, and Walter picked us up, stowed our luggage, and we scooted over to the Bangor Mall for jamocha shakes and curly fries. Walt had something different, and we settled down for a "li'l talkathon." I showed Walt how to sneak down through Bangor's east side to pick up 1-A southbound to Route 46, that comes out on Route 1 east of Bucksport. Walt dropped us off at our little log cabin; he looked around a bit, and then he whizzed up the driveway headed for Parker's Point, while we sorted out our equipment and made the bed up anew. We built a fire in the Jøtul to warm up the stale air and opened the fog deck door to push new air through the cabin; in about an hour it was warming up nicely!

We hadn't named the new boat yet, and I towed it over to Travis Eaton's on the Haskell District Road on Little Deer Isle. There is a beautiful glacial beach there, and Travis backed the Ebbtide on its boat trailer into the water with his New Holland diesel tractor: we had double-checked that the drain plug was in. I lowered the big Johnson, and it started right up. I backed cautiously and swung around to run "straight for Heart Island," as directed by Travis, "so as to clear all them boulders and ledges!" It was nearly high water, and Pam had come down to the

Haviland-Haskell beach to have a little ride in the new boat. It went like a shot, and we even picked up Walter at Parker's Point, where he was out enjoying the bright sunny day. After a little circular spin, we put Walter ashore again and returned to the Haskell-Haviland dock. I towed our peapod over to the mooring that Bill and I had rigged up in the lee of Carney's Island and moored the new boat.

The very next trial, the propeller hub sheared off its rubber bushing. Things went on like that for a while, and we even tried to make a trip to Pond Island with Jennifer's family. The engine performed nicely all the way over, and I put everyone ashore at our favorite picnic spot, forgetting that it was not the best place to moor. I temporarily pushed the Ebbtide off on a fisherman's trigged anchor mooring. One simply figures out a length of anchor rode sufficient to hold the boat in place, while he digs clams or whatever, and then pulls in on the ground line, anchor and all, to retrieve the boat. The wind picked up out of the southwest, and before long the sea was making the Ebbtide dance about. The tide was falling quite rapidly, and the Perrys were walking around the island. The boat threatened to pound on the bottom, and I tried to push it off into deeper water. Mistake number two! I couldn't move the heavy boat by myself, and very shortly she had carried me downwind, and the boat grounded out. About then, the Perrys came around the north end of Pond Island and saw the boat high and dry.

Not to admit to complete failure, I hauled out our two very-much-worn clam hoes and began to search for clams. We were about discouraged when I saw the skeleton of an old wooden coasting schooner lying on the west side of the island. There was a small seashell beach there, and I thought, "If there is a clam on this island they will be in amongst the old ship's timbers!"

After a minute search, I found a tiny clam hole and dug down with my very old and worn hoe, and after several scoops I saw the siphon's head; a little more scratching away and I held aloft a huge *mya arenaria* (soft-shelled clam). Pretty soon, Dan Perry and I were digging away, and we found nearly a third of a bushel of clams. Jennifer and Dan's son Aaron got into the spirit and adventure and dug several clams all by himself. We lined an L.L.Bean tote bag with seaweed and carefully piled the clams into it. We carried our treasure back to the picnic site and found that the tide had turned.

Meanwhile our first-born, Melinda, had realized that we should have been back hours ago. So she called Bill Haviland from her summer camp (our old homestead during the Great Depression); Bill and our neighbor

Corinne Sewall came looking for us. Just as we were loading the Ebbtide for our return trip, the *Cormorant* came out of the fog that was getting thicker and thicker. They got Pam aboard the *Cormorant*, and by then the Ebbtide was almost afloat again, so Bill took our anchor and rowed it off to the full length of the line. Jennifer climbed into the Ebbtide and pulled on the anchor line, while Dan and I pushed the boat out. I managed to get aboard over the transom and "Danzo" made a flying leap onto the bow as Jen hauled us off into deeper water. I managed to get the big Johnson down and started, and I backed her off while Jen continued to haul in on the anchor line. After we had some depth of water under us, I hauled the anchor on board, and we started chasing the *Cormorant.* That's when the propeller acted up again, and we soon lost sight of Bill and crew. He had pounded on his radar, that didn't work on the way out, and got that going, found us again, and we chased him at our best speed. Oddly enough, we broke out of the fog as we got closer to Deer Isle. Once everyone was safely ashore, we moored the Ebbtide on the outhaul overnight, again!

As a grand finale, I made a huge clam chowder. Our son Nathan arrived, and he and I replaced the propeller with a new one that I got from the "girls" in Stonington's NAPA auto parts. That cured the propeller problems, but we had three days of solid rain, and the big Johnson would not start. So I towed it over to the Haskell district, and Travis towed it to the Evinrude dealership in Ellsworth. They fixed the problem, and eventually we circumnavigated Deer Isle with Walter as supercargo and had a very nice picnic on Hen Island, just a few yards east of Heanssler's lobster dealership.

That was the grand finale trip of the summer of 2008 for us. We shot up Eggemoggin Reach in between Pumpkin Island light and along the Haskell district shore to moor the boat after putting Pam ashore and all our picnic and safety equipment. "The very next mornin' the Johnson refused to start! Travis towed 'er over to his place and hauled 'er outta wattah, deah!" The "Gnu *Nessie*" is tucked away under cover, and we will try another trip to the Evinrude dealership in 2009! The New Year may very well be our last boating year. (I'm 81 years young.) But Nathan and Jennifer can handle her as well if not better than I, so we'll keep her! Happy boatin' to all you folks out there who must have a boat!

101. SATURDAY, JANUARY 10TH, 2009

My sister-in-law called me today to tell me that Collis Jones had passed away. He was two months older than I, and back in the Great Depression Days we walked to school together along the Clam City Road. Collis and his siblings, Herb and Vera, lived in the west red building of three that were owned by the town of Stonington at that time. We traipsed up what is now known as Pink Street and along a path that came out at the southeast corner of the old Stonington High School. There was a large granite outcropping just east of the school building.

We were close as brothers for most of our school years. Later in life Collis's family moved up to the old Settlement stone quarry boardinghouse and lived in the first floor's northwest end. There was an old wooden water tank supported upon a wrought-iron base, and a sheet-metal-bladed windmill that drove a water pump. It had all been abandoned after the "Fuller job" was completed on the Settlement quarry. The stone-cutting shed was still standing, neglected and abandoned. The dock derricks had been removed and taken elsewhere, to Deer Isle Granite, possibly.

Collis had the use of a tiny scow that didn't seem to belong to anyone but was used by whoever arrived at the shore of Webb's Cove first! One day he backed into the granite ledge where Pete Knowlton kept his tender, and I jumped into the little scow and drove two planks right down toward the bottom of the cove. We were soon very wet. Not too much disturbed, we hauled the scow ashore, turned her over, and drove the boards back on with a smooth hammer stone. Collis reminded me of that episode for years and years!

When he lived in the old boarding house, we used to row out onto the nearby islands and dig clams together, he in a smaller skiff and I rowing the heavy fifteen-footer (that Dad had made with Garland and me, saving us from the steel-drum boat). One day we got into a patch of ground-up seashells and managed to dig five bushels apiece out of that colony.

We graduated from Stonington High School in 1945, and Collis married Muriel Black. Her father worked in R. K. Barter's fish factory, and he was my boss in the steam-retort room and fish-tank rooms. I didn't see Collis much after we got out of school. But we were friends all our lives.

102. Another Look at the Raising of
Nessie

Today's story will be "The Sinking of the *Nessie* and the Refloating Efforts of Our All-Volunteer Crew." Again, the story would not be complete without the Bell Telephone Company employees who joined me in building a plywood garvey in our tiny Model T Ford-type garage in West Mt. Airy.

Bob Angelow and I assembled the frames in the basement, and once we were happy with the fits and lines, we took it all apart and shoved it out through the basement window, except the frames, which we carted out through the kitchen doorway.

We all worked out of the tenth floor of the Widener building at 9th and Chestnut in Center City Philadelphia. Tom Lo Presti, Brady Marlow and his dad all helped to assemble the V-bottomed craft out in the garage. Bob Angelow captured a serviceable used boat trailer, somewhere in New Jersey. I painted the skiff white, two coats of copper bottom paint, and added green trim to the sheer strake guards, colors of the Italian National flag. Tom Lopresti laughed when we verbally christened the project "Atsa My Boat." I lettered *A.M.B.* on the sides.

We enjoyed several trips to Barnegat Bay, where we caught blowfish, summer flounders, and once in a great while a weakfish. Once, we captured the lead-sheathed telephone cable that crossed Barnegat Bay, without even trying! Releasing it was something else. I seem to remember passing a line under it while the fishing gear snag was unwound, then letting the line slide out from under the cable with a mighty pull by two of us. Several seasons later, Bob Angelow gave me a well-used Mercury 40-horse outboard that we tried out on the *A.M.B.* It would really sizzle.

Eventually, I was transferred to the Oxford Avenue engineering office, and Bob Angelow transferred to another Bell Company title. Tom Lo Presti was promoted to second level, and somehow Brady Marlow was lost in the shuffle. We only saw him at company meetings after that. I sold the *A.M.B.*, trailer and all. But I took the Mercury up to Deer Isle to use on our sixteen-foot carvel-planked skiff that Digger Jones had built for us in a cow barn, while he was stationed with the Air Force in Bangor. Our 30-horse Evinrude had succumbed to corrosion. The power head would still run, but the shift rod had rusted away inside the alloy castings. I finally gave the whole works to Dean Eaton for parts.

Bob Angelow gave me his fiberglass eighteen-foot tri-hulled outboard skiff, complete with boat trailer and three-cylinder 60-horse Evinrude, after the Mercury's lower unit began to leak lubricant.

By that time I was transferred to Rights-of-Way. There were two of us in North Philly, Eugene Weber, known as "Gino," and me, known as "Haskell th' Rascal." I came into the office located at 1347 West Cheltenham Ave., and the office clerks and ladies were having a weight-losing contest. Beverly Devitt was getting on the scales, and I sneaked a big 9½ foot over onto the scale, partly hidden by a layout plans table. I shot Beverly up to 115 pounds or so, and the gals all sucked in their breaths. (Bev didn't weigh 90 pounds wringing wet.) Then Flo saw my foot, and she shouted, "Haskell, you rascal!" And it stuck from that day till now!

My district was everything west of Broad Street, north of Brandywine Street, east of the Schuylkill River, and on out into the boonies. Gino had everything east of Broad Street to the Delaware River and out into the "great northeast." I applied for a notary public's commission and acquired the seal and some instructions, which made some parts of our job easier.

When William Schoettle towed Angelow's old fiberglass skiff to Maine with his little Jeep roadster, I went along as navigator. (Bill has a tendency to take any convenient exit from the Interstate that we were on.) As all things go, the Evinrude ran well for several seasons, but once the underwater shifting drive unit began to miss shifts and eventually failed all together, we hauled the *Nessie* outta wattah early in our vacation.

Kevin Grindle was taking care of the *Nessie* at that time; he was a whiz. He had that place on Little Deer Isle that he called the Dry Marina. He could fix about anything. However, Dean Eaton had told me that repairs to the Evinrude would exceed the cost of a new motor! So we bought our very first brand-new outboard motor. Kevin was selling Tohatsu three-cylinder 70-horse motors, so he removed the Evinrude and fitted a Tohatsu 70-horse three-cylinder onto the *Nessie*. The following spring we had a trial run. It would skim right along, at nearly twenty knots, I think.

Somewhere along there, Kevin got fed up with customer complaints and demands and quit. So he sent us to another young man for service. Ah well! Things went downhill from there.

I towed the *Nessie* down to his place and backed it into a little spot between some trees and a junky machine, to be winterized. In the spring, the bottom was freshly painted with antifouling, and he launched the *Nessie* at the Deer Isle Mill Dam, where a lot of boats get dunked over the season. The Tohatsu fired right up, and I scaled up to the mooring, which Bill Haviland and I had fished up with a gaff. Everything seemed to be hunky-dory. The very next morning, the *Nessie* was not to be seen. Bill and I rowed over to see if she had sunk on the mooring, but didn't see her anywhere. It was high tide.

So I printed out some notices to tack onto the billboards at the island laundromat, Neville Hardy's convenience store, and anywhere else we thought might serve the purpose. Paul Sewall and I spent several hours searching the western shores, but Walter Hardy found the Nessie. He went into Carney's Island's eastern cove, where he had a raft that contained his bait barrel, some traps and other gear, and cruised right over the *Nessie*, which was lying on the bottom. She had sunk on her mooring!

Walter Gottschalk had gone out into that miserable windy and wet rainy weather in his sailboat under power looking for a supposedly drifting *Nessie*. Walter was the first to volunteer to help raise the old scow! His cousin Charlie Brace also volunteered. So Walter Gottschalk rowed our old wooden skiff, standing up using the fisherman's stroke, over to the site. And with Bill Haviland's rowboat we began to winch the *Nessie* up from the deep, using a boat-trailer winch fastened to a stout four-inch-thick plank with a hole bored down through it. Bill and I had been moving very heavy rocks with this contraption spanning the two boats, to improve the beach swimming area and the homemade dock in the process. We simply lifted the rocks with a rope sling, enough to float the two boats over the rocks piled higgledy-piggledy to make a breakwater, actually. (It's worth your life to try to walk on these slippery rocks that we use as a dock.)

Eventually, Walter dove down and unfastened the mooring, and we floated the *Nessie* over to Carney's Island sand bar, where we secured her in place—to sink again where she would be "mostly outta wattah when th' tide went out!"

Sure enough, nearly six hours later, the *Nessie* was high but not dry. Walter and Paul Sewell bailed with five-gallon buckets, spelled by Bill Haviland and me. After she floated, Paul towed the boat over to the Deer Isle end of the causeway bar. Bill Haviland was hollering, "Get her movin'! The leak is gainin' on me!" We grounded her out in the shallows at the bar.

Then Paul and I rowed like fiends down to the Haskell-Haviland dock in Dad's ancient peapod, to race up the stairs to get the Lone Ranger (there will be only one), and we roared up the driveway with the boat trailer in tow. Paul managed to get the *Nessie* up onto the trailer from the clam-flats, with the boat-trailer winch! Water just poured out of a hole in the bottom that was found to be the source of the leak. The four-cylinder Ranger was only a rear-wheel-drive model and could not pull the boat trailer through the mud, as the nose wheel dug right in. Then arrived the complete stranger in my story, driving the homemade high-rise four-wheel-drive Chevy flatbed truck. The stranger wouldn't accept a penny, but he certainly saved our bacon that day. We re-relate "raising Nessie" gleefully over a beer or two to this very day!

We chortle that it was so foggy that no could see our Three Stooges act from the causeway beach. Unfortunately, Paul Sewall has "crossed the bar," in nautical terms. He succumbed to cancer of the brain in 2004 and is sadly missed by everyone who knew him well.

Well o' course! we never got the *Nessie* going again. The 70-horse Tohatsu was repaired, but it resided in my li'l shop for two or three winters. Our son Nathan Tristram declared the *Nessie's* hull too old to be safe. It trembled at high speed on choppy water. Bill Schoettle gave us his nineteen-and-a-half-foot Aquasport, that had been stored in our blueberry field for three or four winters unused. That boat was a really nice hull and would be the source of more nautical stories. So stay tuned; I ain't done yit!

103. Memorial Day, 2009

Memorial Day, 2009. Sometime this morning I remembered climbing an old white-spruce tree that had an osprey's nest in it. Every spring the ospreys flew back from their winter vacation area. Possibly Costa Rica, but it could be anywhere south of my youthful Stonington, Maine, for all we knew. I remember seeing the osprey parents fishing for flounders in Webb's Cove. Once in a great while, they would impale a flounder too large for the big bird to fly off with. I suppose that there is a release method, or else the fish hawk would drown.

Somehow, I got the idea of having an osprey for a pet. I climbed up the scraggly old skunk spruce tree that leaned out over the coarse gravel beach on the south shore of Webb's Cove on the north side of Phoebe Thurston's Point. The heavily wooded point was the southwestern extent of Webb's Cove and the Clam City tote road. The Thurston family settled the subsistence farm sometime before my father's ancestors settled and farmed the Albert Knowlton farmstead. The Ames brothers or their parents had built the granite-block foundation, and the saltwater farmhouse was erected upon the stoneworks. There were four Knowlton families within short walking distances of each other. John Knowlton was the most westerly of the four and was situated downhill from the Tea Hill Road. Captain George Knowlton had a larger house atop the granite monolith that is the bedrock formation for all of Stonington. The Tea Hill Road is paved today as far as Cap'n George's old house. He had a son, Ralph, who lived in an extension to his father's house. He became a dairy farmer and had a small herd of Guernsey cows. Ralph delivered raw milk from house to house, including ours, using a 1939 Pontiac straight-eight-powered sedan, which seemed indestructible. Aunt Net Knowlton lived alone in a smaller farmstead about half way between Albert Knowlton's house and the Ames family's saltwater farm overlooking the Deer Isle Thoroughfare, Russ Island, and all the other islands south of Stonington, from the Clam City Road, in my youth.

Climbing the tree was easy enough, but the ospreys were diving at me, and I had to duck under the nest to avoid being impaled by their sharp talons. Eventually, between diving attacks, I captured a chick and worked my way back down the tree. After dropping to the Old Indian Trail, I hot-footed it for home, to be surprised by my mother's outrage and fear for my eyes! "Now, sir! You just march right straight back up there and put that little chick back in the nest!" It's a wonder that those fish hawks didn't scratch yer eyes out!"

Within sixty minutes, I had the scrawny chick back in the nest. I assume that it survived to begin flying, but I think that in reality the parents only fledge the strongest chick each season. Of course, this was long before *Silent Spring* and the near extinction of ospreys due to DDT weed killer runoff, which was ingested by the flounders in the saltwater breeding areas and transferred to the ospreys. Their eggshells became too fragile to support the broody mother birds, and the osprey populations declined.

If there was any danger for humans eating flounders, Gene Robbins almost eliminated flounders by rigging up an old Muscongus Bay sloop boat to begin dragging for flounders in Webb's Cove and other Island coves until he had exhausted the supply. Perhaps there are flounders in Webb's Cove again by now, but for several years the cove was barren!

However, there were full-grown mackerel schooling there. We caught a boatload one evening, as the summer mackerel season was on at the old fish-factory dock in Stonington. Pam and I took the kids down to the cove, and Ken Jones was cleaning up after a day's hauling his lobster traps. He hollered over to me, "Carroll, you don't have to go down to the fish factory to catch mackerel, there's all you want right here!" and he heaved over several herrings for bait. Within seconds we were catching mackerel as fast as we could unhook them and re-bait the hooks for our children. Then suddenly, the mackerel stopped biting, and we began to catch dogfish, which are definitely not fun to catch. They have sharp spines and twisted around like snakes while I tried to unhook them. I had and still have a long-bladed filleting knife, and I simply sliced the sharks' heads off. That eliminated the danger of being stabbed by the spines.

We returned to the granite-ledge landing place and tied the outboard-powered skiff onto the outhaul and carried our catch up the hill in clam rollers, which were stored in Dad's old workshop-cum-forge. I think that my dad gave almost all the mackerel away. Our three children and Pamela wouldn't eat them.

Deer Isle Haskell Genealogy

With notes by the author, whose ancestors in each generation are italicized.

The First Generation[1]

William Haskell, the immigrant, was born in Charlton, Musgrove, England, 8 Nov. 1618. He emigrated to Salem, Massachusetts in 1635.[2] He married *Mary Tybbot* on 16 Nov. 1643, daughter of Walter Tybbot. William Haskell died 20 August 1693.

Children:[3]

1. *William*, b. 1664, d. 1708, married *Mary Walker* in 1667.
2. Joseph, b. 1646, d. 1727, married Mary Graves.
3. Benjamin, b. 1648, d. 1740, married Mary Riggs in 1677: nine children; married Emma Bond.
4. John, b. 1649, d. 1718, married Mary Baker "of Kettle Cove" in 1685: seven children; first four children were born in Beverly, Mass.
5. Ruth, b. 1654 in Gloucester, Mass., married Nehemiah Grover in 1676: six children.
6. Mark, b. 1658, d. 1691, married Elizabeth Giddings in l685: three children.
7. Elinor, b. 1663, married Jacob Griggs in 1695: six children.
8. Sarah, b. 1660, d. 1691, married Edward Haraden in 1684: one child.
9. Mary, baptized 1660, d. 1737, married Edward Dodge, two or six children (see text).

The Second Generation[1]

William Haskell, b. 1664, d. June 5 1708, married *Mary Walker* in 1667.

Children:[4]

1. Mary, b. 1668 in Gloucester, Mass., married Jacob Davis (1) in 1687.

2. *William*, b. 6 Nov. 1670, married *Abigail Davis* on 8 Sept. 1692.
3. Joseph, b. 1673, married Rachel Elwell in 1696.
4. Abigail b. 1675, married Nathaniel Parsons (1) in 1696.
5. Henry, b. 1678, married Ruth York in 1703.
6. Andrew, b. 1680, d. 1680 as an infant.
7. Lydia, b. 1681, married Ebenezer Parsons in 1704.
8. Sarah, b. 1684.
9. Elizabeth, b. 1686, married Thomas Sargent (1) in 1710.
10. Hanna, b. 1688.
11. Jacob, b. 1691, married Abigail Marcy in 1716.
12. Sarah, b. 1692, d. 10 July 1773, married Daniel Haskell on 31 Dec. 1716.

The Third Generation[1, 2]

William Haskell, b. 6 Nov. 1670, d. 17 Jan. 1731, married *Abigail Davis*, b. Apr. 1762 in Gloucester, Mass., d. Dec. 30, 1730. William was known in Gloucester as Ensign William. He was a fisherman and managed to leave an estate of 2,565 English pounds.

Children:

1. William, b. 1693, Gloucester, Mass., d. 1752 at 59 years, married Abigail Tuttle.[2]
2. *Mark*, b. 10 August 1695, Gloucester, Mass., married *Jemima Tilton* on 3 Dec. 1720, ten children.
3. Elizabeth, b. 29 Nov. 1696, married John Parsons, 6 June 1716.
4. Abigail, b. 16 Aug. 1699, married John Tyler in 1722.
5. Jemima, b. 1704, married Joseph Davis on 21 Sept. 1732.
6. Jedediah, b. 31 July 1708, died as an infant.
7. Kezia, b. 28 Feb. 1710-11, d. 13 May 1732, married Samuel Herrick on 3 Jan 1730-1731
8. James, b. 24 Sept 1712, married Anna Goodhue on 1 Oct. 1739.

The Fourth Generation[1]

Captain Mark Haskell, b. 10 Aug. 1695, Gloucester, Mass. He married *Jemima Tilton*, b. 27 Nov. 1699, Ipswich, Essex, Mass. Her father was

Abraham Tilton and her mother was Mary (Jacobs) Haskell. Jemima Tilton married William Cogswell on 26 July 1718, and Captain Mark Haskell on 3 Dec. 1720. Captain Mark Haskell was the first Haskell to settle on Deer Isle, in 1765.[2]

Further reference to *Captain Mark Haskell:*

While Captain Mark Haskell commanded the sloop *Dolphin*, it was captured by the pirate John Phillips, who claimed to be looking for a man named Tilton. Not finding the man he was looking for, Phillips took prisoner John Fillmore, the great-grandfather of President Millard Fillmore (b. 7 Jan. 1800, d. 8 Mar. 1874).[4, 5, 6]

According to oral history from Eben Haskell to my mother's sister Geneva (Torrey) Howard: Captain Mark Haskell came to Deer Isle's Northwest Harbor and had six slaves brought up from Virginia with an overseer. The slaves dug a foundation hole by hand directly across from Harold and Geneva (Torrey) Howard's house. Geneva got to know Eben Haskell, who had a tannery in Deer Isle Village. Water for the tannery was piped downhill from the Lily Pond.

After the foundation hole was dug out, the slaves erected a crossed-arch, handmade-brick foundation. It is quite possible that the handmade bricks were made at the Crockett's Cove kiln on Deer Isle. (Another colonial source of handmade bricks was the kilns in Penobscot, Maine, not a great distance away and accessible from the sea.) The main floor timbers were hewn by hand and were supported in place upon the brick arches. Smaller floor joists were dovetailed into the main floor timbers at right angles to the main beams. The timber-framed house was erected upon these hand-hewn timbers. The sheathing was most likely hand sawn by the pit-saw method, as the Haskell tidal-powered sawmill was not erected by that time in history. A brick chimney was built on each end of the house and may have had fireplaces on each floor. The kitchen and laundry may have been in the basement, as was the custom in some Virginia houses.

In 1933 and '34, my brother Garland and I played upon the first-floor platform and explored what seemed to be rooms in the basement of the old Captain Mark Haskell house, with Judyth Haskell. Her grandfather Eben was tearing the old house down piece by piece, and only the first-floor platform remained in place. Judyth had a sister Janice. Their father was Ralph Haskell, who was a private yacht captain in 1925. When the Great Depression arrived, he was "put on the beach," as the expression

JUDYTH (HASKELL) HUTCHINSON, SHARON, ROBERT JR.,
ROBERT C. "HUTCH" HUTCHINSON IN FRONT OF THE
STONINGTON TOWN HALL.

goes. He never went to sea again. The old house was lived in by Ralph and his family until he acquired a smaller house on Route 15, next to the old firehouse. Both buildings overlook Northwest Harbor. This house was given to Judyth (Haskell) Hutchinson's daughter Sharon (Hutchinson) long after I left the island, and after her first husband Bobby Hutch died, and before Judyth married Thomas McGuire.

Children:

1. *Francis Haskell*, b. 18 June 1722, married *Elizabeth Wheeler* on 20 Nov. 1745, in Gloucester, Essex, Mass. She died in 1791 on Deer Isle at 75 years.
2. Captain Mark Haskell, Jr., b. 20 Oct. 1723 in Gloucester, Mass., d. 1810, married Abigail Bray on 25 Dec. 1745.

Further reference to Captain Mark Haskell, Jr.:

He built the house, which remains in 2010, much the worse for weather, next to his father's house on Church Street, Deer Isle Village. It is now used by the Heanssler's Service Station, as a warehouse.

Children:

1. & 2. Caleb and Ignatius (sons of Captain Mark, Jr., grandsons of *Captain Mark*) and related events:

Caleb enlisted in the American Army under Cap'n Lunt, and they marched on down to fight the British at Breed's Hill in what is incorrectly called "Bunker Hill" in history. Then Caleb traipsed off to Quebec with Benedict Arnold, the quixotic general who failed to recreate Wolfe's capture of the city. They straggled back through the by-then hostile French Colonial Quebec Province and the dense northern Maine woods, swamps and bogs, to return to Newburyport in rags and nearly starved condition. Day lily tubers saved young Caleb from starvation.

Ignatius was most likely on Deer Isle in 1765 or before. Ignatius's ship (sailing schooner or possibly larger) was on course for Newburyport, Mass., in 1775, where the Haskell families had a shipping business at the time. *Cap'n Mark* and his grandson Caleb went down on that ship.

Sometime after 1770, Ignatius Haskell started building a dam across a small cove which had a narrow seaward entrance. Ira Haskell's photo of the Mill Dam on page 192 of his *Chronicles of the Haskell Family*, first edition (1943), shows a fieldstone structure, which was later faced with cut granite blocks, possibly during the WPA era, when the Little Deer Isle causeway to Deer Isle was improved. My father Leroy Elmer Haskell worked on that project and convinced the supervisor to build it following the curves made by tidal action, "Because if you build it straight it will become a racetrack!" It has been used as a racetrack. I remember the first MG TC roadsters to arrive on Deer Isle, roaring back and forth across the causeway back in 1947-48.

The combination saw- and grist-mill was built upon a barge, according to oral histories passed on to me. It most likely succumbed to competition from the Cushing steam-mill in Winterport, Maine. Theophilus Cushing came down from St John, New Brunswick, Canada, and had the mill built; he had laborers from North Deer Isle working there. The Cushing ancestors came to the Massachusetts Colony in 1638 from Hingham, England. They were carted to Hingham, Mass., directly upon arrival in Boston. Theophilus was my wife's great grandfather on her mother's side. Theophilus had a Civil War monument erected in Winterport, Maine, and it still exists along with his large house.

The Cushing steam-mill burned once and was rebuilt only to succumb to more competition from more modern equipment and technology. There was a tunnel to the river from Theophilus' house. The house was used as a way-station/safe-house to help escaped slaves on their way to Canada. (Perhaps on lumber schooners owned by the Cushing family.)

3. Mary, b. 13 Aug. 1725, d. 4 July 1728.
4. Lucy, b. 5 June 1727 in Gloucester, Mass.
5. Solomon (twin), b. 16 July 1729, died as an infant.
6. Mary (twin), b. 16 July 1729.
7. Jane, b. 26 September 1730 in Gloucester, Mass.
8. Solomon, b. 16 July 1731, d. 11 Sept 1731.
9. Abigail, b. 14 Apr. 1732.
10. Anne, b. about 1734.

The Fifth Generation[1]

Francis Haskell, b. 18 June 1722 in Gloucester, Essex, Mass., d. 1791 on Deer Isle; married *Elizabeth Wheeler* on 20 Nov 1745, who was christened 16 Nov. 1729 in Ipswich, Mass., d. 20 Nov. 1804 at 75 years on Deer Isle.

Children:

1. Francis, b. 29 Mar. 1747, drowned in Boston Harbor when he fell between the ship and the dock.
2. Elizabeth Wheeler, b. 16 Oct. 1748, d. 6 Mar. 1831, married Peter Hardy who built their house in 1795, that still stands in the triangle of route 15 and the old ferry landing road in North Deer Isle.[7] Peter died 7 Mar. 1831 at 87 years. They were buried side by side in Forest Hills Cemetery on the Reach Road, Deer Isle.[8]
3. Jemima, b. 11 Oct. 1750, married Captain Jonathan Dennison on 10 Jan 1768.
4. Frances, b. 28 Feb. 1752, d. 14 July 1842, married Lydia Crockett.
5. Abijah Wheeler, b. 19 Mar. 1754, d. 27 Feb. 1832, married Sara Cole.
6. Jonathan, b. 19 December 1755.

7. Jonathan, b. ca. 1757, d. 20 Dec. 1830, married Dorothy Shute.
8. Solomon, christened 12 Nov. 1758.
9. Hanna (twin), b. 11 March 1761, d. 12 June 1838, married William Eaton.
10. Lucy (twin), b. 11 March 1761, d. 27 Feb. 1847, married Captain Elias Davis.
11. Susan, christened 8 Jan. 1764 at Newbury, Ma., d. 25 Dec. 1836, married Ephraim Marshall.
12. *Tristram*, b. 27 Dec. 1767 at Newburyport, Mass., d. 29 March 1854, married *Martha Marchant*.[8]
13. Elsie Wheeler, b. ca. 1769 on Deer Isle; married Captain Joshua Haskell on 21 Aug. 1785.
14. Abigail, b. ca. 1771 on Deer Isle; married Captain Francis Marshall on 13 October 1796.

The Sixth Generation[1]

Captain Tristram Haskell, b. 27 Dec. 1767 in Newburyport, Mass., d. 29 Mar. 1854, married *Martha or Patty Marchant* (pronounced "Merchant" by the natives) from Merchant Island, south of Green's Landing, now Stonington, Maine. Martha was born about 1775 and died 2 Nov. 1803 at 28 years. Her father was Anthony Marchant, and her mother was Abigail Raynes. Later on, the Merchant Island farmstead was a successful farm, sending produce to Bar Harbor, Maine, during the Rusticator years. The old farmhouse, farm buildings and equipment had been abandoned in place, when my father took me ashore there in 1933 or '34.

Captain Tristram Haskell's second bride was Betsy Barton of Castine, Maine, married 31 Dec. 1805, when he was 38 years old.

Betsy Barton Haskell died, and Cap'n Tristram married Ruth (Weed) Turtle Gray. Ruth was too old to have children, and she died before Cap'n Tristram, who was very lonesome living alone.

Tristram was captain of a mackerel fishing schooner that sailed all the way up to Chaleur Bay, New Brunswick, Canada, and may have brought back a bride or two for one of the crew members, from Arichat, Madeline Island, Nova Scotia, on their many trips to Chaleur Bay. The mackerel schooners stopped overnight in Arichat and possibly longer, on their way north and again on their way back to Southeast Harbor, Deer Isle, which was the center of the salt-mackerel industry until 1889, when it collapsed.

Tristram and Martha's Children:

1. Francis, b. 25 Sept., 1791, on Deer Isle, married Phoebe Carmen on 25 Aug. 1814.
2. David, b. 24 Sept. 1793, married first Hannah Weed, then Betsy E. Weed on 30 Nov. 1828, Judith Weed on 23 Nov. 1862.
3. Tristram, b. 25 Feb. 1795, intention to marry Mary or Polly Small announced on 28 Apr. 1818.
4. Betsy, b. 23 Sept. 1796, intention to marry James Stinson announced on 28 Apr. 1818.
5. *Peter H. Haskell, Sr.*, b. 18 Apr. 1798, married *Susan Eaton* on 10 June 1817.
6. John Raynes, b. 14 Mar. 1800, married Martha Green on 9 August 1821.
7. Abigail, b. 9 Nov. 1801, married first John R. Howe, then married George Poole.
8. Joshua P., b. 28 Oct. 1803, married Mary Stinson on 3 Apr. 1843.

Tristram and Betsy's Children:

9. William, b. 4 July 1806.
10. Barbara, b. 26 June 1808.
11. Washington, b. 26 June 1809.
12. Lucy, b. 13 July 1813.
13. Susannah, b. 12 Oct. 1815.
14. Solomon, b. 27 Oct. 1818.
15. Barbara Barton Green, b. 2 Nov. 1821.
16. Elizabeth, b. 28 Dec. 1824.
17. John, b. 22 June 1828. Dr. Benjamin Lake Noyes interviewed John Haskell, and John told Dr. Noyes that Francis had built a log cabin directly across from the old Deer Isle Town Hall and that a large, white stone was used as the log cabin's doorstep. Ironically when Minerva Young had Colby Weed block the entrance to our driveway with two large stones, one was the white stone door step of Francis Haskell's log cabin! Part of our driveway led off the Haviland family's driveway; its right-of-way was grandfathered. So we had Budget Eaton and his son build a new driveway over 2,000 feet long, all the way down from Route 15, the Old North Deer Isle Road. After Dr. William Haviland bought the contested property and right-of-way from Minerva Young, I had

Brian Billings move the white rock over near our bunkhouse in 1996. We have named the little fifteen-foot driveway section the Minerva Young Memorial Highway.

The Seventh Generation[1]

Dr. Peter Haskell, Sr.,[9] b. 18 Apr. 1798. On 10 June 1817, he married *Susan Eaton.* She married Howard Thomas on 5 Sept. 1869.

Peter Haskell and Benjamin Weed built a house which is still standing in the Haskell District on Little Deer Isle. It was long and narrow and built close to a large rock formation. The front of the house overlooks Eaton's and Pickering Islands. The lawn slopes down to the ocean, and there is a coarse sand beach. There are several boats moored in the waters between Little Deer Isle, Barred Island, and the other islands nearby in the summertime. The house was sold out of the Haskell families sometime after WWII. The white cedar shakes on the roof were removed, and it now has a sheet-metal roof.

Children:

1. Tristram, b. 17 Sept. 1817 on Deer Isle, Maine, d. 26 Sept. 1817.
2. Catherine, b. 25 Sept. 1818, married John Gray on 22 June 1840.
3. Mary H., b. 21 Mar. 1821, married James Joyce Weed on 2 Jan. 1840.
4. Joann H., b. 21 Jan. 1824.
5. *Peter H., Jr.,* b. 6 Jan. 1826, d. 28 Nov. 1894, married *Nancy Eaton* on 22 July 1848.
6. Solomon, b. 27 July 1827, d. 11 Aug. 1897, married Margaret Ann Eaton on 23 September 1849
7. Horace, b. 2 Mar. 1830, d. 19 Jan. 1876, married Charlotte Eaton on 3 Oct. 1853.
8. Elizabeth, b. 30 Apr. 1832, married Peter Andrews on 23 Dec. 1847.
9. Susan, b. 14 Mar. 1835, married Isaiah Valentine Eaton on 6 Mar. 1851, William Blastow on 8 Oct. 1865.
10. Wines H., b. 20 Nov. 1837, married Miranda Ann Billings on 1 Jan. 1860.
11. Cordelia, b. 27 Sept. 1840, married Lewis Black on 27 Jan. 1860.

AUTHOR'S GRANDMOTHER ON HIS FATHER'S SIDE, MARY JANE
(BILLINGS) KNOWLTON HASKELL, MOTHER OF EIGHT CHILDREN: ALBERT
HENRY JR., RAYMOND TELDEN, ETHEL FRANCIS, CECIL NELSON,
AND FLORENCE EMMA BURTON KNOWLTON, ELROY FREEMAN AND
IDENTICAL TWIN LEROY ELMER, AND LASTLY CHRISTIE MAE HASKELL.

The Eighth Generation

Peter H. Haskell Jr., b. 6 Jan. 1826, d. 28 Nov. 1894 on Little Deer Isle in the
house described below. He is interred on the Little Deer Isle Haskell District Cemetery without a stone. He married *Nancy Eaton* on 22 July 1848.

Peter H. Haskell's house on Little Deer Isle: He was in the Civil War,
wounded at the first battle of Bull Run. The surgeon told him that he
could leave, and he took that literally and went back to Little Deer Isle.
So General Sedgwick listed him as a deserter. However, after he got
healed up and feelin' better, he signed up for the navy (bonus for signin'
up)! He got shot up on the *Ethan Allen*, a mortar ship, while bombarding
Charlestown, South Carolina, and was invalided out with loss of hearing

in one ear and partial sight in one eye. His brother Horace was a prisoner of war in Libby Prison. They both died soon after they returned to Little Deer Isle.

Children:

1. Elizabeth H., b. 7 Oct. 1849, d. of Scarlatina 30 Jan. 1855.
2. Louisa, b. 21 Sept. 1851, d. 6 Feb 1855.
3. Peter H. 3rd, b. 19 Oct. 1853, d. in 1910, married Susan Sawyer Cole on 21 Nov. 1878.
4. *Freeman Charles*, b. 22 Dec. 1856, married first Louella J. Eaton on 14 Mar. 1878, then *Mary Jane (Billings) Knowlton* on 17 Dec. 1894.
5. William Davis, b. 24 Apr. 1859, married first Laura E. Howard on 13 Aug. 1884, then married Hattie J. Howard. Lived in Oceanville in what looked to be a driftwood house.

The Ninth Generation

My first cousin Freda Haskell told me that our grandfather Freeman came home from a coasting schooner trip and caught Louella, his bride, in bed with another man, who leaped out of a window and ran for his life (with or without his pants, I was never told)! Estelle Noyes told me that Freeman used to wipe his nose with a bandanna, using it like a strip of cloth, and would run it across his nose holding one corner in each hand. It must have been quite a Hollywood production.

Louella and Freeman had one daughter, Sadie (Haskell), who married a shipyard owner in Camden, Maine.

Freeman Charles Haskell, married *Mary Jane (Billings) Knowlton* in Green's Landing (now Stonington), Maine on 17 Dec. 1894, after Cecil Knowlton. She was the mother of Albert, Raymond, Ethel, Florence, and Cecil Nelson Knowlton, b. Mar. 6 1891. Cecil fell off the powerhouse roof, which was on top of the granite quarry on Crotch Island in 1932. The roof was all ice, and he came down, hit his head on a granite block, and died instantly on 11 Mar. 1932. He was married to Mary Elizabeth Blair, and they had four children.

Freeman Haskell built a house down on the Haskell District shore, and after he married *Mary Jane (Billings) Knowlton*, he left the house vacant. Burton Haskell married Flora Snow and moved in. Somehow it caught on fire and burned to the ground sometime after Pearl Harbor.

Freeman Haskell spoke the Little Deer Isle Elizabethan English with the downeast accent. Little Deer Islanders were called "lordy yous" because they started off every story with "Law you."

Children of Freeman Charles and Mary Jane:

1. Elroy Freeman (firstborn identical twin), b. 18 Mar. 1899 in Stonington, Deer Isle, d. Oct. 4 1984 in Rockland, Maine. On 30 Dec. 1919, he married Christina (Terry) Haskell, b. Mar. 18, 1898.
2. *Leroy Elmer* (identical twin), b. 18 Mar. 1899 in Stonington, Deer Isle, d. 30 Nov. 1990 in the Island Nursing Home, North Deer Isle.
3. Christie Mae, b. 24 Sept. 1900, married Charles Kitridge Hooper on 20 Sept. 1924. She died in childbirth on 18 Dec. 1931 at their Tea Hill house, Stonington, Deer Isle.

The Tenth Generation

Leroy Elmer Haskell (identical twin of Elroy), b. 18 Mar. 1899 in Stonington, Deer Isle, d. 30 Nov. 1990 in the Island Nursing Home, North Deer Isle, married Charlotte Mildred Torrey, b. 20 Sept. 1905, d. 6 Apr. 1986.

Children:

1. *Carroll Madison Haskell*, b. 29 Dec. 1927, married Pamela Jean Haviland, b. 6 Nov. 1930 in Germantown Hospital, Philadelphia Pa. Married on 11 May 1957 at First Unitarian Church on Chestnut Street in Philadelphia, Pa.
2. Garland Leroy, b. 13 Jan. 1929, d. June 24, 1966, married Katherine Benton, b. Sept. 8 1934. One son: Garland Leroy Haskell, b. July 20 1958, married, lives in Arvarda, Colorado.
3. Leon Curtis, b. 23 July 1934, never married, lives in Darby, Pa.

The Eleventh Generation

The author, Carroll Madison Haskell, married Pamela Jean Haviland on 11 May 1957 at First Unitarian Church on Chestnut Street in Philadelphia, Pa. They now reside in West Mt. Airy, Philadelphia. Carroll and Pamela have two daughters and a son.

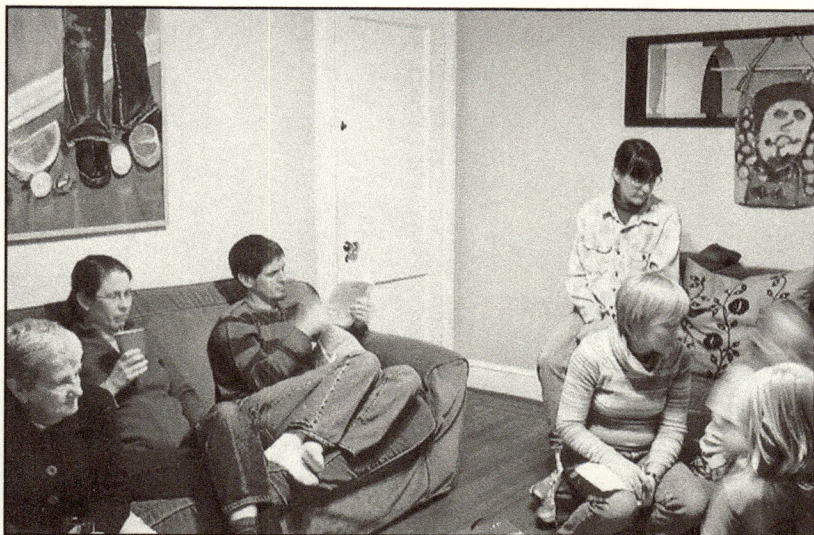

FROM LEFT: GRAMMIE BENSON, JENNIFER HASKELL PERRY, NATHAN HASKELL, MELINDA HASKELL ADAMS, LISA BENSON HASKELL, ANNA ADAMS (IN MOTION), GRETA HASKELL.

Notes to the Genealogy

1. Researched by Judyth (Barton) Reitze at Salt Lake City, Utah.
2. Winthrop A. Haskell has done extensive research on the Haskell families. I have used some of his notes with his permission and encouragement. He lives with his bride Gertrude in Karlsruhe, Germany.
3. Judyth (Barton) Reitze found a discrepancy between the records of the Salt Lake City Mormon Church and the book *Chronicles of the Haskell Family* by Ira Haskell cited below. Reitze found in the Salt Lake City Mormon Church archives that William was born 26 Aug. 1644 and that he married Mary (Brown) Walker. Was William her second husband? She was born in 1649 and died 12 Nov. 1715. William died 5 June 1708. Other than that, the Salt Lake City Mormon Church Archives and Ira Haskell's research agree.
4. Ira J. Haskell, *Chronicles of the Haskell Family*, Lynn, Mass.: Ellis Printing Company (1943).
5. Ibid., p. 189.
6. http://www.whitehouse.gov/about/presidents/MillardFillmore.
7. Researched by Dr. William A. Haviland.
8. George L. Hosmer, *An Historical Sketch of Deer Isle, Maine*, copyright 1905 by Abel Hosmer, Oakland, California, page 63. The *Historical Sketch* is in error stating that they died on the same day: "He was for several years a coroner, and he and his wife died upon the same day, in 1831, and were buried in one grave, having lived together in wedlock over sixty years."
9. Judyth (Barton) Reitze's genealogical chart shows Peter H. Haskell's title as "Dr."

Carroll Haskell reading from his manuscript.

www.ingramcontent.com/pod-product-compliance
Lightning Source LLC
Chambersburg PA
CBHW022005080426
42733CB00007B/476